DEATH VALLEY NATIONAL PARK

Death Valley National Park

A History

Hal K. Rothman and Char Miller

UNIVERSITY OF NEVADA PRESS RENO & LAS VEGAS

University of Nevada Press, Reno, Nevada 89557 USA
Copyright © 2013 by University of Nevada Press
All rights reserved
Manufactured in the United States of America
Design by Kathleen Szawiola

Library of Congress Cataloging-in-Publication Data

Rothman, Hal, 1958–2007.
Death Valley National Park : a history /
Hal K. Rothman and Char Miller.
pages   cm.
Includes bibliographical references and index.
ISBN 978-0-87417-925-5 (pbk. : alk. paper) —
ISBN 978-0-87417-926-2 (e-book)
 1. Death Valley National Park (Calif. and Nev.)—
History. I. Miller, Char, 1951–   II. Title.
F868.D2R67   2013
979.4′87—dc23   2013007479

Only the desert has a fascination—to ride alone
—in the sun in the forever unpossessed country—
away from man. That is a great temptation.

—D.H. LAWRENCE,
letter to Catherine Carswell,
September 20, 1922

CONTENTS

LIST OF ILLUSTRATIONS

FIGURES *(following page 68)*

Timbisha artisan
Timbisha march
Mining shaft
Twenty-mule team
Furnace Creek Inn
Peck-Judah Company
Scotty's Castle
Death Valley sign
Civilian Conservation Corps work crew
Lonely road
Devil's Hole section
People and hills
Sand dunes

MAPS

PREFACE
Char Miller

Death Valley National Park is one of the most complex and intriguing of all desert national parks in the United States. Located in the heart of the Mojave Desert, the park's 3.3 million acres of staggering dimension and arid beauty epitomize the concept of desert preservation. Though not the first national park in a desert, it is the most quintessential, with a history that is exceptionally diverse in its geological record, human activity, and cultural and natural resources.

This book details the history of this unique landscape, which nearly one million people visit each year. It began as an administrative history of Death Valley National Park, which Hal Rothman wrote under contract with the National Park Service. Rothman planned to revise the text into a book, and in 2003 the University of Nevada Press agreed to publish the manuscript once completed. However, Rothman was diagnosed with amyotrophic lateral sclerosis (ALS), also known as Lou Gehrig's disease, before he was able to complete the revision. His death in February 2007 was a devastating blow to his family and to his colleagues in western and environmental history, a paired field of inquiry he had done so much to advance through his many books and articles; his teaching and research at the University of Nevada, Las Vegas; and his brilliant tenure as editor of *Environmental History.* So prolific was he that there have been three posthumous books, *Blazing Heritage: A History of Wildland Fire in the National Parks, Playing the Odds: Las Vegas and the Modern West,* and *The Making of Modern Nevada.* This volume is the fourth.

At an environmental history conference in the spring of 2011, acquisitions editor Matt Becker approached me about revising and updating the manuscript. I evaluated the project and the two peer reviews that had already been completed for it and went to work. By early 2012 the manuscript was finished.

Like all works of scholarship, this history of Death Valley National Park has benefited from the help of an array of colleagues. Key thanks go to Daniel J. Holder, who served as Hal Rothman's principal researcher. This book also could not have been completed without the invaluable aid of leaders of the Timbisha Shoshone people and National Park Service employees who provided critical insights into this arid land and the people who have inhabited it over time. These individuals and others have also helped identify some of the environmental pressures, cultural tensions, and political debates that have framed the National Park Service's management of the site since its establishment on February 11, 1933.

The completion of this book owes a great deal to the generous support of

Lauralee Rothman and the historians in the Pacific West Regional Office of the National Park Service. The staff at Death Valley National Park was instrumental in securing recent reports, illustrations, photographs, and other data necessary to the book's successful revision. Lisa Crane at Special Collections of the Claremont Colleges' Honnold/Mudd Library unearthed some of the tourist brochures that grace these pages. My gratitude goes out as well to the staff of the press, including director Joanne O'Hare, Matt Becker, Michael Campbell, Kathleen Szawiola, and Annette Wenda, and to the three readers of the manuscript whose incisive commentary proved critical to turning the manuscript into a book. As Rothman and I did with our first collaborative project, the coedited volume *Out of the Woods: Essays in Environmental History,* so with this, our last: *Death Valley National Park: A History* is dedicated to our families.

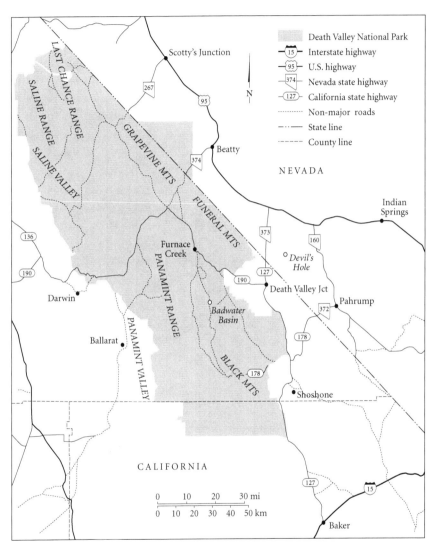

Death Valley National Park

Legend:
- Death Valley National Park
- 15 Interstate highway
- 95 U.S. highway
- 374 Nevada state highway
- 127 California state highway
- Non-major roads
- State line
- County line

Map labels:
Scotty's Junction
LAST CHANCE RANGE
SALINE RANGE
SALINE RANGE
SALINE VALLEY
GRAPEVINE MTS
FUNERAL MTS
267
95
Beatty
374
NEVADA
Indian Springs
136
373
160
Furnace Creek
Devil's Hole
190
127
190
Darwin
Death Valley Jct
Pahrump
372
Badwater Basin
PANAMINT RANGE
Ballarat
PANAMINT VALLEY
178
BLACK MTS
178
Shoshone
CALIFORNIA
0 10 20 30 mi
0 10 20 30 40 50 km
127
15
Baker
N

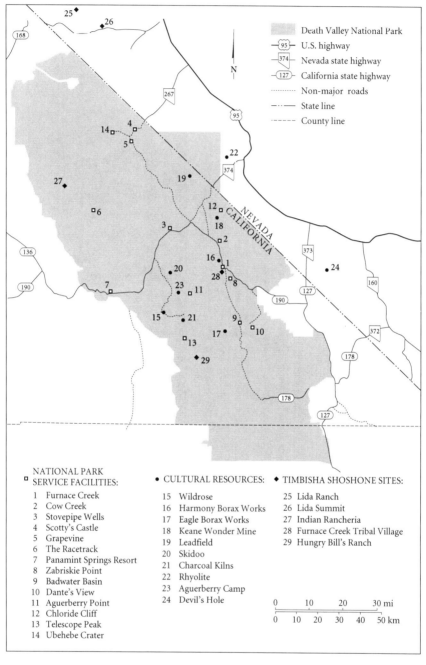

168		
267		
95		
374		
136		
190	127	
190	373	
160		
372		
178	127	

NEVADA
CALIFORNIA

N

Death Valley National Park
95 — U.S. highway
374 — Nevada state highway
127 — California state highway
.... Non-major roads
— · · — State line
— — — County line

□ NATIONAL PARK
SERVICE FACILITIES:

1   Furnace Creek
2   Cow Creek
3   Stovepipe Wells
4   Scotty's Castle
5   Grapevine
6   The Racetrack
7   Panamint Springs Resort
8   Zabriskie Point
9   Badwater Basin
10 Dante's View
11 Aguerberry Point
12 Chloride Cliff
13 Telescope Peak
14 Ubehebe Crater

● CULTURAL RESOURCES:

15 Wildrose
16 Harmony Borax Works
17 Eagle Borax Works
18 Keane Wonder Mine
19 Leadfield
20 Skidoo
21 Charcoal Kilns
22 Rhyolite
23 Aguerberry Camp
24 Devil's Hole

◆ TIMBISHA SHOSHONE SITES:

25 Lida Ranch
26 Lida Summit
27 Indian Rancheria
28 Furnace Creek Tribal Village
29 Hungry Bill's Ranch

0		10	20	30 mi
0	10	20	30	40	50 km

Timbisha Shoshone sites, National Park Service facilities, and
cultural resources at Death Valley National Park

DEATH VALLEY NATIONAL PARK

Introduction

Not far from the small outpost of Death Valley Junction near the Nevada state line, California Highway 190 quickly drops in elevation. The above-sea-level landscape seamlessly changes as the miles pass, becoming more colorful, more jagged, more ornate, and more spectacular as the descent continues. Even the casual traveler can see the difference, feel the change, and intuit the special nature of what is to come. To people from a culture shaped in humid places, defined by forests and prairies, this journey into the Mojave Desert is a revelation. It forces the concept of arid landscapes into the traveler's perception and demands that the viewer come to grips with the desert. The landscape's power is so great that it is little wonder that acclaimed author David Darlington calls the Mojave "the definitive American desert."[1]

Inside the signs that indicate Death Valley National Park's boundaries, the distinctions become even more pronounced. The elevation markers tell the story: 3,000 feet at the park boundary, 2,000 feet at the turnoff to Billie Mine and Dante's View, 1,000 feet just before the 20-Mule-Team Borax loop, sea level at the Furnace Creek Wash, and finally 190 feet below sea level at the Furnace Creek Visitor Center. During the descent, a marvelous scenic view unfolds. The world seems elongated and stretched, made grander by the clarity of the vista. Distances are telescoped; miles seem inconsequential. Features far away appear so close that every detail is visible. The Panamint Range to the west and the Cottonwood Mountains strike up into the sky in spectacular fashion. Stone gray without the sun, they turn a bright gold as light streams in at sunrise. They reveal a singular beauty, a mystical power that easily overwhelms unsuspecting visitors.

Death Valley National Park is one of the most complex and intriguing of all desert national areas. Few of its peers can claim as diverse a human and natural history; in few other desert parks is the variety of geological, human, and natural stories so broad. Located in the heart of the Mojave Desert, the park's 3.3 million acres testify to the complexities of preserving such a vast, arid, and culturally rich landscape.

Death Valley is the American desert, a landscape so stark and forbidding, so dramatic and stunning, as to demand new tools for understanding. Here is nature foreboding, the expanse of desert seems to say, a world in which humans can endure only with caution and careful planning, with respect for the physical world and appreciation of its limits and resilience. As the great environmentalist John Muir once observed, nature was not created for human dominion, and the Mojave's combination of expanse, grizzled landscape, upthrust mountains, and rolling desert sands confirms that sentiment with remarkable clarity. Of all the places in the American West, Death Valley may be the most intimidating. Certainly, its name contributes to its image as the place that modernity and its accouterments have not yet and may never thoroughly tame.[2]

In this, Death Valley enjoys peculiar status. The desert has long been a mystifying landscape for the peoples of the Old World—the Europeans, Africans, and Asians who came to demographically dominate the humid climates of the new continent. These people came in great numbers, some by choice, others coerced, and they brought a shared fear of the desert. Although it could be endured and even tolerated, for there were many ways to live in it, the desert was rarely comfortable. It demanded adaptability and humility, traits often short among the human species.

Many newcomers to the Americas feared its deserts. In part, this stemmed from their faiths, Christian and animistic alike. The biblical connotation of the desert as wilderness, derived from the story of Moses and the Israelites and their forty-year sojourn, remained a dominant form of expression throughout the first three centuries of Old World inhabitation of the New World. The African Americans whom Europeans brought to the continent as chattel absorbed this perspective, for it was not far from their own thoughts about nature, derived from their natal lands, mostly in West Africa.[3]

These Euro-, Afro-, Asian Americans, a biologically composite people who shared a complex of disease immunities, foodstuffs, skills, and goods through trade, likely reviled the desert on first encounter. Deserts are hot, dry, sandy, frightening, and unyielding. Unlike the fertile river deltas in the eastern half of the United States, the wet and lush environments of the mid-South, or even the prairies east and west of the Mississippi River, the desert had little to offer either colonists or the United States before the twentieth century. Thomas Jefferson's vision of the yeoman farmer as the nation's backbone held sway while the

United States remained primarily an agricultural society. Long after that attitude crumbled, this vision of what made nature useful dominated the national psyche. In this view, deserts were formidable obstacles that stood between migrants and their destinations. Travelers from any European-based society passed through the desert, commenting on its lack of trees, weird rock shapes, unusual plants, and always the heat, but typically only the unusual and the reclusive, the strange and the anomic, settled along the occasional stream or water hole that dotted the arid West.[4]

Yet the desert was also entrancing, a refuge from the outside world, and it attracted many who sought its solitude. Native peoples had long made their home in it, learning to wring their livelihood from its special and sometimes scant resources. Desert cultures maximized available resources. They found ways to use the sun and thirst-producing aridity to create homes, drawing life from springs and seasonal seeps. Such people used elevation to contravene the limits of nature and made accommodations with a physical world generously described as harsh. Later, miners came in search of riches buried in the earth; they exploded across the landscape in great rushes of energy, building cities overnight that often disappeared just as quickly. They paved the way for the fringes of their society: people unafraid of the loneliness, solitude, and physical hardship of the remote desert or even those who preferred to live apart from the norms of their day.

They all found the desert and made it their own, for it offered solace and shelter, a minimalist existence for those who chose it. In the process, they created an image of the desert as full of the eccentric and bordering on the bizarre. Deserts became the hiding place for the desperate, where those who stepped away from US society could feel comfortable. Many took this option, from miners and outlaws in the nineteenth century to the deranged killer Charles Manson in the twentieth. For all it lacked, the desert could provide shelter.[5]

The people who preceded these Old World invaders in the desert well knew the ways the desert could shelter and provide. The Southwest's deserts remain home to people who preceded the arrival of Old World peoples by centuries and even millennia. Some settled in permanent communities: the Pueblos of the Rio Grande and Tohono O'odham of Arizona. Others, such as the Shoshone and Paiute people of Death Valley, moved seasonally from place to place. Their adaptation to the oft-rigorous climate and the seasonal cycle of plant maturation and animal movement kept them fed and clothed. They found sustenance in the desert's limited opportunities; when it did not sustain, they developed social mechanisms to protect their survival as a group.[6]

The Death Valley Shoshones typified this relationship to place. Part of the Western Shoshones, the people who took the name "Timbisha" when they received federal recognition in the 1980s had long lived in an area that stretched from Death Valley to the eastern slope of the Sierra Nevada. Well established in the desert before the first wagon trains arrived, the Shoshones faced the onslaught of a new culture. These newcomers curtailed options for the Shoshones over time. Despite being well adapted to their harsh environment, the Timbisha could not overcome the ways in which US politics and power restricted their activities.[7]

As the flood of US citizens first swept through and then to the desert, Native peoples faced assaults on their choice locations, their ways of living, and, in the end, their very being. American expansionism, embodied in the concept of Manifest Destiny, drove this westward movement, but geographic obstacles often disrupted the national ambition of continental conquest. Large sections of the continent were too inhospitable to provide the independence and wealth this settler society believed landownership brought. The desert in particular stymied the plans of the grandiose, the megalomaniac, even the ordinary. As people who relied on wood as their primary source of fuel and shelter, Euro-American travelers looked at the sparse vegetation and the dry landscape, wilted from the searing heat or penetrating cold, and calculated that this arid terrain would not provide the Promised Land they sought. Most simply passed through, continuing on to places that their outlooks told them offered fitter futures.[8]

Such travelers sometimes left accounts of these regions they so poorly understood. Deserts were wastelands, they wrote, eerie and frightening, and hard to reconcile with nineteenth-century notions of beauty or usefulness. The eyes that taught them value in land showed them little they could use in the desert. What could people do with such lands? What value did they have for an agricultural society? Most who visited those arid regions expressed fear and disdain. One of the first recorded groups of Anglo-American travelers into the region, faced with its limited water and vegetation that compelled the party to suffer hardships and death, bestowed the name "Death Valley," a mark of their despair and a warning to subsequent travelers.[9]

That caution would be increasingly set aside during the late nineteenth century as the nation's principal economic activity shifted from agriculture to industry. Below its windswept and stark surface, Death Valley held some glittering possibilities for this new order. Industrialization turned the once-despised desert into a resource: the minerals essential to its functioning offered great wealth to those who found and controlled them. Deserts turned out to be storehouses of gold, silver, copper, zinc, oil, magnesium, bauxite, and, in Death Valley, borax. As long as industry flourished and the veins were not exhausted, the desert offered the possibility of a livelihood. Towns appeared and disappeared, seemingly overnight. Some, such as Rhyolite, Nevada, grew from nothing to ten thousand people within the space of two years, only to recede into oblivion. Others persisted, shells of their heyday, for many years. Some continue on.

The miners who flocked to the deserts were instrumental in shaping the way late-nineteenth-century Americans and their twentieth-century descendants defined the desert. They were repelled and attracted: in the 1880s, miner Thomas W. Brooks recognized the "horror to all who traveled that part of the territory," but observed that even such a dismal land promised "to be one of the principal sources of wealth of the country." Death Valley would be "a blessing of wealth and happiness to many; and to the healthseeker, and the lover of sublime beauty and grandeur, the work of nature's God, they, too, could go and bathe the body and feast the eye."[10] Such ambivalence has remained a powerful force in our cultural perceptions of Death Valley.

The growth Brooks anticipated never matched his expectations. Death Valley became a thriving mining region, but a permanent population that might have transformed the entire area did not materialize. Among Euro-Americans, the "stickers," as writer Wallace Stegner referred to westerners who stayed put, never took hold in this very tough place.[11] Their options in the valley were too few, they required too much capital, and the sites were too far from urban markets to depend on them for sustenance. If US citizens sought to root themselves in the soil, the Mojave Desert proved particularly inhospitable.

But it was that very inhospitableness that attracted a new kind of visitor to the deserts of eastern California—tourists. Those with ample means often derived from the wealth that the Industrial Revolution generated also had the time to travel, and with the laying down of the transcontinental railroad grid, they had as well the opportunity to head west. Most of these late-nineteenth- and early-twentieth-century travelers made their way to the Pacific Coast and its more bucolic valleys. Some of the more adventuresome, like J. Smeaton Chase and Edna Brush Perkins, deliberately sought out these arid wildlands. Chase spent two years crisscrossing the Golden State's "dreamy, dreary" deserts astride his long-suffering mule Mesquite. His poetic travelogue, *California Desert Trails,* contains rich insights into desert biota, the striking beauty of "Sand, Mountain, Sky, Silence," and the complicated dynamics of living in "this pure bit of Arabia that has somehow fallen into our territory." Although she did not stay as long, feminist activist Edna Perkins, seeking a short-term respite from her "militant mission to free the world," set off for California, intrigued by what her atlas designated as a "great empty space just east of Sierra Nevada Range and the San Bernardino Mountains vaguely designated as the Mojave Mountains." As the Santa Fe train pulled out of Needles, California, she and her friend Charlotte Jordan were transfixed as "hour by hour great sweeps of blue-green brush led off to mountains blue and red against the sky. We passed black lava beds, and strange shining flats of baked clay, and cliff-like rocks." Hooked, the women found a guide to take them into the valley, and as they stood finally on a promontory facing south and caught their first glimpse of its vast extent, its white floor, Perkins wrote: "We knew that the valley was sterile and dead, yet we saw it covered with a mantle of such strange beauty that we felt it was the noblest thing we had ever imagined." In giving voice to the landscape's "terror and beauty," she contributed to the language, the cultural expression that ever since has drawn so many to Death Valley—the place and the park—to stand still as Perkins did "in the companionship of greatness."[12]

The overwhelming vastness of space and sky that these writers evoked and that nurtured a budding tourist business in the Mojave led others to note the value its isolation contained for military purposes. Frontier fortifications from which the US Army had sallied to enforce national sovereignty across the Southwest may have disappeared by the early twentieth century, but not the idea that these arid lands could serve other militaristic ends. Beginning in earnest in World War II, as the nation developed its capability to fight globally, and continuing throughout the Cold War and beyond, the California and Nevada deserts became home to training camps, experimental laboratories, and live-fire zones in which the nation tested its most dangerous weapons. Within a hundred miles of Death Valley, 126 atmospheric nuclear tests took place between 1951 and the cessation of such activity in 1963; underground testing continued until 1992. In the 1980s, Congress selected Yucca Mountain, east of the national park boundary, as the site for the nation's high-level nuclear-waste storage facility; although authorized in 2002 during the George W. Bush administration, and then defunded in 2010 with the support of Senate majority leader Harry Reid (D-NV) and President Obama, the "radioactive politics" that hover over the site means that Death Valley National Park has not yet escaped the threat of being the closest national park to what would be the nation's most toxic waste facility.[13]

The social impact of the military in and on the desert has been profound. Defense spending fueled much of the region's post-1945 economic activity: at its peak, atmospheric nuclear testing provided more than nine thousand jobs. Towns such as Mercury, Nevada, and large installations such as California's China Lake Naval Air Weapons Station and Fort Irwin Military Reservation attested to the importance of the military in the regional economy and its population growth. This federal dominance was typical of places that remained outside the primary patterns of western settlement and lacked the attributes that an agricultural society valued.

Partly spurred on by the expanding military presence in the desert, a remarkable cultural shift occurred that altered the face of Death Valley and the rest of the Mojave Desert. During the second half of the twentieth century, and drawing on an earlier generation's fascination with the desert as desert, more Americans began to change their attitudes about these stark landscapes. Part of this transformation stemmed from the solitude that could be found in the desert's vast emptiness as life became more physically dense, a yearning to which Edward Abbey's *Desert Solitaire: A Season in the Wilderness* (1968) spoke powerfully. Moreover, the swift population growth in the proximity of the Mojave during and after World War II and the related sprawling expansion of Los Angeles and its environs played a catalytic role in giving people a different vision of this landmass. Technology had helped make the desert more palatable and available. Earlier in the century, the first automobiles had made the region accessible in new ways; jeeps, dune buggies, and all-terrain vehicles later attracted an even wider cut of the public. The vehicles took people off the main roads in relative comfort, creating a new meaning for the term *exploration.* In the later 1990s, widespread use of cellular telephones and the emergence of global positioning system (GPS) technology took some of the risk out of the desert experience, opening the possibility that more people would come to experience its clear skies, penetrating heat, and staggering vistas.[14]

Altered as well was the desert's very character. Between 1945 and 1980, the population in the Mojave Desert more than quadrupled, and after 1980, the growth continued at an even greater pace. Subdivisions spread out toward the formerly remote places such as Death Valley, from Greater Los Angeles to the west and from Las Vegas to the east. Once sparsely populated towns such as Pahrump, Nevada, now grew rapidly, ballooning from 24,631 in 2000 to 36,441 ten years later, an influx that makes greater demands on the desert's limited resources. Water in particular became the first pressing need; poor air quality followed in the wake of the desert's urban development.

At Death Valley, the National Park Service (NPS) played an integral role in addressing the desert's century-long transformation, and the evolution of its struggle to meet its many and varied responsibilities is the central theme of this study: its failures to fully appreciate the desertscape it would manage; its lengthy battles to gain control over mining claims, high-value scenic and cultural sites, and all-important water rights; its mission to protect natural and cultural resources and to maintain a healthy biodiversity; the social tensions that resulted from its inability fully to appreciate the needs of the Timbisha; and the enduring hope that what had originally been designated as a national monument would become a national park. Each of these stories, among other conflicts and controversies, underscores why the National Park Service's management of Death Valley is integral to and reflective of the historically fraught relationship between Americans and nature, our troubled passion to possess the unpossessed.

CHAPTER I

Before the Monument

The land that in 1933 became Death Valley National Monument had a long human history that preceded the arrival of the first Europeans in the New World. In that lengthy story, the environment's fundamental characteristics determined the fate not only of pre-Columbian peoples but also of each of the cultures that succeeded them. At its core, Death Valley stretched humanity, for no human culture easily adapted to its harsh climate, lack of water, and often sparse food sources. The populations that best adapted, those closest to the land, had nothing to rely on save the place. Adaptability was crucial to their survival. Later cultures saw in Death Valley sources of raw material that developers could barter in an industrial society. Their connections to the land and concern for it were not as deep, for they did not have to be.

This second, later, vision of a place that could provide natural resources in exchange for the goods of an industrial mainstream indirectly led to the creation of Death Valley National Monument. The creation of single-purpose mining towns that exploded and then receded created a new context for the desert's development. As more Anglo-Americans encountered the region, including such writers as George Wharton James, Mary Austin, Dix Van Dyke, and Edna Brush Perkins, and as its natural-resource advantages seemed to be exhausted in the rise and fall of the prices of raw materials, Death Valley acquired a new significance, entering the pantheon of the nation's special places.

More than 10,000 years of human history predated that transformation. People began to inhabit Death Valley and the Mojave Desert between 11,000 and 8000 BCE. Before this era, the evidence of human occupation in Death Valley is scant. Scientists cannot date with certainty nor clearly ascribe to human endeavors artifacts from the late-Pleistocene period, before 10,000 BCE. Possible archaeological objects from the succeeding Lake Mojave period, 10,000 to 5000 BCE, have been found near the shores of now-dry pluvial lakes around the Slate Range, southwest of the park, and provide the most compelling evidence of early human habitation. Scientists suggest that this choice of locations indicates an adaptive strategy focused on lakeside resources. Others question that reasoning, suggesting that archaeologists have tended to search for early sites primarily along the shores of pluvial lakes, finding there exactly what they expected. In this view, artifacts and the few faunal remains associated with the Lake Mojave period suggest a more generalized hunting-and-gathering adaptation, providing a direct challenge to explanations that focus on lake resources. Around 7000 BCE, hunters and gatherers who resembled the people archaeologists designate "Archaic" moved through the region, fashioning their existence from its intermittent offerings. Typically without domestic animals, intensive horticulture, or permanent dwellings, these people knew their environment well and took advantage of all it offered.[1]

During the Lake Mojave period, the Death Valley region contained widespread xeric juniper parkland, more abundant large fauna (including some now-extinct creatures), and more plant life than are now present. This relative abundance of resources allowed well-documented human occupation throughout the Great Basin, that now-rain-starved region comprising portions of Nevada, western Utah, southeastern Oregon, and California east of the Sierra, as well as part of northern Mexico. Two distinct dry environments constitute the Great Basin: the Great Basin Desert to the north, a cold, high-elevation desert dominated by sagebrush, and the Mojave Desert to the south, a low-elevation area typically home to cactus and creosote bush. Across this more southerly area, a variety of cultural complexes, including Clovis, Lake Mojave, Cougar Mountain, Lind Coulee, and Silver Lake, established communities. In Death Valley, artifacts such as spear and dart points, crescents, gravers, distinct scrapers, drills, leaf-shaped knives, and a few heavy core tools suggest consistent occupation during an extended period.[2]

During the subsequent Pinto period, 5000 to 2000 BCE, Great Basin inhabitants first encountered environmental conditions that resembled the contemporary era. The changes began as the Pleistocene lakes in the Mojave dried up. Some scientists argue that the desert was too dry for extended human habitation from the beginning of this era for as long as 2,000 years. There is no firm confirmation of Pinto sites in Death Valley prior to 3000 BCE, but the later Pinto Basin Complex offers the clearest articulation of the era's characteristics. Researchers disagree about the traits of Pinto-period artifacts, especially the spear and dart points that might help articulate period boundaries, but a consensus of thought posits habitation of the Pinto Basin Complex until about 700 BCE. These items appear similar to the Lake Mojave period, but the occurrence of milling stones serves to differentiate them. The similarities suggest a generalized hunting-and-gathering strategy during the era, with people inhabiting the desert during wetter periods and retreating to its fringes or oases in drier times.[3]

Although the Gypsum period, 2000 BCE to 500 CE, remains largely devoid of material cultural remains, evidence of culture and lifeways suggests intensive desert occupation and a broadening trade with coastal California and Southwest communities. Such exchanges later became more frequent. Hunters introduced the bow and arrow late in the era, allowing them greater food success, and a rich ritual life developed. Large spear and dart points overlap with Pinto points in time and morphology, suggesting a continuation of earlier hunting practices. Knives, scrapers, drills, and other small stone tools characterize period artifacts. In addition, archaeologists have found stone and shell beads, slate tablets, incised and painted pebbles, and split-twig figurines at Gypsum-period sites. They have also discovered milling stones, including mortars and pestles, at these sites. In the eastern Mojave, the influence of Pueblo culture of the Colorado Plateau region as the Gypsum period ended became evident. Figurines, pit houses, and Basketmaker III ceramics typify this influence, and the introduction of agriculture may have resulted from contact and trade. The inhabitants of the western Mojave seem to have experienced few of these developments, continuing their patterns of hunting and gathering. Researchers have found sites from this era near Death Valley at lower elevations—near current water sources and ones that now are either dry or too salty for human use—and in the mountains.[4]

During the Shoshonean period, beginning about 1200 CE and continuing until European arrival, ancestors of the Numic-speaking Paiute and Shoshones first inhabited the southwestern Great Basin. When contact with the Spanish occurred, the Panamint Shoshones and Nevada Shoshones regarded the Death Valley area as their territory, even as it served as the border between the two groups. The appearance of small Cottonwood Triangular and Desert Side-notched arrow points and locally made plainware ceramics marks the Shoshonean period. Scientists categorize such plainwares as Paiute and Shoshone utility wares. They include several varieties of knives, drills, gravers, scrapers, manos, metates, pestles, mortars, Olivella shell beads, bone beads, pendants, occasional pointed tools, incised stones, and baked and unbaked clay figurines. Large villages in valleys or along valley boundaries and smaller hunting-and-gathering camps near specific resources, at lower elevations and in the mountains, characterize human habitation during this time.[5] These groups remained in the region and greeted the first Europeans and Americans who arrived after 1800 CE.

By the nineteenth century, the Native peoples of the Mojave faced the ever-growing European presence in the New World. Spain and Mexico had seen little of value in the Mojave Desert; Spanish soldiers and settlers passed through it when necessary, as did the first Anglo-Americans, who arrived in the 1820s. When trappers and mountain men such as Jedediah Smith and Peter Skene Ogden explored the Great Basin, Death Valley and its environs offered little to these fur-trapping commercial entrepreneurs. Only with the 1838 formation of the US Army Corps of Topographical Engineers and its subsequent search for railroad routes to California did the expansionist nation look seriously at the region.[6]

The quest for a transcontinental nation gave meaning even to stark deserts, and government-sponsored expeditions and gold seekers dominated exploration throughout the 1840s. In early 1844, during his second exploration of the Far West, Captain John C. Frémont and thirty-nine explorers skirted Death Valley's perimeter. After nearly a year on the trail, Frémont was eager to reach the southern part of the Old Spanish Trail and begin his return to St. Louis. Traveling south, Frémont and his men turned east at Los Angeles. On April 27, he and his party camped at Frémont Springs, known as Salt Spring on contemporary maps. Frémont made mention of the region's paradox in his journal entries: "Throughout this nakedness of sand and gravel, were many beautiful plants and flowering shrubs, which occurred in many new species, and with greater variety than we had been accustomed to see in the most luxuriant prairie countries; this was a peculiarity of this desert."[7] This was a fitting assessment by one of the more inventive minds of the first half of the nineteenth century.

The clamor to reach California during the 1849 Gold Rush brought the next wave of Americans into Death Valley. Most of the parties entering the valley between 1849 and 1851 sought a shortcut to the goldfields. During the winter of 1849–50, at least five groups came to the area. None had declared this southern approach their first choice; all took the difficult Spanish Trail because they started late in the migration season or experienced delays along the way, making their departure from Salt Lake City too close to winter to be assured of clearing the Sierra Nevada passes before snowfall. While the lure of gold remained strong, the memory of the Donner Party disaster of 1846–47 that left more than forty dead lingered, and none wanted to wait for spring.

One of these gold-hungry groups gave Death Valley its name. During December 1849, a group of Kansans, Georgians, and others left their Utah camps for the final trek to California. Near the Las Vegas springs, two groups decided to travel directly west, following a shortcut they thought led them directly to the California fields. One group, led by Captain Edward Doty and consisting of about three dozen men from Knoxville and Galesburg, Illinois, called themselves the Jayhawkers. Another group, the Bugsmashers, included more than a dozen men who hailed mostly from Georgia and Mississippi. Three families, those of Asabel Bennett, J. B. Arcan, and Harry Wade, trailed behind with a few stragglers, most prominently William Lewis Manly. All the travelers entered Death Valley between December 22 and December 27, 1849, likely at the same place, Furnace Creek, and all faced the same obstacle, the Panamint Mountains. The Bennett group went south to Bennett's Well, while the Jayhawkers turned north and followed Emigrant Wash to the southwest. Eventually, the dry, vast, and seemingly empty area ensnared both parties.[8]

Hemmed in by snowpacks that covered the western Panamint Mountains, the separated parties rejoined and searched for a trail leading west. Unable to find an exit from the valley floor, they separated into smaller parties. A number stayed near Tule Spring, while others, including Manly and John Rodgers, searched for an escape route. After five weeks, the two men returned, reporting an exit to the south. Manly's account, penned some fifty years later, notes that three members of the party died of dehydration before he returned. Other accounts claim that only William B. Robinson expired during a separate search for a western route. Despite the differences, no account disputes the severity of their situation. Had Manly and Rodgers not returned with a way out, the party faced dire circumstances and even death. The groups reassembled and left the valley floor just north of Searles Lake at Providence Spring. Upon leaving their base camp, someone in the party reportedly commented, "Good-bye Death Valley," giving the region its foreboding name.[9]

The party left considerable physical evidence behind. The remains of a large camp stood at Furnace Creek Spring. At Jayhawker Spring to the east, either Robinson or Rood scratched the initials "W. B. R." and the year, "1849," in the lava rock. Rood inscribed "WB Rood" on a boulder near the trail between Cottonwood Canyon and Emigrant Canyon. The ill-fated 1849 party left traces at Six Springs and Bennett's Well as well. Reaching the California settlements a few weeks later, members of the party reportedly announced that large silver-ore deposits lay in the mountains surrounding Death Valley, spurring more prospecting activity in the Mojave. These rumors inspired prospectors to chance the difficult eastern Mojave and added to the knowledge that Americans possessed of the desert, setting the stage for further exploration.[10]

During the 1850s, the federal government's reconnaissance of the nation's newest acquisitions lands acquired after the Mexican War reached Death Valley. The US Army Corps of Topographical Engineers took the lead in surveying the West, performing cadastral surveys to measure, mark, and delineate land and collecting information about plants, animals, Native peoples, geology, and anything else its teams encountered. The topographical engineers preceded railroad surveying parties intent on finding a route for the transcontinental railroad. Talented scientists supported the surveying expeditions that spread across the West.

Crossing California's mountains and desert proved the greatest obstacle, and agents of the government and private companies sought safe avenues of passage. In 1853 the Pacific and Atlantic Railroad Committee retained Lieutenant Tredwell Moore to find a railroad route through eastern California and the Sierra Nevada. Although Moore did not find such a route, his expedition did map the upper reaches of Death Valley. George H. Goddard, a British artist, cartographer, and amateur naturalist who served as Moore's assistant, collected more than six hundred geological and biological samples during their stay. Three years later, the General Land Office sent a cadastral survey team, led by William Denton, to subdivide the region into quarter sections for future homesteaders. At nearly the same time, Allexey W. von Schmidt led another survey team into Panamint Valley, west of the Denton team. In 1857 a self-styled colonel from Virginia, Henry Washington, extended the cadastral survey into the center of Death Valley. All the surveys extended the definition of "suitable for homesteading" to marginal lands, but none so egregiously as Washington's. Washington marked nearly one million acres from the sink of Death Valley to the crest of the Amargosa as potential ranch and farmland, submitting a bill for more than forty thousand dollars for his work. This sum, greater than the surveyor general's annual budget, was paid before anyone challenged the veracity of Washington's claims. Despite the ludicrous expense, these surveys, published as part of the US surveyor general's 1857 map of California, provided the first detailed topography of Death Valley. By the end of the 1850s, US society had learned a considerable amount about the eastern Mojave.[11]

As more and more people determined that the region merited further attention, the mapping of its features continued. The creation of the Nevada Territory in 1861 necessitated a clear boundary line between this new state and California. As long as Nevada remained part of the distant Utah Territory, a defined boundary meant little; territorial status anticipated statehood, and the federal government had to address the question of boundaries. That year, Lieutenant Joseph Christmas Ives commanded the United States and California Boundary Commission that attempted to draw an accurate map of the California-Nevada border between Death Valley and Lake Tahoe. Washington's earlier map had already been found wanting. The Ives Party used camels as pack animals because of the arid conditions. Starting near the Colorado River, Ives and his team completed only about one-third of the project before cost overruns aborted their mission.

After the Civil War, the US military reestablished its mapping program in the West, beginning the era of the "great surveys." Lieutenant George M. Wheeler, Clarence King, the one-armed Major John Wesley Powell, and others began systematic explorations of the West and Southwest. In his late twenties, Wheeler was ambitious and precocious. In 1869 he asked to begin a large survey project in the Southwest. Army officials assigned him the task of exploring and mapping lands south of the Central Pacific Railroad in California and in eastern Nevada. Assembling one of the era's most impressive expeditions, Wheeler started in northern Nevada, bringing along the pioneer photographer Timothy O'Sullivan, reporter Frederick W. Loring, and an array of scientists, topographers, meteorologists, and other specialists. The expedition twice crossed through the heart of Death Valley. Wheeler divided his men into two parties that explored separately but rendezvoused frequently. Characteristic of Wheeler, the plan was grandiose, and unfortunately its timing was atrocious. The expedition spent the summer in the Mojave Desert, an interminably hot and difficult venture. Many of the men suffered sunstroke, as Loring, who nearly succumbed himself, reported. Wheeler emphasized Death Valley's harsh and arid character, and his party described the region in terms of its "utter desolation" and lack of water and vegetation. Rather than open the desert up for settlement, Wheeler's party further reminded the nation of its limits.[12]

Wheeler's expedition simultaneously was a success and a failure. The expedition collected some of the more accurate barometric readings of the below-sea-level elevations in Death Valley. Losing two guides during its stay, its members also discovered just how treacherous the area could be. The expedition did not help the image of the federal government in the West. California newspapers vilified Wheeler for his perceived shortcomings as a leader. Nor did the data Wheeler's men collected please government officials or the scientific community. The army realized that more exploration and mapping around Death Valley were necessary.

After the Wheeler expedition, exploration of the West continued at an accelerating pace. The government dispatched a parade of surveyors to investigate the region. Allexey von Schmidt returned to Death Valley in 1872 and finished the boundary-line survey from Lake Tahoe to the Colorado River. Captain A. B. McGowan and Lieutenant Rogers Birnie undertook additional military surveys in 1875. By 1877 the detailed mapping of Death Valley reflected solid understanding of the area's topography. Within two decades, naturalists emerged as an important source of knowledge about Death Valley. The Department of Agriculture's 1891 regional biological survey made the first significant contribution to understanding the complexity of Death Valley's natural history. Led by noted nineteenth-century biologist and naturalist C. Hart Merriam, the expedition explored the Death Valley region. Botanist Frederick V. Colville, ichthyologist Charles H. Gilbert, and Merriam all published findings beyond their Department of Agriculture reports. Some ethnographic interviews, conducted with Death Valley Native Americans by Merriam, were in print before the turn of the twentieth century.[13]

These exploratory initiatives spurred expansion, for they provided the crucial knowledge that prompted settlement and economic development. In this, explorers were national scouts, carriers of the knowledge the nation craved as it sought to fulfill its conception of Manifest Destiny.

Mining opportunities grew directly out of the surveys, which illustrated the possibilities for wealth that existed in the ground. Such opportunities proved the primary attraction for most Anglo-Americans. Gold seekers in late 1849 had sparked mining interest in southern Death Valley and the eastern Mojave Desert. In the Panamint Mountains, two men found what they suspected was a large deposit of silver and carried samples out of the region. Legend suggests that one melted the ore to fashion a rifle sight. Other miners repeated this story, and the Lost Gunsight Mine became an oft-told legend, another of the many fabled lost mines that dotted the West. Like many such stories, later travelers could never verify it. The accounts suggest that if the mine existed, it might have been somewhere in the Panamint Mountains or Argus Range.[14]

The push to mine Death Valley's wealth began in the decades after the California strikes. Fueled by rumors of the Lost Gunsight Mine, the discovery of gold at Salt Springs near the Amargosa River, and the 1855 opening of the Comstock Lode on the Sierra Nevada's Washoe Front, mineral exploration in the Death Valley area preceded with alacrity. It began, as did most mining in the West, with the grit, determination, and outright good fortune of individual prospectors. E. Darwin French and Samuel G. George led two groups of prospectors through Death Valley in 1860. While prospecting, French and George discovered gold and silver mines in the Coso and Slate Ranges and an antimony mine in Wildrose Canyon; these findings received significant publicity, but ultimately proved not very profitable.[15]

The increase in the number of prospectors led to greater tensions between Native Americans and miners, as social systems with different cultural and economic values collided. Incoming Euro-American miners imposed their cultural template on the area, upsetting Native Americans' patterns of life. In response, desert dwellers acted to protect their traditional lands against miners, who often behaved with little respect for Native rights. At times during the growing tensions, miners feared real or imagined Native American attacks, and many abandoned claims at Salt Springs, at Coso, and in the Slate Range.[16]

In a reprise of a pattern common throughout the Intermountain West, these conflicts led to federal intervention. Miners sought help from the national government, which provided troops to maintain order while its representatives pressured Native peoples to cede their potentially mineral-rich lands. While the Death Valley area did not experience the full-scale onslaught seen in the California Gold Rush or the Comstock Lode, its Native peoples felt the heavy hand of Anglo-American society upon them. After the Ruby Valley Treaty of October 1, 1863, the western bands of the Shoshone Nation generally cooperated with US authorities, but their compliance helped them little. Especially in the California desert, far from northeastern Nevada where the federal government and the Shoshone representatives negotiated the treaty, the United States rarely kept the promises it made.[17]

Without support for treaty conditions and provisions, prospectors enjoyed de facto control of relations with Native Americans in and around Death Valley. The 1863 treaty had expressly guaranteed their rights to prospect and mine, resulting in an intimidating chaos. A revolution in population happened in a brief time. By 1870 most Native peoples had fled the mining areas or been subdued, for the onslaught of miners and the people that accompanied them made life hard for Native Americans. After their departure, miners worked without fear of attack. Prospectors flocked to the desert in greater numbers. In 1873 three significant mineral finds occurred west of Death Valley: at Panamint; at Darwin, on the west side of the Argus Range; and at Lookout, on the Argus's east side. Venture capital secured before the national economic downturn of 1873 allowed the construction of kilns at Wildrose Spring to supply charcoal for smelting to regional mines, and miners continued development even as the national economy threatened to collapse.[18]

Mineral excavation brought new settlements to Death Valley that had little to do with mining, yet evolved in response to the miners' needs and fostered economic opportunities for Native Americans. Andrew J. Laswell, a Kentucky native, was Death Valley's first Anglo-American homesteader. Laswell and his partner, Cal Mowrey, started a hay ranch in 1874 at Bennett's Well to supply feed for animals working at the mines. Later in that decade, William L. Hunter started the Hunter Mountain Ranch, where he kept animals for a pack-train venture at Cerro Gordo. During the 1870s and 1880s, Native Americans, including Hungry Bill, a Panamint Shoshone, and George Hansen, known as Indian George, returned to Death Valley ranches abandoned as a result of tension with miners. Kentuckian William Johnson had started a truck garden on the west side of Death Valley and planted fruit trees in the canyon later named for him. Hungry Bill and Hansen replanted the gardens, terraced and irrigated several additional acres, and planted more peach trees. Hungry Bill's brother, Panamint Tom, started a ranch in Warm Spring Canyon, while Indian George began another ranch at the mouth of Hall Canyon.[19]

The search for mineral wealth continued even as other Americans followed the explorers and prospectors to Death Valley. Prospectors canvassed the region in search of minerals, staking claims and luring more miners with every success. In this, their experience mirrored the unorganized model of mining common in the California Gold Rush: miners were in search of a strike, yet lacked the ability or the resources to dig deep beneath the surface. Their limitations impeded their success and undercut their capacity to form and maintain communities. Those new populations would last only as long as miners could easily find accessible resources.

Some extractive endeavors demanded greater organization and capital. After initial discoveries, silver and lead mines required enormous investments of capital, altering the regional terrain. Panamint, on the west side of the Panamint Range, became the most famous but least productive of the silver-lead districts of the late 1870s. After silver discoveries in Surprise Canyon, Nevada's US senators William Morris Stewart and John P. Jones bought the Panamint mines for more than $250,000, organized the Panamint Mining Company, and started Death Valley's biggest nineteenth-century mining rush. Stewart had been deeply involved in the Comstock Lode as an attorney. In the Senate, he became the champion of the 1866 mining law that gave prospectors almost complete run of the public domain. He later served as president of the Sutro Tunnel Company, an important effort to support the Comstock's development, before leaving politics temporarily in 1874 to pursue new mining opportunities. Jones had made his fortune in the Comstock and was purported to have spent as much as $800,000 securing his Senate seat. Eliphalet P. Raines, a smooth-talking southerner, brought Jones into the mining district, and the junior senator persuaded his equally avaricious colleague. By the time the two were finished, the Panamint Mining Company was worth $2 million in capitalized stock, but at its peak the yield from claims barely met the costs of capitalization.[20]

Despite the limited economic success, a city of two thousand grew from a small tent camp. The community included more than fifteen saloons, a newspaper, butcher shops, barbershops, bakeries, assayers, jewelers, and pharmacies. Three stage lines served the town. It took the name Panamint City even as the mines began to yield less silver, and within two years of its founding, the community started to recede; by 1877 the silver had played out, extinguishing the town's reason for existence. For a time during the 1870s, the area held the most significant California desert mining districts. The mines at Darwin and Lookout each had produced $2 million during their heyday. Miners established lesser extractive ventures at Chloride Cliff and Lee in the Funeral Mountains, on the east side of Death Valley.[21]

Borax became the next mining bonanza in Death Valley. Widely used in the United States for softening water, in medical treatments of eyes and wounds, and as an aid to female complexion, the nation imported borax until its discovery in the California desert. Californians long searched for a domestic source, first finding the material in abundance in the state's northern half. Operations there failed eventually, leaving a void in the market. Two southern California mining entrepreneurs, Dennis Searles and E. M. Skellings, discovered borax near Argus in the early 1870s. However, serious commercial development failed to occur, as falling prices for silver combined with the panic of 1873 to thwart hopes for launching a substantial borax market.[22]

The most productive borax mining operations in Death Valley history began ten years later. Isadore Daunet, a French immigrant who had spent more than half his life roaming the US West, noticed a white crystalline mineral when he crossed Death Valley in 1875. Unable to determine its value, he discarded his samples. In 1881 Daunet heard a rumor that another miner, Aaron Winters, sent similar samples to William T. Coleman, a San Francisco mining entrepreneur. Coleman's representatives reportedly paid Winters $20,000 for all claims with the intention of starting a borax mine. Daunet enlisted help from three friends, raced to Death Valley, and staked a claim on 275 acres of borax-laden land near Bennett's Well, twenty-two miles south of Furnace Creek. By the time Coleman's team arrived, Daunet's Eagle Borax Works was in operation. By June 1883, Daunet had incorporated his company, married, and even found a way to lower the exorbitant shipping costs that cut into his profit. Soon after, Daunet's operation collapsed because of simple bad luck, and one year later, he was nearly bankrupt. Borax prices fell, his wife secretly filed for divorce, and the despondent Daunet took his life on May 28, 1884.[23]

By that time, Coleman had started the Harmony Borax Works at Furnace Creek. Between 1884 and 1888, his company worked the Harmony operation in rotation with the Meridian Borax Company, located at a higher elevation east of Death Valley at Resting Springs. Harmony was a large operation, with two 3,000-gallon dissolving tanks, eight 2,000-gallon settling tanks, and fifty-seven 1,800-gallon crystallizing tanks. It operated about eight months of the year; summer heat interrupted the operation by making it impossible for the borax to crystallize. Between June and October, workers shifted operations to the Amargosa, where the slight difference in temperature allowed production to continue even during the summer's extreme heat. Transportation of the borax proved the most difficult problem facing Coleman's operation. Enormous wagons hauled loads of borax 165 miles to the railhead at Mojave, California. This system allowed Coleman to move more than 2.5 million pounds of borax out of Death Valley every year and later led to the creation of the popular image of the twenty-mule-team wagons.[24]

Even during America's Gilded Age, which favored business at every turn, many operations closed, and Harmony Borax eventually became one of those failures. The aggressive economic climate had negative consequences for men such as Coleman, who searched constantly for ways to monopolize the borax industry. Soon after starting the Harmony and Meridian operations, Coleman's field teams discovered a new and richer type of borax, which became known as colemanite.

Other miners claimed colemanite deposits near Calico, south of Death Valley, and significantly closer to the Mojave railroad. Coleman bought out all the claims he could afford and purchased a soap factory in Alameda, California, intending to convert it into a colemanite processing works. The combined stress of all these interests and poor yields drove Coleman into bankruptcy in 1889.

Coleman's longtime rival, Francis Marion Smith, acquired all of his assets and consolidated the various holdings into the Pacific Coast Borax Company in September 1890. Smith's first move was to shut down the Harmony and Meridian operations and hold them in reserve to the Calico mines. He opened a Wall Street office and hired Joseph Mather to run the East Coast operation. Mather selected his son, Stephen T. Mather, who later became the National Park Service's first director, to head the company's advertising and promotion efforts. Mather received the credit for conceiving the "Twenty-Mule-Team Borax" product name. Long before 1916, when Congress established the National Park Service, Steve Mather knew a great deal about Death Valley.[25]

Workers eventually depleted the borax at Calico, forcing Smith and his company to search elsewhere for the mineral. His field teams developed colemanite borax reserves at Old Ryan, on the east side of Death Valley in 1903, and opened the Lila C. Mine. With great difficulty, Smith built a railroad to serve the Lila C., but its completion cost more than $3 million and came after two other railroads had already reached the mining district. Although Smith's railroad successfully hauled enormous quantities of borax, it precipitated the end of his empire.

Within a decade, borax revenues significantly diminished, and Smith experienced Coleman's fate. As early as 1910, he was engaged in an elaborate pyramid scheme, acquiring new loans to pay old ones. In December 1910, he formed United Properties of California, a holding company designed to consolidate his assets and provide his creditors with the illusion of greater stability. Even these maneuvers did not slow the decline. In 1913, as the borax operation began to collapse, Smith's holding company became insolvent. The Death Valley railroad was only one of a number of grandiose failures. Although he never succeeded in reclaiming industry dominance, Smith's title as the "Borax King" persisted long after his death in 1931.[26]

Old Ryan, the town at the heart of the colemanite boom, never grew as did its early-twentieth-century peers such as Rhyolite, but when the Lila C. played out, a new site on the west side of the Greenwater Range overlooking Furnace Creek Wash attracted attention. By 1915 prospectors had filed a number of claims in the area. The operations exceeded two hundred tons a day by 1919, about twice the output of the Lila C. A town, New Ryan, sprang up, marked by claim jumping that required adjudication by the courts. After 1934 the mines at Old Ryan and New Ryan became the most profitable operations for Borax Consolidated.

In the end, however, the more than $30 million in product that came from the area could not supersede competition from new producers such as the American Potash and Chemical Company. By 1927 Borax Consolidated closed its mining operations in the Death Valley area.[27]

Gold extraction still retained the characteristics of the individualist phase of mining even after the development of the borax operation. Unlike borax, which required elaborate processing, gold could be sold as it was located. It became the last hope of the small miner, the iconic prospector of the Old West with his burro and his gold pan. Death Valley held promise for such people. Gold had been the original attraction at Death Valley, but borax had temporarily superseded it. Two men who became the region's most famous personalities, Jean-Pierre "Pete" Aguerreberry and Frank "Shorty" Harris, set off a new rush when they made a different kind of strike at Harrisburg.

The two were as different as prospectors could be. Aguerreberry, born in southern France in 1874, immigrated to the United States in 1890. A novice miner, Aguerreberry arrived in Death Valley fifteen years late and met Shorty Harris at Furnace Creek Ranch. Harris had already achieved prospecting fame in the nearby Tonopah, Nevada, gold boom. In 1904 he found surface ore in the Bullfrog Mountains, and a gold rush quickly followed. Following his discovery, Harris, whose ore deposits assayed at $700 per ton, went on a three-week celebratory drinking binge. In a stupor, Harris supposedly sold the Bullfrog gold mine for $1,000 and three barrels of whiskey. Before leaving Bullfrog, Harris helped found the boomtown of Rhyolite, just west of today's Beatty, Nevada. In August 1905, he and Aguerreberry headed to Ballarat, another mining strike, to try to make new fortunes there.[28]

On their way to Ballarat, the men stumbled across a new strike. Harris hurried down the trail toward town, while Aguerreberry stopped on a well-traveled trail near the flat of the head of Blackwater Canyon and found ore on a large barren cropping. The two staked claims and continued to Ballarat, where the legend grew. In the new mining town, Harris loudly talked in the saloons of his find. Reports of assays of more than $500 a ton attracted even more attention. Harris and Aguerreberry returned to their stakes and found more than twenty miners working. Within ten days, as many as three hundred men scoured the area; after two months, more than five hundred were at the site. Harris and Aguerreberry retained some control of the strike as a result of their land claims. Aguerreberry had filed claims on the north side of the hill, which he called Eureka. Harris filed his claims on the south side, which soon became a three-hundred-person tent city called Harrisburg. Miners had to import water from Emigrant Spring, Blackwater Spring, and Wild Rose Spring. As was typical of mining booms, the town and claims were short-lived. After a two-year ownership battle with investors,

Aguerreberry gained permanent control of the Eureka site, working his claim alone for almost forty years, until his health no longer permitted the physical demands of mining. He died on November 23, 1945.[29]

Success at Ballarat led to another significant gold strike. In December 1903, Jack Keane, an unemployed Irish miner, and Domingo Etcharren, a Basque butcher, left Ballarat to prospect for silver south of Chloride Cliff. After several months of working a single ledge without success, Keane stumbled on an immense vein of gold not far from where he had been toiling, leading him to name the claim the "Keane Wonder Mine." News of the find spread fast: by the following summer, more than five hundred miners worked the area near Keane. Keane and Etcharren filed eighteen claims to protect their interests.[30]

In the pattern of such strikes, offers to buy the Keane Wonder Mine poured in. J. R. Delamar paid Keane and Etcharren $10,000 for an option to purchase the mine for $150,000 at the end of one year. Delamar developed the Keane during that period, bringing in thirty workers and building an assay office, a general office building, and a wagon road across the desert that reached within one mile of the mine; he spent most of his capital in development and at the end of the year lacked the money to complete the purchase. The partners took back the property, complete with improvements, and looked for another buyer. The process repeated itself in 1906, when L. L. Patrick purchased the option. Before he could complete his extravagant development plans, his one-year bond expired. John Campbell, a speculator from Goldfield, Nevada, then purchased the mine for $250,000, and this sale served as the high point in the Keane Wonder Mine's history.[31]

At Skidoo another version of Death Valley's mining story took place. As at each of the other mines, the owners predicated their operation on hope and a little bit of luck, in this case generating one of the two largest-producing gold mines in Death Valley. A pair of miners originally headed for the Harrisburg strike found the gold that initiated the rush in March 1906. John L. "Harry" Ramsey and John A. "One Eye" Thompson went on to file twenty-six claims under the name Gold Eagle. Bullfrog, Nevada, mining millionaire E. A. "Bob" Montgomery soon bought most of the claims. The operators founded the Skidoo Mines Company, and as was typical, a town followed. Within one year, seven hundred people called Skidoo home. Two years and $500,000 in investment later, the mine produced its first significant yield. Skidoo Mines Company paid $200,000 for a water pipeline to supply the growing town site and power a mill, becoming the linchpin of the mine's productivity.[32]

After the turn of the twentieth century, lead and copper replaced gold and silver as the main mineral interests in the desert. As part of the early-1900s mining boom in Nevada and California, towns such as Leadfield, on the Titus Canyon road, boomed in Death Valley. Early in the new century, Clay Tallman, a Rhyolite attorney who later became commissioner of the Department of the Interior's General Land Office, brought the first ore samples out of the area. Assayers valued the finds at $40 a ton. Miners filed lead and copper claims in the area as early as 1905, but the high cost of shipping ore from the canyons doomed these early ventures. In March 1924, prospectors Ben Chambers and Frank Metts came to Titus Canyon and staked out claims on numerous lead deposits. They sold their claims to John Salsberry, who formed the Western Lead Mines Company. As 1925 ended, he had increased the number of claims owned from the original twelve to more than fifty. Eighteen men started building an automobile road out of the canyon. Workers added a boardinghouse and pipeline from Keane Spring by January 1926, the same month that Leadfield received its name. Six mining companies operated in the town, and shares in the Western Lead Mines Company sold for $1.57 each.[33]

As Leadfield prospered, C. C. Julian, who became president of the Western Lead Mines Company, arrived. A flamboyant oil promoter from the Los Angeles area, Julian was already deeply immersed in the town's biggest financial scandal in the 1920s, an oil-stock swindle, and he sought refuge in the desert. In his colorful style, he advertised the sale of stock in a venture he called Jazz Baby, manipulating the value of the stock on the Los Angeles Stock Exchange. To increase investor interest, Julian often brought visitors to Leadfield. They typically came by train from Los Angeles to Beatty and then traveled the final fifty miles over his newly completed road from Rhyolite to Titus Canyon. Julian gave potential investors an outdoor feast, with an orchestra playing in the background, and then offered a mine tour. As March 1926 ended, he had sold more than three hundred thousand shares of company stock, at an average of $3.30 a share.[34]

Then the California State Corporation Commission began investigating Julian for selling stocks without a permit. At the same time, Leadfield investors learned that one of the richest lead veins had bottomed out, heralding the town's end. In January 1927, the post office closed, and the community became a ghost town. Julian moved to Oklahoma, but faced indictment there for mail fraud in 1933. He fled to Shanghai, China, where he committed suicide a year later at the age of forty. His legacy, the Titus Canyon road, built at an estimated cost of $60,000, heralded a future that promised better access to the outside world for everyone in Death Valley.[35]

By the time Julian's world collapsed, the nature of mining had radically changed. In the late nineteenth century, prospecting made sense for social and economic reasons; by the early twentieth century, the larger economic conditions in the nation and scope and scale of investment demanded much greater returns than a prospector could provide. A regional society based in three-hundred- to one-thousand-person tent cities rushing around the western desert in search of the next strike promised little permanence. As mining grew in value, it precipitated an important transformation clearly evident in many of the Death Valley–area strikes. Although prospectors still made significant initial finds, more often they looked to quickly sell them to large companies with the capital to support sophisticated operations. In this respect, the prospectors were heirs to a tradition that started on the Comstock and continued throughout the West. As mining required greater technological intensiveness, miners became scouts for great finds that they soon sold to large companies for as much as they could negotiate. The discoverers of the Keane, Leadfield, Harrisburg, and Skidoo mines all followed this pattern, allowing for the extraction of wealth, but doing little to establish a permanent desert presence.[36]

On occasion, these prospecting entrepreneurs pointed toward a different future, one that had little to do with actual mining. In this respect, Walter Scott, better known as "Death Valley Scotty," took a prominent role in shaping Death Valley. Born in 1872 near Cynthiana, Kentucky, the fourteen-year-old Scott ran away to join two brothers in Nevada. He worked as a water boy on a survey crew, as a laborer for the Harmony Borax Works, and even as a roughrider for "Buffalo Bill" Cody's Wild West Show. Among his many and often wild contentions, he claimed to have been one of Cody's close friends and drinking companions but said he left the show in 1902 to chase a mining strike after he and Cody had a falling out.[37]

A flamboyant man, Scotty was a compulsive attention seeker, con artist, and showman. On July 9, 1905, a three-car Atchison, Topeka, and Santa Fe Railroad special train, the Death Valley Coyote, bolted out of La Grande Station in Los Angeles. In the last car stood Scott, waving a roll of currency after claiming to have struck it rich in a secret Death Valley mine. His stunt broke the record for travel time between Los Angeles and Chicago, establishing him as an archetypal early-twentieth-century celebrity. It was an era of "firsts," and Scott's travel record gave the con man–turned-celebrity new entrée to the wealthy. Among the many whom Scott attempted to pull into his mining schemes was Albert Johnson, a Chicago life insurance magnate who had grubstaked Scott the previous fall. When Scott shook free of all the attention from his train event, he quickly went to meet with the enterprising Johnson. The meeting began a relationship that lasted the rest of Johnson's life.[38]

Scot's celebrity was short-lived: the public quickly perceived Scott as a scoundrel. Still, Johnson stuck with him. He enjoyed Scott's company and continued to invest in his schemes despite public derision and evidence that no mining potential existed in any of Scott's operations. Johnson found Scott fascinating, telling his corporate business partner, Robert D. Lay, that "Scott is such an uneasy fellow, and so shrewd, too, that you don't know half the time whether he is just talking or is telling you something. He is good company though, and a nice fellow to be with. He has them all guessing, me with the rest."[39]

Johnson was just as entranced with Death Valley when he first visited it in 1906, later referring to it as "a place of his heart." This powerful affinity for place was characteristic of affluent men of his time. Many of his class and background found ranches, farms, or summer places that became precious to them, and during the twentieth century's first decades, they purchased and transformed such locations. While such transactions were often the epitome of self-interest, they also seeded a nascent preservationism. Some individuals, such as geologist Wallace Pratt, eventually made gifts of their holdings to the National Park Service; others, such as Chicago industrialist Walter Paepcke at Aspen, created communities that captured the national imagination. Johnson's effort shared elements of both categories. In subsequent years, he acquired more than fifteen hundred acres in Death Valley. The Steininger Ranch, developed in the 1880s as a grape, vegetable, and fig farm, became his most important component. Nestled in a spring-fed valley, it became the site of Death Valley Ranch.[40]

For several years, Johnson used the Steininger site as his camp, residing in several canvas-tent platforms erected by his workers. The campsite stood on the north side of Grapevine Canyon at an elevation of three thousand feet. In a 1909 photograph, the Steininger Ranch included an irrigated pasture for grazing horses, with a grove of cottonwood trees along a nearby stream. Several buildings within the grove formed the ranch headquarters. In 1922 Johnson built three simple frame and stucco structures, the largest of which was two stories high and ninety-six feet long. He preferred this unadorned style of architecture, which was consistent with the religious fundamentalism that guided his life. He had asked noted architect Frank Lloyd Wright to design the buildings, but the staid Johnson found the resulting drawings too esoteric. Johnson's wife, Bessie, raised in Northern California, preferred Stanford University's mission-revival buildings. She convinced her husband to remodel the ranch in "provincial Spanish," as she called the popular style of the time, with an old Stanford friend, engineer Matt Roy Thompson, as head of the construction.[41]

While construction proceeded in Grapevine Canyon, Johnson had a small, finely crafted bungalow, garage, and shed built on the Lower Grapevine tract. The bungalow served as a residence for Scott and as a sometime retreat for Albert Johnson when he visited the ranch from his Los Angeles home, a place to escape the attention naturally drawn to the fantastic desert castle. Throughout the 1920s, he struggled with claimants for Grapevine Canyon and other nearby lands, winning some major battles but finding control of the region elusive.[42]

The ever-enterprising Scott capitalized on the construction of Johnson's house to announce to the world that he was building a castle in Death Valley. After a decadelong hiatus, he again became standard fare in the country's newspapers. Johnson reveled in the attention, collecting scrapbooks of Scott's coverage. Work on the complex of buildings continued in Upper Grapevine Canyon for the next five years. Johnson suffered large financial losses in the Depression of 1929, which along with a land dispute with the government led to an end to construction in 1931. The Johnsons managed to complete an ornate residence, which featured the main castle building with its annex, hacienda, chimes tower, powerhouse, stable, garage, and gas house. Collectively, the structures became known as Scotty's Castle.[43]

Johnson considered restarting work on the castle several years after the Depression, but never continued. He and his wife continued their frequent visits until Bessie Johnson died in an automobile accident in 1943. When Albert Johnson died five years later, his will deeded the property to the Gospel Foundation of California, a charitable corporation founded by Johnson in 1947 to "carry on the work of the Lord." The Gospel Foundation gave tours through the castle and provided accommodations for guests. It allowed Scott to live at the ranch and later at the castle until his death in 1954.[44]

Scott's flair put Death Valley on the map in a new way, and people in great numbers flocked to see the castle complex. As a result, a small sightseeing business began, typical of the local versions of the tourist industry that dotted the West in the early twentieth century. At Stovepipe Wells, what had been a private development turned into a small hotel. When the Bullfrog gold strike began in 1906, Rhyolite merchants subscribed to a fifty-six-mile road to connect their enterprises to the new strike. Eventually, the road continued to Skidoo. Bullfrog's preeminent millionaire, Bob Montgomery, had his crews build from one direction, while James R. Clark and his workers graded the other way. At the juncture, Clark built the Stovepipe Road House at a well to attract the growing number of passersby. By 1907 the small dugout there had tents for groceries, an eatery, a bar, lodging, and a bathhouse. Clark also installed a telephone on the line from Skidoo, the first in Death Valley. He later conceived of a resort for the spot, but neither he nor Smith, the "Borax King," ever made the investment to develop "Old" Stovepipe Wells.[45] Death Valley remained too remote and frightening to attract the tourist trade.

Yet tourism continued its rise in importance in the Southwest, and businessmen did not overlook its allure for the Death Valley region. Because mining was a boom-bust economy, drawing thousands one year and leaving remnants scattered across the desert the next, those who imagined the desert's next big score wanted greater permanence. They tied their plans to the democratization of travel resulting from the automobile. As Americans spread out across the country in their Tin

Lizzies, the possibility of bringing enough of them to Death Valley to sustain a tourist business took shape.[46]

One such visionary was a young electrical engineer from West Virginia, Herman W. "Bob" Eichbaum. He had arrived in the region in 1907 and helped build the electrical plant at Rhyolite. After the mine shuttered, he moved to Southern California, keeping Death Valley and the Amargosa River in mind. In 1925 he returned to the desert to build his dream hotel at Stovepipe Wells. To give his hotel a chance of success, Eichbaum needed to construct a road; the state ultimately permitted him to build from Darwin Falls, where the road from Dunes Valley ended, to his property. Drifting sand hindered his efforts, so in the end he moved the resort operation to the road's end and took its name from what is now called Old Stovepipe, five miles away. There he constructed a collection of bungalows that opened as Death Valley's first resort on November 1, 1926. The fifty-bungalow operation sported a searchlight that assisted lost travelers, a restaurant, general store, and filling station. Within a few years, Eichbaum added a swimming pool, tennis court, makeshift golf course, and airfield. After Eichbaum died suddenly of meningitis in 1932, his wife, Helene, continued the business.[47]

Eichbaum's capture of the toll-road franchise spurred competitors and led to rivalries between different segments of the Death Valley population. Frank Jenifer, general manager of Borax Consolidated's Tonopah and Tidewater Railroad, had advocated tourist development in Death Valley as early as 1905. The crusty innovator sought to revive the railroad's sagging fortunes, but only after the decline in borax prices did his superiors pay much attention. Enlisting the support of the Union Pacific Railroad, which had taken over the old San Pedro, Los Angeles, and Salt Lake Railroad, Jenifer had plans drawn for a resort at Furnace Creek. Finally, the borax company agreed to build it, creating the Death Valley Hotel Company, with Jenifer as president.[48]

Close ties between the National Park Service and Pacific Coast Borax led the agency to offer assistance to the company's Furnace Creek Inn. When the inn opened in 1927, Stephen T. Mather and his second in command, Horace Albright, recommended the new resort hire Beulah Brown, a skilled manager from Old Faithful Lodge in Yellowstone, who brought the lodge staff down to Death Valley in the winter months and returned with them to Yellowstone for the summer. Such support did a great deal to establish the difference between professional operations such as the Furnace Creek Inn and independent ones such as Eichbaum's Stove Pipe Wells.[49]

In the field of visitor services, Mather's National Park Service valued professionalism and national presence. Throughout the first two decades of agency history, Mather and Albright favored larger national business concerns over smaller local ones, believing that the national operations offered better and more consistent service to park visitors. The two National Park Service leaders worked with companies they deemed reputable to provide visitors with high-quality experiences, and they made their expertise available outside the park system as well. Among those they favored were railroads: at Glacier and Yellowstone, Grand Canyon and Zion, visitors enjoyed railroad-owned lodges inside park boundaries.[50] Because the Furnace Creek operation modeled itself on these National Park Service advantages, it may have stimulated agency interest in Death Valley as a possible park site.

That would make sense, for by the time the National Park Service expanded its sphere of influence in the 1920s, Death Valley had receded from its prominence as a mining center in the previous half century; the frenetic activity that intermittently transformed the region slowed, and population dwindled. With its obvious economic potential exhausted, something else could be done with the region. Tourism was one such possibility.

CHAPTER 2

On the Periphery

At its establishment in 1933, Death Valley National Monument was an anomaly among US national park areas, an enormous reserve in a region that many Americans did not regard as special. Most Americans thought of the national parks as places of monumental scenic grandeur, and many still treated the nation's desert areas as wasteland, far less valuable than the scenic mountains and great chasms that had defined the nation since the time of Thomas Jefferson. Following the 1872 creation of Yellowstone National Park, scenic and spectacular national parks became the norm for landscape preservation, a formula that was institutionalized with the 1916 establishment of the National Park Service. Influenced by the romantic art movement of the late nineteenth century that had begun in the United States with the Hudson River School of painters, was personified in the American West by artists such as Thomas Moran, and was explained by thinkers such as Clarence Dutton, Americans embraced the spectacular as a vivid reflection of their society's virtue.[1]

Scenic parks dominated the Park Service's goals throughout the seventeen-year tenure of the National Park Service's first director, Stephen T. Mather, and his right-hand man and later successor, Horace M. Albright. Californians both, Mather and Albright appreciated the impact of spectacular scenery on the public imagination. Despite their intimate knowledge of the California desert, the two men pushed for the creation of mountaintop parks throughout the nation, as these areas' distinctiveness made it easy to garner public support for them.[2]

In this formulation, desert park areas such as Death Valley were an afterthought. The late-nineteenth-century definition of natural beauty tended to exclude deserts, despite a body of literature—from George Wharton James to

Edna Brush Perkins—that extolled these dry lands' "endless solitude." As the 1930s began, Congress had not seriously considered Death Valley for inclusion in the national park system, and would not until a vision of nature different from the one current in the early twentieth century had emerged.[3]

Ongoing mining in the area, an extractive process that was anathema to the National Park Service conception of America the Beautiful, further muddied park possibilities at Death Valley. Only rarely did the National Park Service tolerate commercial use in any form. Inholdings and prior land claims pushed the limits of agency forbearance; temporary grazing in Yosemite National Park during World War I, for instance, had ignited passionate objection. This powerful definition made it difficult to consider Death Valley for any category of national park area, much less worthy of the coveted national park status.[4]

Mather ran the early National Park Service as he had his business career, using his business connections to further public-service objectives. Mather's frequent travels were replete with meetings with local officials, landowners, and business leaders, at which he talked, persuaded, even cajoled them into supporting national park projects. After making his fortune promoting Twenty-Mule-Team Borax, Mather remained closely connected to the mining industry and to the Pacific Coast Borax Company. Yet Mather rarely promoted Death Valley, feeling that his personal history in the borax industry compromised his credibility in this particular instance. His reticence was unnecessary. Even during the heated 1920s, when the Teapot Dome scandal toppled Secretary of the Interior Albert B. Fall, Mather's informal lobbying and his offers to take political and civic leaders on area tours did not contravene the era's standards of conflict of interest. Mather's fear of tarnishing his reputation stalled efforts to make a park in the California desert. Instead, throughout the 1920s, he promoted national parks in the eastern half of the nation and Utah's scenic wonderlands.[5]

Changing economic conditions made a park area at Death Valley a possibility. In 1926 Pacific Coast Borax, which held countless mining claims in the area, including one at the mouth of Furnace Creek Wash, closed its mining operations in Death Valley. Borax reserves had diminished significantly, so much so that in February 1927, the company opened a hotel at the mouth of Furnace Creek Wash. To lure tourists, it purchased a gasoline-powered passenger car for the Death Valley rail line, imported tour buses similar to the ones the Union Pacific Railroad used in the Utah national parks, and developed an impressive winter-visitor business. Although logistical problems abounded, tourism gained momentum, and the company considered further investments in the recreational property. It hoped to benefit from the national park imprimatur; the Atchison, Topeka, and Santa Fe Railroad enjoyed a near monopoly on tourism at the Grand Canyon, while the Union Pacific controlled the nearby Utah park trade, and the borax company leaders recognized the advantages of a national park designation. Pacific Coast Borax officials sought to persuade Mather that Death Valley would make a fine addition to the national park system, and they invited him to inspect the region.[6]

Although he had worked for Pacific Coast Borax, Mather had never explored Death Valley in any systematic way. Excited at the prospect of the area's inclusion but still wary of the appearance of a conflict of interest, Mather invited Albright and a number of agency officials to join him. In January 1927, the group, along with Pacific Coast Borax representatives, toured Death Valley and its environs. The National Park Service people raised questions about boundary lines, the effect of national park status on mining claims, the scarcity of water for service facilities, and the obvious displeasure some residents felt at the prospect of having a national park area in their backyard. Privately, Mather still worried that his ties to Pacific Coast Borax would lead to charges of improper influence if he championed the area for the national park system. The region's diversity and its scientific and scenic potential impressed the National Park Service group, but mining claims inside the proposed park still gave the director pause. Despite the enthusiasm of Pacific Coast Borax, much of the region's best land was beyond federal jurisdiction, ensuring that park establishment would require either the generosity of powerful interests or congressional appropriation. Neither seemed likely. In 1927 Death Valley lacked the combination of features and public land that typically simplified the park-origination process.[7]

After Herbert Hoover's presidential election in 1928, the chances of adding Death Valley to the national park system improved. As with many members of his social class, Hoover was an avid conservationist who enjoyed the outdoors and was a strong supporter of national park initiatives. After Mather's poor health forced him to leave the agency directorship in January 1929, Hoover replaced the agency's founder with Albright. Thorny, acerbic, and extraordinarily proficient, Albright proceeded with plans for Death Valley. He had been the National Park Service's inside man throughout the 1920s, bringing a decade of experience and close relationships with influential figures to the task of guiding national park proposals through Congress. He had a personal stake in the creation of a national park area in Death Valley, but existing mining claims remained an obstacle that continued to challenge agency assumptions about the site's value. Albright recognized that Pacific Coast Borax's cooperation in any park endeavor was crucial. The company appeared to have decided that tourism was its future in Death Valley, but Albright felt compelled to assure Pacific Coast Borax leaders that any federal legislation would allow mining in Death Valley to continue. In return, he hoped that the company would continue to offer the project its enthusiastic support.[8]

During the 1920s, the National Park Service expanded in size, theme, and geographic reach. Well established by the end of the decade, the agency could plan its future with a greater degree of certainty. Throughout this period, Albright pushed the agency past its emphasis on spectacular scenery. Most of the places in the public domain that fitted nineteenth-century definitions of beauty already were in the park system. Although Albright announced in 1930 that he believed he was "rounding out the park system for all time," he also recognized that to continue to grow, the National Park Service needed new definitions of national park area–caliber features. The desert offered precisely the opportunities he coveted. Mather's affection for Death Valley and Albright's desire to commemorate his predecessor combined with Albright's political skill to put the area squarely in the agency's plans.[9]

After Mather died in 1930, Albright moved to consolidate the National Park Service's strategic position in the federal government. A lifelong Republican who was closely identified with the Hoover administration, Albright was keenly aware of the legislative tools available for national park area establishment. Chief among them was the Antiquities Act of 1906, which allowed the president to proclaim national monuments from unallocated public land. Albright had relied upon the Antiquities Act throughout his tenure as Mather's chief assistant. He advocated its liberal use during the 1920s even as he developed close relationships with Congress that led to greater support for legislatively established parklands. Long before he became director, Albright had become a master at encouraging the political process to yield desired results.[10]

In 1930 Albright demonstrated the agency's growing interest in Death Valley. Since its founding, the National Park Service had devised a successful strategy for assessing park lands; time and again, it sent one of its trusted representatives to view prospective areas, following up with detailed reports and then using the reports to persuade its friends in Congress. Albright followed this strategy at Death Valley. He sent Roger W. Toll, superintendent of Yellowstone National Park, and Charles Goff Thomson, Toll's counterpart at Yosemite National Park, to conduct detailed studies of eastern California. During the 1920s, Toll had become the agency's leading evaluator of national park proposals. He and Albright pursued similar objectives for the agency, and the new director could count on Toll and Thomson to provide him with the positive endorsements needed to carry out the National Park Service's mission. No surprise, Toll and Thomson urged national park or monument status for Death Valley. Albright requested temporary withdrawal of the area, a technique by which the General Land Office temporarily excluded new claims until final disposition occurred. Hoover signed the withdrawal directive, Executive Order 5408, on July 25, 1930.[11]

Albright continued to generate momentum for Death Valley's inclusion in the park system. In February 1931, he instructed Sequoia National Park superintendent Colonel John R. White to provide another report on Death Valley. White found Death Valley impressive, calling the view from Aguerreberry Point as spectacular as any in the park system. During his visit, he met Walter Scott, "Death Valley Scotty," and toured Scotty's Castle. He also encountered Herman W. "Bob" Eichbaum, the owner of the Stove Pipe Wells Hotel. White shrewdly divined the level of support for such a project, and his report focused on how to operate a park after its founding. He suggested the possibility of dividing any park into upper-, middle-, and lower-valley management districts and pointed out possible difficulties with local residents and mining concerns. In response, Albright opted to again recommend national monument status. Late in 1931, he drafted legislation that permitted continued mining in Death Valley even after its establishment as a national monument. "We thought Death Valley deserved protection at once, except perhaps for mining, and that in time the mining authority might be repealed," Albright later recalled. "No new mines were opened," he reported in his memoirs, an inaccurate assessment of the result of this endeavor.[12]

The establishment of Death Valley National Monument on February 11, 1933, resulted from the change in political fortunes that cast the Republican Party from power in 1932. Albright's strong affinity for Death Valley and the desert made him persist, but until conditions changed, he found little support. After Hoover's resounding defeat in November 1932, Albright conceived a plan modeled on Theodore Roosevelt's aggressive lame-duck period of national monument proclamations, most prominent among them the 1909 Mount Olympus National Monument on the Olympic Peninsula of Washington State. As 1933 began, a powerful sense of loss permeated Hoover's cabinet and executive staff. Albright felt certain that the new administration would not retain him, and he looked for ways to strengthen his agency and accomplish a number of long-sought goals before his departure. Hoover saw himself as a strong conservationist, and Albright recognized the exiting president's desire to offer the nation a conservation gift as he departed office. Staunch in his views, Hoover shared the values of the Progressive Era's professional classes, and he found solace in the opportunity to leave a legacy that he believed people would admire.[13]

After the 1932 election, Albright prepared the necessary paperwork in anticipation of the president's outgoing objective. In the last month of the lame-duck period, Hoover proclaimed five national monuments, three of which—Death Valley, Saguaro, and White Sands—were the first desert parks. These "representative area" national monuments broadened the park system and allowed it access to a wider array of public lands than was common during the 1920s. Hoover had left the national park system and the nation richer in its conservation heritage.[14]

For all these benefits, when Roosevelt's New Deal began the National Park Service was short on resources. The Depression had reversed the advances the agency had made during the 1920s, and in the early 1930s, budgets were flat or declining. National monument proclamations rarely included appropriations, Congress typically doling out park budgets in a lump sum, with allocations for some specific projects. As a result, the agency had to reallocate existing resources for management of new park areas. In a cost-saving measure, larger parks often managed new smaller ones. Death Valley National Monument became the responsibility of Sequoia National Park superintendent John R. White, even though he already administered General Grant National Park in addition to Sequoia. White immediately assessed the new monument and informed Albright that even though he thought that Death Valley was too large for management with the resources available for national monuments, the park needed to be larger to serve agency purposes. Several areas north and east of the original monument boundaries merited inclusion, he wrote. White also recognized the crucial need for access. Following agency practice, White argued for a main entrance road and improvement of existing roads to scenic viewpoints. "In Death Valley we have inherited not an area in embryo but one ripe for development."[15]

White faced a complicated management situation at the new Death Valley National Monument. Not present on a daily basis because of his other commitments, he understood that the new park contained a range of issues that demanded on-the-ground management. Death Valley's 1,697,112 acres made it very large by national park system standards. The National Park Service arrived atop a layer of animosity. The family of Bob Eichbaum, who died suddenly in early 1932, and Walter Scott, at the north end of the valley, resented Pacific Coast Borax's move into tourism. To these rugged entrepreneurs, the company and its shiny tour buses seemed to have stolen the best of their business. White noted that increasing visitation threatened scarce water sources, many of which Pacific Coast Borax controlled, and filled the few camping sites. He estimated that five thousand cars and nine thousand visitors entered Death Valley National Monument between October 1932 and May 1933; another one thousand visitors arrived during the summer of 1933. All of them relied upon the new park's limited resources and facilities.[16]

Located at his headquarters in Sequoia, White decided that he needed a representative at the new park on a daily basis. In 1934 he created a Death Valley administrative plan, appointing engineer Theodore R. Goodwin to serve as onsite manager. Highly motivated and capable, Goodwin became the lead administrator at Death Valley, supervising acting custodian Tom Williams, one of the "dollar-a-year men," the volunteers so common in national monuments during this era. With a pattern of authority established and a full-time National Park Service representative at the monument, White could begin to contemplate facility development.[17]

In the National Park Service's short history, national monuments typically received significant support under distinct circumstances. When Congress designated an area for national park status, such as Zion in the 1910s, or when public-interest demand forced first the creation of facilities and then the reclassification of the monument, such as occurred at the Grand Canyon between 1902 and park status in 1919, the agency was able to commandeer development resources. The interest of Frank "Boss" Pinkley of the Southwestern National Monuments Group also furthered development. Pinkley was a vociferous and even contentious advocate, and he was able to scare up resources for the areas he supervised.[18] At its inception, Death Valley fell into none of these categories, greatly limiting its developmental potential.

Conversely, the presidential decree established Death Valley National Monument at a fortuitous moment in national park history, when the ascendance of Franklin D. Roosevelt inverted not only the National Park Service's premises but those of the entire federal system as well. Roosevelt's New Deal became one of the most revolutionary programs in US history. An unprecedented intervention into national economic and social affairs, it redefined the role of the state in society. The Depression had left as much as one-quarter of the nation's workforce unemployed, precipitating a crisis in public confidence. The institutions of the United States seemed to have failed, and thousands of Americans simply gave up. Many citizens, once economically stable, starved, begged, or rode the rails; all felt that economic and political circumstances had tarnished the nation's promise. When Roosevelt moved into the White House, he brought an ebullience that the dour Hoover could not muster, and the programs he espoused produced a spark of optimism. The New Deal injected huge amounts of federal money into the economy, creating jobs by the thousands, providing guarantees that became the basis of the social "safety net," and building a range of projects that reshaped the national landscape.[19]

The National Park Service became one of the primary beneficiaries of the New Deal, and this changed the trajectory of Death Valley National Monument. The only significant source of money and labor for national park development in the 1930s came from New Deal programs, and that funding became the backbone of physical improvement throughout the park system. National parks and monuments benefited from the Emergency Conservation Work (ECW) program and its subsidiary, the Civilian Conservation Corps (CCC). At Death Valley National Monument, as at most new parks, CCC work transformed the area. The CCC provided funds for two camps of laborers to implement White's administrative plan.

Workers built trails, roads, firebreaks, and buildings, creating the beginning of the monument's physical plant.[20]

Most important, CCC labor provided Death Valley National Monument with the infrastructure necessary to support the increasing levels of visitation. White actively championed the road-building program, making it his leading priority. He understood that visitation at Death Valley followed newer patterns of travel. Unlike the Grand Canyon, where officials planned and developed the facilities in response to people arriving predominantly by train and Fred Harvey motorcars, at Death Valley people arrived nearly exclusively by personal vehicles. During 1933, the first year of New Deal programs, Goodwin and the CCC workers completed forty miles of oiled road from the Furnace Creek boundary to the Stove Pipe Wells Hotel. During the following season, CCC workers graded almost three hundred miles of road inside the monument; Goodwin continued the improvements throughout 1935 and 1936. During 1936 more than one hundred additional miles of roads were graded and oiled. The demand for infrastructure, in the form of new roads and road maintenance, fell entirely on the National Park Service. Pacific Coast Borax felt no obligation to help maintain government roads.[21]

Visitation continued to increase, exacerbating management concerns. In 1934 White reported 22,377 registered visitors at the Furnace Creek Checking Station, an increase of 150 percent from the previous year. Furnace Creek totals reflected only a portion of the growing visitation, since the monument suffered a lack of monitoring elsewhere. Recorded visitation doubled again to more than 50,000 the following year, creating more conflicts about use of space. The growth led to a struggle with Pacific Coast Borax, an uncomfortable reality apparent to both White and Goodwin. Goodwin learned that the borax company had made an effort to develop all the monument properties to which it held mining rights. Pacific Coast Borax possessed claims but not fee-simple patents to most of this land, yet it treated mining claims inside the monument as company property. The most notable result was the disposal of mining refuse in dumps visitors could see. In the most egregious incident, the company created a road and trash dump only a few miles south of the Furnace Creek Inn. The company clearly did not hold title to the tract, and White sought to compel more responsible behavior. He urged Frank Jenifer, general manager of the borax company's Death Valley operations, to realize that the monument's establishment had created new circumstances, and while the company was entitled to mine and was an important partner of the National Park Service, it needed to be more sensitive to agency values. White also requested a full-time position from the agency to be dedicated to monitoring the mining company's activities.[22]

The economic circumstances of the Depression and the public's increased reliance on New Deal programs created a climate in which the expansion of the monument's boundaries became an easier task. The Depression and the New Deal softened historic resistance to federal landownership across the West, and executive orders enlarged many park areas. Death Valley's original boundaries had not fulfilled agency aspirations, as White pointed out when President Hoover established the monument. The original proclamation had omitted Wildrose Springs, Saratoga Springs, and the trail access to Telescope Peak, all desirable inclusions. Between 1934 and 1937, the National Park Service prepared justifications for adding the additional lands to the national monument. Agency officials pointed to scenic and management advantages that stemmed from the additions. In 1937, with Executive Proclamation 2228, 50 Stat. 1823, President Franklin Roosevelt added 304,789 acres to the monument.[23]

With infrastructure development under way and with the successful reformulation of boundaries that better accommodated the agency's mission, White and Goodwin next turned to questions of staffing. The agency could get all the short-term project labor it required, but even during the New Deal, securing funding for permanent personnel positions remained difficult. As visitation grew, Death Valley's lack of staff became a critical issue, even before Roosevelt expanded the monument's boundaries. The 1937 enlargement made those needs even more immediate. In 1936 Goodwin and former acting custodian Tom Williams, now acting chief ranger and a paid employee, constituted the entire permanent staff. The following year, the monument received funding for one permanent and two seasonal rangers. White focused on obtaining new staff positions, especially an assistant superintendent who could reside in Death Valley and focus on its management. Goodwin informally filled that role before official appointment; on April 14, 1938, he became superintendent of Death Valley National Monument.[24]

Active mining activity within park boundaries made Death Valley distinctive in the park system. Mining claims presented one of the most difficult management problems the National Park Service faced. The General Mining Act of 1872 allowed prospectors to claim tracts with purported mineral value from any part of the public domain at almost no cost. The establishment of a national park or monument did not override existing claims, and Death Valley's establishing legislation grandfathered mining claims into the monument. The federal government lacked the personnel to oversee the thousands of claims, and as mining played out, these lands often drifted to other uses. Many such claims became de facto inholdings throughout the national park system, lands within park boundaries that were privately controlled and not subject to agency strictures.[25]

At Death Valley National Monument, those working some claims that preceded the monument's establishment decided that some sites had greater value as service locations for tourists than as mining claims. In 1937 two men operated a filling station and campground on a mining claim adjacent to the main highway between Lone Pine and Death Valley. Although the Department of the Interior recommended that the General Land Office and National Park Service cancel the claim, the instance was only one of many potential issues for the National Park Service.[26] The agency was vulnerable to legal but what it regarded as inappropriate uses of land within or near monument boundaries, and it needed a strategy to curtail such activities.

In this, Death Valley was not alone. The need for a proactive position stemmed from increasing National Park Service frustration with misuse of lands within and near national park areas. At Carlsbad Caverns, Charlie White established the tourist camp he called "White's City" on a homestead claim at the entrance to the park; Secretary of the Interior Harold L. Ickes was negotiating for the purchase of Grandview Point at the Grand Canyon from William Randolph Hearst at about the same time. Inholdings posed a very real and largely insoluble management problem for the National Park Service, and throughout the system, park managers sought a comprehensive strategy for their elimination. Most would have quickly settled for some measure of control. When it recommended against the filling-station land claim, the Department of the Interior provided the agency with an important precedent to act against such claims. White praised the department's action, saying it would "decide whether it is possible for any squatter or other person to occupy, possess, and use Government land without complying with the provision of the law."[27]

Such circumstances revealed one of the most common gaps in US land law, the difference between the terms of the law and actual practice on the lands in question. Throughout the West and especially in the nation's remote areas, people used land claims to secure their control of acreage that they had little intention of using in the way the law allowed. Only in rare circumstances, such as Richard Wetherill's homestead claim on archaeological ruins in Chaco Canyon, New Mexico, in 1906, did the government act against fraudulent attempts to circumvent land law. The General Mining Act allowed an even greater degree of latitude than did the Homestead Act, limiting the Interior Department's response even more.[28] Yet in the middle of the Depression, in a rare era in which westerners gratefully accepted federal control of land and even asked the government to take more, the National Park Service learned that the courts could remove claimants from their land who did not use their claims in accordance with the law. This was an important lesson at Death Valley National Monument, for it offered the National Park Service an important way to diminish outside impacts inside park boundaries.

Even before the creation of the National Park Service, private ownership inside park boundaries, typically located near the very best features, vexed the Department of the Interior. At Death Valley, the National Park Service faced an even more complicated pattern of private ownership. Shortly after the monument's establishment, the National Park Service identified mining claims, homestead patents, confirmed patents that had been sold, and patents that resulted from exchanges of scrip with the government as categories of private ownership within monument boundaries. Mining claims and homestead patents required development, and the government could challenge them when officials had the combination of resources to vest in a case and the will to pursue it. Confirmed patents were beyond government control. There was little the National Park Service could do about them, and in most cases, they damaged the monument.

At Death Valley, such claims typically sat above water sources and often included important historic features such as mines and mining towns. The result mirrored the relationship between land and water throughout the arid West: whoever owned the water source enjoyed de facto control of the surrounding land for miles around. It also hampered the National Park Service as it sought to establish its presence. When the agency acquired new areas, its officials assiduously worked to ensure that the public knew the area was part of the national park system and that the agency would be providing needed services to travelers. Private ownership made the recognition the National Park Service craved from the public far more difficult to attain. The result was a powerful desire to end private claims; as part of his management obligations, White had received authority to pursue their acquisition.[29]

The inholdings inside Death Valley National Monument were substantial. The Pacific Coast Borax Company alone held 10,951.12 acres of patented claims, including 520 acres at Furnace Creek Ranch and another 160 acres around the inn. Other mining companies held claims throughout the monument, typically the claims that miners and prospectors had sold during the various rushes in the desert. Many were in the Panamint Mountains and in and around the defunct mining boomtown of Skidoo. A few sites were in the southern portion of Death Valley. Elsewhere in the monument, Adolf Nevares owned 320 acres at Cow Creek with valuable water rights, and the Stove Pipe Wells Hotel sat on 80 acres owned by Helene Eichbaum, Bob Eichbaum's widow. She also held a tract at Hell's Gate, where Daylight Pass opened into the monument with a magnificent view. Individuals also had claimed countless other tracts inside Death Valley's boundaries.[30]

One of the most significant concerns was Nevares's land, which the agency considered essential for Death Valley National Monument. A limestone fault on the property created a number of potable warm springs, and the property seemed an oasis, a rare spot of abundant water in the desert. Goodwin intuited that Nevares's springs provided much of the water on which the National Park Service relied. Knowing Nevares, he recognized the monument's vulnerability to diversion under the doctrine of prior appropriation, the first-in-time, first-in-right precept that underpinned western water law. Goodwin also recognized the possibility for a small hydroelectric facility in the five-hundred-foot drop from the springs. By any estimation, the Nevares property was crucial to the development of Cow Creek, one of the monument's principal residential and maintenance facilities.[31]

Acquiring inholdings proved difficult during the 1930s, for despite the largesse of the New Deal, appropriations remained lean. In 1934 Nevares, known for being difficult in negotiations, offered his property to the government for twenty thousand dollars. The National Park Service had already recognized how crucial his holding was and wanted to make an effort to acquire it. Although there were few buyers during the 1930s, Nevares sought outside offers in the hope of inflating the National Park Service's offer. Goodwin requested fifty thousand dollars to acquire inholdings, but a congressional appropriation did not follow. As a result, an excellent opportunity to buy the Nevares property escaped. The land remained out of National Park Service reach for the next twenty years, with the agency facing an ever-angrier and more recalcitrant landowner. Without a source of adequate funds, the agency typically relied on exchanges to address the question of inholdings. In the climate of the era, a few small exchanges, such as an eighty-acre exchange that gave the National Park Service a tract that surrounded the Stove Pipe Wells Hotel, were all that was possible. Although such exchanges furthered specific park goals, they did not eliminate the need for a comprehensive program of acquisition of inholdings.[32]

After the opportunities supported by the New Deal began to fade later in the 1930s, Death Valley's physical expansion slowed. Following the 1937 addition, few occasions to acquire land appeared. The pattern of exchanges continued in a limited way and the agency pursued Nevares's land, but monument boundaries changed little. Growing emphasis on science in the post–World War II period led to a new addition in 1952 that while small in size was significant for what it preserved. National Park Service scientists discovered unique biological areas beyond monument boundaries, including Devils Hole, a small spring in Ash Meadows, Nevada. The astute Goodwin lobbied for another boundary extension, realizing that the small size of the tract belied its significance for preserving a significant part of the desert. On January 17, 1952, Truman issued Presidential Proclamation 2961, adding forty acres around Devils Hole to Death Valley National Monument.[33]

The 1952 proclamation furthered expansion in additional ways. It included authorization to acquire inholdings within monument boundaries, permitting the agency to resume such efforts. Between 1950 and 1957, inholdings became a focus of park acquisition efforts. Goodwin consistently faced this question until an automobile accident in 1953 severely injured him. His successors, Edward E. Ogston, who served as acting superintendent until Goodwin formally retired in 1954, and park superintendent Fred W. Binnewies, continued to pursue myriad parcels within monument boundaries through exchanges and purchases. Goodwin had begun an active program to combat fraudulent acquisition attempts and eliminate illegal claims. Many Death Valley residents still used the 1872 Mining Act's broad protection to claim land with no intention of using it for mining. In June 1952, for instance, M. C. Williams filed notice of his intent to develop a mill on five acres in Wildrose Canyon. Goodwin believed Williams and David Adams, proprietor of the Wildrose Station, were conspiring to acquire water rights from the mill claim. The National Park Service previously had denied Adams a special-use permit for a swimming pool. Williams intended to bulldoze a large stand of trees and shrubs to clear a pad for construction of the mill. Agency personnel acted quickly, soliciting legal advice from attorneys at the Department of the Interior and Bureau of Land Management (BLM). Superintendent Goodwin informed Williams that the National Park Service would determine what activities were suitable inside monument boundaries.[34]

Monument designation did not prevent further mining claims inside Death Valley, for the authorizing legislation contained explicit provisions to allow placer and mill claims. Williams had filed a claim with the Inyo County assessor, but the law required a National Park Service special-use permit for surface development inside the monument. Existing regulations thwarted Williams's development goals. Nor could he get access to water without agency assistance. Goodwin used the circumstances to announce that the agency would apply the doctrine of prior appropriation to claims on all local water sources. This judicial philosophy, "first in time, first in right," awarded water to users based on their priority date, the moment from which they could demonstrate their use of water began. The National Park Service and its CCC contingent had developed and used most of the water sources inside the monument. The agency's claims superseded most mining claims and were second only to Native American claims and some existing mining rights, and so preceded any associated with the proposed mill, a reality that persuaded Williams to abandon his plan.[35]

In essence, the National Park Service now had begun to use the very laws that had hampered the monument to its advantage. Barring a change in statute, the agency could do little about existing and even new mining claims. Yet mining was a water-intensive process, and it could use its control of water to hinder non-park activities within park boundaries. If such a proactive strategy was to succeed, establishing agency water rights was sure to be an essential component.

Because of its enormous ramifications, Williams's mill claim filing was the extreme among the land disputes at the monument. National Park Service officials handled other situations, especially those involving an exchange of interests, with greater ease. Horace Albright's long relationship with Pacific Coast Borax and its successor companies facilitated land exchanges with the monument's leading private landowner. In 1931 Pacific Coast Borax had diversified by helping create the United States Potash Company. When Albright left the National Park Service in 1933, he became vice president of US Potash, and the former agency director remained a powerful advocate of park goals. As Death Valley's borax became less of a commodity and tourism grew in importance, the borax companies and the National Park Service often worked closely together to achieve complementary goals, most significantly development of Pacific Coast Borax's resort at Furnace Creek.[36]

The mining company and the National Park Service found it easiest to agree over questions of infrastructure, as the unusual bifurcation of land created natural affinities on most questions concerning development. Even when their needs did not dovetail, the two organizations could usually broaden any discussion to reach an equitable agreement that furthered both sets of objectives. The question of access to the monument's facilities offered a prime example. The remote location and primitive transportation infrastructure affected Pacific Coast Borax's resort areas as much as they did the National Park Service's tourist facilities. The obvious solution was air travel, which began across the desert during the 1920s. Throughout the era of propeller aircraft, air travel consisted of a series of interrelated short flights. Scheduled commercial routes and charter flights crossed the region, stopping with some regularity at Death Valley and other locations.

Airports represented one of the National Park Service's key dilemmas, an opportunity that brought the National Park Service's mandates to increase park use and to protect resources into direct conflict. Simultaneously, air facilities juxtaposed ideals of preservation (solitude, quiet, and human scale) with those of access (reaching the parks easily). Demands for airports within national park areas began in 1944 and gained momentum after the war. During the late 1940s, the National Park Service embraced the concept of airstrips near park areas as a convenient way to attract new visitors. Some resisted this approach, seeing it as an inherent compromise. Others believed that the agency's health and future depended on an avid public, and airports provided one more way to build extensive public support. The airport dilemma reflected every inherent tension in the National Park Service's organic legislation.

The National Park Service had coexisted with an airstrip at Death Valley since the monument's creation. Pacific Coast Borax built the Furnace Creek Ranch airstrip during the 1930s on its property. The National Park Service had little control over decisions the company made on its own acreage, but it held one important trump card. The existing airstrip was too short to accommodate postwar commercial airline traffic. At the company's request, airport engineers from the California Aeronautics Administration (CAA) surveyed the airstrip in 1948 to see if the company could lengthen it. At about the same time, Bonanza Airlines sought landing rights at Furnace Creek, a portent of more visitors by air if Pacific Coast Borax could improve its facilities. After meeting with Goodwin and National Park Service engineers, a CCC engineer requested an official survey for a forty-four-hundred-foot extension, but the grade at the site the National Park Service proposed was too steep for CCC standards. At the same time, Pacific Coast Borax still needed to ensure that the Furnace Creek Inn had a dependable and legally protected water source. In response to the airstrip rejection, the company offered an exchange of airport lands for a permanent easement between the Furnace Creek Ranch and the Furnace Creek Inn, which contained the water rights the company sought. National Park Service director Newton B. Drury supported the exchange.[37]

Under Drury, the most preservation-minded agency director, the National Park Service routinely conceded that aerial views of the national parks might be valuable for attracting tourists, but insisted that airfields remain outside park boundaries. In 1947 the agency had prohibited the landing of planes in national park areas except in emergencies, at the same time permitting existing landing strips to continue in operation. In a 1950 policy decision, National Park Service regulations became obsolete. Interior Secretary Oscar L. Chapman received authority to sponsor airport development within park boundaries. Chapman, a proponent of the Echo Park Dam and the Colorado River Storage Project who forced Drury to resign the NPS directorship, was not the agency's staunchest ally on questions of intrusive use.[38]

Airports remained a difficult issue for the National Park Service throughout the early 1950s, but the great need for access to Death Valley National Monument, added to the small size of the Furnace Creek airport already in existence, made objections moot. Drury's successor, Conrad L. Wirth, recognized air access as an important component of his plans for park-area development. Negotiating a fine line between development and protection, Wirth did not support airports within parks. The thirty miles of new runways constructed during his tenure were near but outside of park boundaries.[39]

The airport at Death Valley fell into a different category. The 1947 decision grandfathered the little airport in, but as the Civil Aeronautics Administration fashioned plans for a national network of airports, it was not among the sites considered. A 1952 illness of Senator Pat McCarran (D-NV) helped bring political influence to bear on the issue. While recuperating, McCarran spent time at Furnace Creek, where park superintendent Goodwin discussed the airport project with him. Before he left, McCarran made the project his own, promising to secure passage of two bills in Congress, one restoring the Death Valley airport to the *National Airport Plan* and another inserting an appropriation for the National Park Service's share of construction. By September negotiations between the agency and Pacific Coast Borax were under way, and the Death Valley airport was part of the National Park Service's national list of priorities.[40]

The renovated Death Valley airport depended on more than an exchange of land. Although the National Park Service assigned the project high priority, Congress deleted four hundred thousand dollars in funding from the agency's 1952 budget request. Undaunted, the National Park Service completed the land exchange with Pacific Coast Borax, relying on McCarran's promise to secure the needed funding. After the parties completed the exchange, the agency acquired 230 acres inside the monument, offering in return only a total of 20 acres of perpetual easement and water rights. On June 20, 1951, Representative Clair Engle (D-CA) introduced House Bill 4515 to authorize the land exchange. Its counterpart in the Senate, Senate Bill 1730, drew the promised support from the powerful McCarran. Congress approved the exchange on March 24, 1952. The monument upgraded the airport and airstrip during 1952 and 1953. In 1954, just months before his death, McCarran personally welcomed a Bonanza DC-3, the first commercial airline to arrive at Furnace Creek Airport.[41]

Even as the monument modernized its infrastructure after World War II, the National Park Service continued to rely on land acquisition to mitigate the impact of the enormous visitation increases on Death Valley. Visitation reached 212,710 in 1949 and rose to 300,142 in 1956, a number that severely tested its resources. Mission 66, the ten-year capital development program created to overhaul the national park system, played a significant role in fashioning the agency's response at Death Valley National Monument. During Mission 66, the National Park Service usually received what it asked for, and even the most remote parks acquired full-fledged physical plants, temporarily reducing management problems to questions of personnel.[42]

Mission 66 was the most thorough development program ever proposed for the national park system. It reflected the influence of NPS director Conrad L. Wirth, a landscape architect. When Wirth ascended to the directorship in 1951, the park system was at its nadir. The capital development of the New Deal era let the agency provide facilities to 1930s levels of visitation, but postwar growth had swamped the system. Wirth conceived of Mission 66 to refurbish the national park system in time for the fiftieth anniversary of the founding of the NPS in 1966. He succeeded with Congress, where congressional representatives fell all over one another to increase the allocations to the national parks. Beginning in

1956, Wirth's Park Service engaged in a decadelong one-billion-dollar building program that put new facilities almost everywhere in the system. Visitor centers, new park headquarters, and staff housing were prominent features of the program.[43]

As part of the Mission 66 program, and in response to the enormous increases in visitation, the agency initially sought a new visitor center. Furnace Creek was the most logical location, for it had become the central area of the monument because of the presence of the Furnace Creek Ranch. The land in the vicinity belonged to US Borax, formed by the merger of Pacific Coast Borax and US Potash on June 1, 1956, and the National Park Service needed this new entity's cooperation. The company proved a willing partner. In 1957 the National Park Service sought lands near the Furnace Creek Ranch to which the borax company held subsurface mineral title. As always, the long-standing relationship and Albright's insistent presence ensured that the agency and the company would negotiate successfully; both parties had specific goals that a land exchange could attain, and their long history together made accommodation a genuine possibility. After the merger, US Borax diminished its direct interest in the resort, leasing its two hotels, the Furnace Creek Ranch and Inn and the Amargosa Hotel, to the Fred Harvey Company. This longtime purveyor of southwestern tourism seemed a much better vendor to capitalize on the burgeoning tourism in Death Valley.[44]

In this case, the land exchange worked to mutual benefit. The exchange helped the borax company because the resort needed rights-of-way and water rights near its inholdings; in exchange, the National Park Service received important lands for the visitor center. US Borax owned 90 acres just north of the Furnace Creek Ranch, an ideal location for a new visitor center and campground from the National Park Service's and the company's perspectives. After negotiations, the agency acquired 440 acres of US Borax inholdings in exchange for 200 acres of easements and water rights in Texas Springs and Furnace Creek Wash, which included Travertine Springs. On July 2, 1958, Congress ratified the exchange.[45]

Despite this example of smooth cooperation, inholdings remained a primary management issue at Death Valley. Fred Binnewies brought strong credentials to this difficult and complicated task. A National Park Service veteran who came from a seven-year stint at Bandelier National Monument, where he negotiated the difficult Cold War climate in the immediate vicinity of Los Alamos, he was a practiced diplomat and a creative manager. His efforts led to the acquisition of a number of private inholdings throughout Death Valley. In the 1954 season, the National Park Service purchased the 160-acre Thorndyke property near Wildrose for $16,250 and 80 acres near Hell's Gate from C. E. Fuller for $1,500. The government also acquired title to Hungry Bill's Ranch in Johnson Canyon during this period. In 1957 the agency paid $14,500 for 160 acres at Saratoga Springs. These efforts completed the acquisition of the most visible and most important inhold-ings, and the acquisition of private lands inside the monument subsequently slowed.[46]

Scotty's Castle, the most prominent inholding in Death Valley, remained beyond National Park Service reach throughout this era. Before his 1948 death, Albert W. Johnson had transferred the property's ownership to the Gospel Foun-dation of California. Walter Scott, "Death Valley Scotty," continued to live at the castle until his death in 1954. After his passing, the Gospel Foundation admin-istered the property for visitors. Interpretation and other issues concerned the National Park Service, but the expense of a purchase remained beyond reach. Throughout the 1960s, park superintendents were left hoping that Congress would authorize new funds to purchase Scotty's Castle.

Mission 66 marked the end of an era not only for Death Valley National Monument, but for the National Park Service in general, capping a long period in which landscape architects provided the dominant influence on agency plan-ning and activity. Wirth's 1964 departure accelerated a shift in agency emphasis away from facilities construction and toward the newly developing profession-alized sciences such as ecology. For the monument—fundamentally left behind throughout the era of development—the shift in emphasis to ecology had important consequences. It elevated the resources of the desert in contrast to the high-elevation scenery that had so shaped the National Park Service mentality throughout the age of park development. If Americans appreciated ecology more, the desert stood a chance of becoming at least a partial focus of their new enthu-siasm for the environment. In contrast to the first thirty years of park history, the environmental revolution of the late 1960s promised a more prominent future for Death Valley National Monument.

CHAPTER 3

Changing the Meaning of Desert

The 1960s were a heady time for the National Park Service. Mission 66 had finally given the agency the facilities to accommodate the tremendous growth in tourism that followed World War II. Because of a divergent set of forces, the National Park Service began to move in new management directions. Two significant changes—the GI Bill that trained so many specialists at the college level and two reports, the Leopold Report on the condition of wildlife in the park system and the National Academy of Sciences or Robbins Report—compelled a new vision of National Park Service management.[1] In a way never before possible, the agency embraced science as a guiding administrative force, its people focusing with renewed vigor on resource management as a core mission.

In the late 1960s, American culture began to change its perspectives on the question of the environment. Support for environmental protection had been building since the early twentieth century, but as late as 1968, environment, conservation, and ecology did not register on the Brooking Institution's assessment of problems facing the new Nixon administration; the following year, the environment became the leading concern of the respondents in that survey. This transformation reflected the enormous change in US society wrought by postwar prosperity and its power to transform social expectations. Along with the demographic transformation caused by the "baby boom," this prosperity created an enormous population with ideas and values that altered national society at every stage of life. The idea of a "quiet crisis" in the environment, in Secretary of the Interior Stewart L. Udall's phrase, and a strong pull away from material prosperity at all costs led to new questions concerning the environment. A much stronger emphasis on preservation, on resource protection from any kind of use, resulted.

This was very different from the conservation that marked the early twentieth century, for its focus was aesthetic as much as cultural. Despite the National Park Service's long involvement with preservation, it was uncomfortable with some of the new movement's goals.[2]

Designated wilderness became a measure of the National Park Service's discomfort with the environmental revolution. When it came time to apply the Wilderness Act of 1964 to Death Valley, the idea of wilderness became a dominant concern, for its impact on the regional population and for the limitations it placed on NPS discretion in management. Unlike any preceding environmental legislation, the Wilderness Act permitted the reservation of land for a single purpose. Wilderness designation required stringent management and limited administrative prerogative to the least-intrusive tool for the job, in most cases eliminating motorized travel and equipment. The National Park Service had not been enthusiastic about the passage of the Wilderness Act, because its regulations made park-level management more difficult and managers complained about the law's inflexibility. At the same time, the wilderness concept was extremely popular with the public, albeit often in a symbolic fashion.[3]

Wilderness required a legislatively mandated review process that had the complicated effect of making wilderness of places that park planners had previously ignored. Because the statute required roadlessness as a prerequisite, only areas of more than five thousand acres that remained undeveloped qualified for federal wilderness assessment. Although of all federal land-management agencies the National Park Service's mandate most closely resembled the goals of the Wilderness Act, the agency initially balked at ceding discretion of its backcountry. The agency soon discovered that designated wilderness offered advantages. Wilderness designation of lands beyond its boundaries could insulate national parks from the clutter that often surrounded them. Even more, adjacent wilderness provided a permanent viewshed for national park areas, protecting an important asset with little direct agency investment.[4]

This seemed particularly true at Death Valley, one reason the agency recognized wilderness designations there as an asset for monument managers. New mining claims in surrounding areas remained a real threat to its aims, and lands adjacent to Death Valley and other park areas posed an ongoing threat that had the potential to affect resource management. As every superintendent beginning with Theodore R. Goodwin had noted, the desert had the potential to change very rapidly. The number of inholdings, the possibility of new mining claims, and countless other potential intrusions repeatedly threatened the monument. Designated wilderness might provide Death Valley with a way to forestall development of these lands or, in ideal circumstances, to prevent it altogether.

In 1971 the National Park Service assessed the possibilities for wilderness designation at Death Valley National Monument and assembled a corresponding management plan. The 1972 *Death Valley Wilderness Proposal* led to public hearings in Las Vegas, Nevada, and San Bernardino, California, two years later, which generated 1,771 oral and written responses. On May 15, 1974, NPS regional director Howard Chapman submitted the agency's proposal for the park's future management in the Preliminary Wilderness Study and Draft Environmental Statement for Death Valley to National Park Service director Ronald H. Walker and Secretary of the Interior Rogers C. B. Morton, and seven months later the Nixon administration forwarded it to Congress for its consideration. In its final form, the proposal designated 1,908,000 acres in and around Death Valley—almost 95 percent of the monument—as wilderness. The National Park Service remained confident that the proposal would pass; throughout the early 1970s, Congress favored environmental protection and wilderness, and it designated new areas with some frequency. Despite the positive circumstances, Congress took no action on the Death Valley wilderness proposal during the remainder of the 1970s.[5]

Industry opposition provided a primary reason for congressional reticence. The National Park Service had added a stipulation to the legislation that prohibited new mining claims inside monument boundaries. The effort to exclude claims was part of an ongoing struggle. Since the 1930s, Death Valley had grappled with land uses that were not compatible with National Park Service goals. Most of those, in particular mining claims, had preceded the monument's creation, but many occurred even after its 1933 establishment.[6] The Antiquities Act of 1906, the authorizing legislation for the national monument category, did not expressly forbid mining. The compromises necessary to create the monument in 1933 permitted mining to continue. By the mid-1970s, mining had become much less important at Death Valley National Monument, replaced in economic significance by tourism. Broad national environmental sentiment in favor of parks and monuments encouraged agency attempts to curtail future claims, but powerful resistance from mining companies remained. The pressure stalled wilderness designation. Agency officials hoped the delay would be short, but a full generation passed before the formal declaration of wilderness in Death Valley.

Another consequence of the new emphasis on resource preservation led to greater concern for the integrity of Death Valley National Monument. Mining interests were politically powerful by comparison to the National Park Service. Especially during the Depression, when a great deal of small-scale and seemingly desperate mining by individuals inside monument boundaries took place, the agency clearly saw an attack on mining as counterproductive. By the 1950s, large-scale mining inside the monument had subsided; the mining companies with substantial acreage had become tourist purveyors as early as the 1920s and now saw Death Valley in different terms. The changing environmental emphasis that developed in the nation's society during the 1960s gave the National Park Service a vision of possibilities that had not previously existed. To many who made agency policy, this looked to be the first genuine opportunity to eliminate mining within Death Valley's boundaries.

Although mining in the national monument appeared to be in abeyance, with individual owners and companies abandoning many claims, a sudden revival in the early 1970s shocked the National Park Service. In 1970 Morandex, a Canadian company, considered purchasing the Cooper Lode claims of Grand State Mining. Suddenly, a number of companies expanded mining operations on old claims. Most stunning was the revival of open-pit mining, begun in 1971 by Tenneco Oil Company, which started the Boraxo Pit on the former Clara claim near Ryan. Miners had not worked the claim since the 1920s, and its revival did not bode well for the monument. For the first time in more than a generation, a major corporation used its legal right to mine inside Death Valley.[7]

The pit proved profitable, and other companies eyed similar opportunities. By 1973 workers were mining 130,000 tons a year from the fifty-one-acre pit, a fifteen-million-dollar annual business. By National Park Service accounts, the Boraxo Pit's tailings pile was visible to travelers who entered Death Valley from the east; company officials disputed this contention. Mine management was an issue as well. The pit flooded on more than one occasion, creating a potential environmental hazard as well as a use that contravened park objectives and necessitated a response from the monument. Death Valley officials could do little as the company explored other borax deposits near Ryan and planned a mill near Death Valley Junction, inside Nevada, to avoid California's stringent environmental regulations.[8] The plan yielded a significant profit, and a new surge of mining activity in Death Valley seemed likely to follow.

Some other park areas faced similar situations, and regional managers looked for ways to limit the impact of mining on the sites they supervised. The legislation for some Alaska parks permitted mining, and in the age of activist environmental sentiment in both political parties, some park advocates in Congress sought legislative remedies. In 1973 Senator Barry Goldwater (R-AZ) and Representative Morris Udall (D-AZ) introduced identical bills to repeal the authority for mining in most national park areas. Although an amendment eventually limited the legislation to Organ Pipe and Coronado National Monuments in the legislators' home state, the bill was prima facie evidence that the toleration of mining in national park areas was ending. Udall and Goldwater represented different political philosophies as well as parties, and their alliance on this issue proved that Goldwater's libertarianism and Udall's Great Society liberalism could coincide.

Although their effort benefited only Arizona's national park areas, their concurrence on a bill limiting an activity so important in their home state gave Death Valley National Monument superintendent Jim Thompson considerable hope.[9]

Still, Thompson and his staff faced an onslaught of mining activity in the 1970s. Talc-extraction operations in the Panamint Range's south end and in the Ibex Hills posed one major issue. Production teams used bulldozers to explore for talc outcrops, leaving waste piles and visible road scars. The Tenneco open pit had already created its own issues, most notably a stacked waste dump of more than one million tons. Pfizer's Galena Canyon operation "obliterated" six acres of desert for every ten thousand tons mined, while the Tenneco open pit used only one acre for the same quantity. In the estimation of monument management, these impacts were too great to tolerate. Exploration roads throughout Death Valley scarred the landscape. With little regulation, companies often started many roads where one would have sufficed. A requirement to annually assess claims often led to damages unrelated to mining. Faced with these mounting threats, the monument fought back. Beginning in 1972, personnel increased enforcement of mining regulations and emphasized application of the permit system that gave the National Park Service some measure of oversight.[10]

Tenneco's presence in Death Valley provided the primary obstacle to National Park Service goals. The open-pit mine visibly contradicted the widely held presumption of mining's imminent demise inside the monument, and Tenneco's political power provided cover for every individual claimant who wanted to keep working a defunct claim. Tenneco's operation seemed headed for a collision with the staff's management objectives. The company's mining claims were valid and its methods legal, if not compatible with Death Valley's direction in the 1970s. The National Park Service had no legal way to resist such actions, for the work took place well within the boundaries of existing mining claims. Frustrated, Thompson and other monument officials sought short-term defensive strategies without investing too much in the prospect of a long-term remedy. They had been disappointed too many times to believe that they could bar mining from the monument.[11]

The primary effort became a three-year program to bring mining into compliance with National Park Service regulations by issuing special-use permits for mining operations. These permits, monument officials thought, would help Death Valley control surface activity and road access. From a low of 50 permits in 1973, the monument issued 194 in 1974 and 135 in 1975. The tool "afforded an excellent management tool for dealing with miners in a mutually constructive way," observed James Thompson, for it made clear monument expectations and reminded mining companies and their officials that they operated within a national park area. The need for more stringent regulations was obvious to the superintendent, but special-use permits were the best he had to offer.[12]

Thompson's efforts ran hard against the rapid growth of mining inside monument boundaries. By the middle of the 1970s, the success of extractive operations in Death Valley enticed more new mining within its boundaries. In 1974, even though monument personnel twice cited the company for permit violations, Tenneco expanded its open-pit operation to more than two hundred acres. Because of the expansion, mining operations became clearly visible to visitors traveling on a nearby road. Since the mine operated under a National Park Service permit, the agency could fashion only limited responses. The monument considered rerouting the adjacent paved road. In 1975 a second mine, the Sigma Pit, opened. A stream of trucks removed about 220,000 tons of borate from Death Valley that year, about 80 percent of domestic colemanite production. Tenneco contemplated further development, assessing the viability of its claims near Zabriskie Point, almost in a direct line with the visitors' entrance to Furnace Creek. The company requested a special permit to operate an open-pit mine in that area and asked for access by road. One company official later recalled the move as strategic, an effort to deter competitors, and at the same time increase company leverage in its ongoing land-exchange negotiations with the National Park Service. James Barker, one of the principals in the Tenneco operation, remembered that the company's goal was to exchange the Zabriskie Point claim for land that was "out of sight [and] out of mind."[13] This tactical decision had far-reaching ramifications. It set the stage for a larger battle over the very existence of mining not only in Death Valley, but throughout the national park system as well.

Tenneco's Zabriskie proposal aroused national opposition and ignited a confrontation between environmentalists and the mining industry. At the crowning moment in an era of aesthetic environmentalism and affluence, Americans widely supported environmental protection goals and believed that the nation was sufficiently well off that it could set aside some of its resources for preservation purposes. The creation of the Environmental Protection Agency in 1971 was one reflection of this aspiration. Another marker of changing sentiment was the passage of the 1973 Endangered Species Act, which empowered the government to protect species threatened as a "consequence of economic growth and development untempered by adequate concern and conservation" (16 USC 1531). In this emerging context, mining seemed yet another threat to be controlled, especially in national parks, which seemed inviolable in an age of apparent bipartisan political environmentalism. The worry over more development inside park boundaries rallied the environmental community at a time when it typically could count on Congress for support.[14]

By 1976 mining in Death Valley pitted Tenneco against the monument, a juxtaposition that for the first time put the company at a disadvantage. Superintendent James Thompson fought the company's expansion plans, arguing that the full-scale open-pit mining was not the intent of Congress when it permitted mining in Death Valley in 1933. Instead, he averred, legislators envisioned that "single-blanket jackass prospectors" would continue to mine on a small scale, as they had since the 1860s. Tenneco superintendent Greg Sparks countered that mining had been an integral part of Death Valley throughout the twentieth century and that the open-pit mine's existing location was the most suitable spot in the monument for such activity. Besides, the pit was unobtrusive. Nor was the desert unique in Sparks's view, a perspective that Thompson roundly attacked. "The idea that if something isn't green, it's worthless, shows no respect or understanding for desert ecology," Thompson told an Associated Press reporter. The open pit was "like a mole on your face. It's in one spot, but it affects everything."[15]

As congressional legislation to curtail mining remained under discussion during 1976, the tension at the monument increased. The National Park Service perceived an acceleration of mining activity inside Death Valley. Mining companies responded to the prospect of legislation by aggressively trying to expand development, identifying and exposing additional mineral fields, and by increasing the transfer of stockpiles to areas outside of monument boundaries. The issue drew the attention of the national media. The *CBS Evening News* featured a segment with bulldozers moving material into dump trucks in Death Valley, the reporter intoning above the din: "This is your national park." At the same time, National Park Service advocates increased their pressure to halt mining. In February 1976, the Sierra Club sued the National Park Service, the Department of the Interior, and Secretary of the Interior Thomas Kleppe, asserting that the federal government had not fulfilled its statutory management obligation to prevent surface disturbance. California's Division of Mines and Geology rushed a special report into publication that supported mining, and the monument countered it with an opposing report. The issue became so intense that in July, a congressional delegation risked the summer heat to visit the monument to assess the issue.[16] Such a physically uncomfortable junket ensured that some action would soon follow.

After the visit, monument staff felt certain that legislation to limit mining would pass Congress, and they correctly assessed this important shift in legislative and national sentiment. In October 1976, passage of the Mining in the Parks Act upended the existing structure of mining in national park areas. The law closed the national park system to new mining and regulated existing claims with increased vigor. It added new assessment requirements that reduced the number of viable claims. The standards now required that mining operations be conducted in a manner that minimized damage to lands, a direct acknowledgment of the impact of open-pit mines. The act also required the recording of mining claims within the park system and established a process for invalidating unrecorded and unworked claims.[17]

Passage of the act quickly changed the character of mining in Death Valley. Instead of compliant toleration, extractive companies faced an energized staff that aggressively opposed new mining ventures. The American Borate Company, which acquired Tenneco's holdings in 1976, sought new permits to expand surface mining, but encountered a monument staff prepared to litigate. The profits available in mining also diminished. Confounded, the company drew back and focused on its existing operations. "It was good for the park that [Tenneco/American Borate] was a big company," Barker reflected twenty-five years later. "A small company might have had to fight on; it might have needed the operation." To a large conglomerate, this one relatively small entity had given it a public relations black eye. Eventually, such pressure mitigated large-scale mining at Death Valley, removing the greatest single obstacle to eventual national park status at Death Valley National Monument.[18]

The Mining in the Parks Act had significant management consequences for Death Valley National Monument. After two generations of accepting mining with little ability to slow its advance, the monument could now take a posture more in line with widespread National Park Service expectations. The act created an entirely new management obligation, energizing the monument's response. Although Tenneco's actions prompted the legislation, the reality of mining extended far beyond its operations. In 1973 Death Valley counted more than 7,125 acres in private hands within its boundaries, as well as a considerably larger amount of state-held land, also susceptible to mining development. Five major mining companies owned more than 4,412 acres; private claimants, many of whom had not prospected in years, held the rest. In 1975 there were 384 unpatented and 207 patented claims in the monument, with more than 100 waiting to be negotiated. US Borax held 66 percent of the patented claims. The 1976 act allowed for more stringent enforcement, but it also demanded a vast commitment of staff time and resources.[19]

A chance to make serious inroads on their largest and most persistent problem propelled Death Valley's staff members forward. The law gave the monument many new tools for regulating mining, and in a move that further bolstered its arsenal, the National Park Service won a court decision in August 1977 that would have been impossible to secure but a few years earlier. US District Court judge M. D. Crocker of the Eastern District of California issued a permanent injunction against surface mining on the Billie Mining Claim.[20] The decision stunned the mining industry and strengthened the monument staff's morale and sense of mission. Although the decision did not halt mining on the Billie claim, it restricted it to belowground activities, more expensive and less lucrative than the increasingly popular open-pit mining. This was a major triumph for Death Valley and a portent of the power contained in the Mining in the Parks Act.

Thereafter, the National Park Service exerted considerably greater control over mining in Death Valley. In 1977, the first full year that the law was in effect, the monument rejected six new mining proposals, two for a lack of information about impact in their proposals and four because of the questionable validity of the claims they intended to develop. The monument had assented to only two of five plans of operation for existing mines by year's end, with the others continuing under temporary authority. At the end of the one-year period for recording claims specified in the act, the agency had 860 claims. In 1978 the National Park Service evaluated the unrecorded mining claims and found that only 27 were valid. Following the process to reclaim abandoned property, the agency returned many inholdings to public ownership.[21]

By 1978 the future direction of mining inside Death Valley was clear. The National Park Service used the 1976 statute to limit its impact. Between its efforts at assessing plans of operation, administering approved plans, and assessing claims, the management of mining became a primary endeavor of the monument staff. Compliance checks of approved mines yielded no major violations in 1978, but mining companies remained well aware of the implications of National Park Service oversight. The monument filed reports on the environmental impact of mining and wrote another study that assessed possible solutions to the need to purchase hundreds of mining claims that year. In 1979 the emphasis on minerals management continued. Mining again became an underground rather than a surface activity as a result of the new regulations, and the National Park Service then pressured the mining industry to take measures to avoid ground subsidence. The agency established more than eighty subsidence-monitoring stations for underground mines in 1979, further accentuating its increased regulatory authority. That year, it compelled reclamation at the Boraxo mine and other locations and judged more than 300 claims to be invalid, ensuring that mining in Death Valley proceeded in accordance with statute and National Park Service policy, not at the whim of mining operators. The change in power represented a major shift in monument management, perhaps the most noteworthy in the history of Death Valley.[22]

The shift in relations appeared temporary when the four-year moratorium on surface disturbance ended in 1980. The next year, Death Valley personnel experienced a "record workload" that resulted from the filing of new plans of operation for surface mining. Monument staff recognized that the legislative climate had also changed; under the new Reagan administration, further legislation restricting mining was at best unlikely. It fell to the monument to maintain its management policy in the face of an increasingly hostile regulatory structure. The NPS Regional Office offered money to support Denver Service Center staff and a Rocky Mountain Region mining engineer during the year, and Death Valley was able to use the law to restrict future surface disturbance. The monument also sought to eliminate inactive mining claims, making inroads throughout the 1980s. By 1990, even though Death Valley National Monument still contained significant inholdings—including 3,084 acres in patented mining claims—its staff had made considerable strides in resolving inholdings and mining claims.[23]

At Devils Hole, a second battle that highlighted the impact of the environmental revolution on traditional western extractive activities led to increased appreciation for Death Valley National Monument. Changes in agricultural water use prompted a transformation in the way governing agencies allocated the region's water resources. Until the 1960s, Amargosa Valley residents engaged in small-scale agricultural activities that had only a limited impact on the region's scant water supply. As the decade ended, the growing demand for agricultural products brought Spring Meadows, Inc., owned by Francis L. Cappaert, to the area. The company acquired 5,645 acres in Ash Meadows in an exchange with the Bureau of Land Management. The company eventually owned more than 12,000 acres, along with the majority of the water rights in the Amargosa Valley. A large-scale cattle operation, the first of its kind in the vicinity, took shape. In the economically depressed Amargosa Valley, residents looked at the operation with hope. They saw a self-contained entity that employed as many as one hundred people, ran cattle and horses, and raised its own feed. Residents welcomed the economic activity, for it seemed to offer new and better economic options for the region.[24]

The cattle enterprise drew considerably more water from Ash Meadows than did any earlier operation in the area. Such actions affected the complicated network of springs, in whose waters biologists had been monitoring a number of species for more than a generation. By the 1960s, Ash Meadows had earned a reputation as one of the most ecologically diverse places in North America. A range of desert fish, primarily pupfish and dace, could be found in its springs and Devils Hole, where the opening into a large underground limestone cavern is the only habitat of the Devils Hole pupfish. Studies of that species began in the 1930s, leading to the addition of Devils Hole to Death Valley National Monument in 1952. Ten years later, National Park Service monitoring of water levels in the area began; as pumping associated with Cappaert's ranching activities increased, the water levels in Devils Hole and other springs in the area fell, endangering the pupfish.[25]

The potential demise of an Ice Age relic population such as the pupfish attracted considerable public attention. Scientists such as Dr. James Deacon, a biologist from the University of Nevada–Las Vegas, arrived annually to assess the Devils Hole pupfish population and the condition of the single shelf on which it reproduced. The National Park Service and these scientists worked to establish a direct connection between the cattle operation and Ash Meadows' diminishing water levels. Scientific studies established that when pumping slowed or ceased, the water levels rose.[26] Although not incontrovertible evidence of direct impact, scientists argued the correlation was strong.

These studies created a setting in which environmentalists could lobby for protection for the pupfish. Scientists became catalysts in making the public aware of the issue, and the media soon took up the cause of the pupfish, once again bringing national attention to Death Valley National Monument. The environmental community loudly opposed Spring Meadows' use of water, initially pointing to the Endangered Species Act of 1966, the predecessor to the 1973 act of the same name, as justification for a halt to the pumping. In May 1970, after a series of articles in *Cry California,* the journal of California Tomorrow, which lamented the pupfish's fate, the Department of the Interior formed a pupfish task force. The agency appointed as its chairman James T. McBroom, assistant director for cooperative services in the Bureau of Sport Fisheries and Wildlife. The task force's goals included the creation of a management plan for the area that would protect pupfish and their habitat, a special groundwater study, reclassification of BLM lands in the area to protect water levels, investigation of the legality of existing water claims, and assessment of potential sites to which to transfer the pupfish. The task force recognized that it had to proceed with a plan to restore water to the springs and had to create an alternative in case the preferred plan could not attain the desired result.[27]

Deeply invested in traditional western extractive endeavors, the local community regarded the existence of the federal task force as tantamount to a declaration of war. From the perspective of many Amargosa Valley residents, the university scientists and federal officials were meddlers interfering with the region's livelihood. The appearance in the area of a US Geological Survey team to study regional groundwater conditions heightened the community's fears. The animosity became so great that at least one Amargosa Valley resident took pleasure in catching pupfish and feeding them to her cat.[28] A battle began that foreshadowed the struggles between extraction and ecology that would characterize the New West of the late twentieth century.

With the species' survival at stake, the task force acted quickly. It produced an initial June 1970 white paper that presented scientific solutions to the pupfish question, raised funds for the groundwater study and contracted with the

US Geological Survey to undertake it, and persuaded the Interior Department's assistant secretary for public land management to declare that seventy-three hundred acres of Ash Meadows were inappropriate for exchange, disposal, or sale. Although the task force failed to sway the Nevada state engineer, who continued to grant irrigation permit applications throughout 1970, a year later a combination of public opinion and political action changed the tenor of the dispute. Early in 1971, Senator Alan Cranston (D-CA) proposed the creation of a thirty-five-thousand-acre Devils Hole National Monument; others proposed a national wildlife refuge for the same land. Finally, on August 17, 1971, the US Department of Justice, acting on behalf of the Department of the Interior, asked a federal district court to order Spring Meadows to stop pumping water from three Ash Meadows wells to protect federal water rights in the area. The legal action attracted attention from the environmental community and the national press. The *Wall Street Journal* and *NBC News* both sent representatives to Death Valley National Monument to report on the situation. Just before the scheduled September 2, 1971, hearing, the federal government and the company reached an agreement that permitted pumping to continue until September 9, 1971, but prohibited it throughout the rest of the year and during all of 1972.[29]

The agreement blended different categories of assumptions, and as they proved incompatible, it collapsed. Although the agreement's restrictions were temporary, from Spring Meadows' perspective, they might as well have been permanent. The rules halted the company's business for an eighteen-month period without providing a mechanism to pay its expenses or provide additional water. The competing perspectives defied compromise. In the Interior Department's view, the 1952 inclusion of Devils Hole in Death Valley National Monument reserved unappropriated water rights to the land in question. This doctrine, never before tested in court, asserted that water rights came bundled with the land when the terms of an executive proclamation expressed a purpose for the property that required water to fulfill. Spring Meadows lacked perfected water rights when Congress added Devils Hole to Death Valley, and the department contended that under the doctrine of prior appropriation that governed most western water rights, its claim took precedence. Cappaert and his attorneys disagreed. In their view, the addition of Devils Hole to the monument did not specifically reserve any water rights, and any existing federal rights were included in the land exchange that brought Cappaert to the Amargosa Valley.[30] At its core, the battle was as old as federal involvement in the West, a question of state or federal precedence in law.

The courts were the only venue for a permanent resolution. On June 5, 1973, after an Interior Department request, a US district court limited pumping from wells connected to Devils Hole, ruling that federal interest in preserving the

Devils Hole's pupfish population created implied water rights that superseded Cappaert's claim. The Ninth Circuit Court of Appeals concurred, agreeing that the inclusion of Devils Hole in Death Valley National Monument reserved water rights to administer the area under the proclamation's terms. Cappaert appealed to the US Supreme Court, which ruled in favor of the government on June 7, 1976.[31] The water supply at Devils Hole was finally secure, protected by the very act that had included it in Death Valley National Monument.

The decision sent shock waves across the West. To farmers and ranchers, it seemed to permit the US government to claim water used for generations in many of the seventeen western states that depended on federal water compacts; it appeared as if the court ruling made their economic position tenuous. It also provided another piece of evidence for rural westerners that the tone of the time was against them and sharpened their antifederal sentiment. "There goes the neighborhood," wrote J. R. McCloskey, publisher of the *Mineral County (NV) Independent* in a typical regional assessment. "The high court did not officially declare the citizens of Nevada as an 'endangered species,' but it certainly established them as such."[32] While hyperbolic, McCloskey's comments reflected the growing dismay rural westerners felt about the environmental revolution. A few years later, such sentiments culminated in the Sagebrush Rebellion, a complicated backlash that fused antigovernment feelings across the region with the private–property rights movement.

The *Cappaert* decision was a major triumph for the National Park Service, and it produced ongoing ramifications. The Supreme Court ruling established precedent that in combination with the Mining in the Parks Act further increased Death Valley National Monument's significance. Yet protecting the victory required outside help. With the water levels under Devils Hole falling again in the early 1980s and plans in place for constructing more than twenty thousand homes in nearby subdivisions, the Nature Conservancy, one of the most successful conservation land-acquisition entities, stepped in. In the aftermath of the *Cappaert* decision, this land's original owners had offered to sell it to the US Fish and Wildlife Service, but its director declined to support a purchase. Once sold to developers, however, the USFWS changed its tune. The Nature Conservancy offered to purchase the land and hold it until the wildlife agency could secure federal funding for government purchase. An unusual emergency listing by Secretary of the Interior James Watt, always hostile to conservation goals but bound by statute in this case, inhibited the landowner and opened the way for the Nature Conservancy to step in. After a complicated funding arrangement, the land was transferred to the USFWS as a wildlife refuge in 1984.

Death Valley National Monument still faced enormous internal and external challenges. One of the most significant was the region's explosive growth and the resulting impact on local resources. The increasing influx of new residents in the California and Nevada deserts prompted calls for more comprehensive protection for Death Valley. Between 1970 and 1990, California grew by almost 14 million people. Las Vegas alone quadrupled in size in two decades to 1.8 million residents in 2005, and Tehachapi, California, zoomed from 11,957 to 32,653. These many new residents increased their use of the desert, aided by technologies such as automobile air-conditioning and with the evolution of all-terrain vehicles and other off-road motorized transportation. Since its establishment, Death Valley National Monument had received de facto protection because of its remote location. By the late 1970s, that physical security no longer sufficed; even the legal protection of national monument status, buttressed by the Mining in the Parks Act, seemed inadequate.[33] As elsewhere in the Southwest, national park proponents marshaled arguments in favor of a change to greater protective status.

The combination of the new enthusiasm about environmentalism and the impact of growth led to new land acquisitions in and around Death Valley. Chief among these was one of the most important acquisitions in the monument's history, the purchase of Scotty's Castle in 1970. Since Albert Johnson's death, the Gospel Foundation had managed what was for them an expensive operation far from their primary activities. It long had negotiated with the National Park Service for acquisition, but the agency lacked the funds. Money from the Land and Water Conservation Fund, established in 1964 as a mechanism for the federal government to acquire habitat, park, and recreational land, enabled the National Park Service to purchase the castle for $850,000. This sale served as a catalyst for a concerted effort to acquire other pieces of private property within the monument. Nearly a decade later, on January 23, 1979, the National Park Service purchased Stovepipe Wells Village from Trevell, Inc. Donations also helped the National Park Service acquire other private holdings. In 1978 the monument received a donation of the Harmony Borax Historic Site. In 1992 the Conservation Foundation provided fourteen hundred acres of patented mining claims.

Three years later, Edwin Rothfuss arrived at Death Valley to become superintendent. A geologist and a veteran of more than twenty years in the National Park Service, Rothfuss brought considerable experience to a difficult situation. He previously served as a law enforcement ranger at the Everglades, a naturalist at the Grand Canyon, the first district ranger at Island in the Sky at Canyonlands National Park, chief of interpretation and resource management at Virgin Islands and Mammoth Cave National Parks, and chief naturalist at Glacier National Park. After eight years at Glacier, Rothfuss took his first superintendency at Mount Rushmore National Memorial. Three years later, regional director Howard Chapman called to offer him the top job at Death Valley National Monument.[34]

Death Valley had severe problems beyond its land-acquisition and mining issues, and Chapman's offer included three specific actions that the new superintendent must tackle. First, burros were overrunning the monument, driving out other species and damaging water sources throughout the region. The National Park Service had a plan to resolve the problem, but any such program ran the risk of challenges from outside activists. Death Valley needed a superintendent with the courage to implement the agency's plan and the skill to keep it out of court— and out of the newspapers. The second issue reflected the monument's ability to manage its lands. The 1976 Mining in the Parks Act had limited extractive operations, but Chapman wanted the new superintendent to work with the monument's mining engineer to phase out mining inside its boundaries. Finally, Death Valley faced dire personnel problems. Chapman told Rothfuss that he wanted someone who could motivate personnel and create better career opportunities for them. The prospect of Death Valley had not initially enticed Rothfuss, but the challenges were exciting, as he recalled later: "I can't refuse that, so that's why I went to Death Valley."[35]

When he arrived in August 1982, however, Rothfuss discovered that Chapman had described only the most visible issues. Death Valley's physical facilities were abominable. Housing was "in sorry shape," the maintenance area was impossibly deficient, and Stovepipe Wells "looked like it needed to be condemned. . . . It was a disaster." Morale among monument staff was low. Many staff members lived in mobile homes, "hot tin boxes in the desert," as Rothfuss called them, forcing them to endure brutal summer heat with no relief. Inadequate schools made life difficult for children of staff members. The distance that students in the older grades had to travel to reach classes also affected their families. The staff seemed stagnant as well. A large portion had spent many years at the monument. When they sought other posts, they usually found few options. After a number of years, many felt that they could not leave and that the rest of the National Park Service did not appreciate their skills.[36]

Rothfuss learned that the inability of staff members to transfer within the agency reflected larger issues: a lack of respect for the monument within the National Park Service and a parallel inability to secure funding for its operations. Death Valley was "not held in the highest esteem," he recalled, especially by the National Park Service's Washington office and the Western Region that directly supervised the monument. After several months at Death Valley, Rothfuss confronted Chapman, telling him that he felt that the regional director was ignoring Death Valley and its needs. The crippling lack of staff and resources for needed programs seemed inexplicable to the new superintendent. Chapman first blanched at the remark and then candidly explained the problem to Rothfuss.

When National Park Service director George B. Hartzog Jr. appointed Chapman regional director, he expressed his personal philosophy that no area that permitted mining belonged in the national park system. Chapman felt Hartzog did not want him not to expend resources on the monument. Rothfuss realized that as long as that perception existed in the regional office, his task of effectively managing Death Valley remained difficult, if not impossible.[37]

Chapman's words crystallized an ongoing problem for Death Valley National Monument. Despite a generation of greater national appreciation of arid regions and the monument's features, desert parks remained outside the National Park Service's normative values. Continuance of mining within the monument remained a major part of the dilemma. Nearly a decade after the Mining in the Parks Act, the transformation it caused had not penetrated even the next layer of agency management. The difficulties extended beyond perception. One look at California's political culture showed that most political support for national parks went to Yosemite, Sequoia, King's Canyon, and Redwood. Mountaintops and gargantuan trees dominated the state's perception of its national park legacy, considerably narrowing a primary avenue of outside support. Rothfuss needed a strategy to redefine the meaning of Death Valley National Monument within the national park system and within California's congressional delegation.[38]

Other desert national park areas shared Death Valley's predicament, and nearly all similarly struggled for resources. Chief among these common concerns was a sense that the National Park Service did not appreciate desert parks. Managers came to refer to the issue as the "big-tree syndrome." In the perception of desert park managers, "parks with big trees could do no wrong," Rothfuss averred, and as a result, desert parks did not receive an equal share of agency resources. The enterprising superintendent recognized the raw material from which to form a community of interest, and he organized other key staff members of desert parks. By the late 1980s, Rothfuss helped convene the Desert Parks Conference, which created a venue to allow the desert parks to devise common strategies to alleviate their common concerns.[39]

On the local level, improving staff morale at Death Valley became a primary goal, and Rothfuss moved housing and schools to the top of his action list. Transfers for employees who wanted to leave became another priority. A nationwide agency program existed that sought to eliminate mobile homes for park staff, and Death Valley annually applied for funding. Secured money eventually built new houses at Cow Creek and Stovepipe Wells. Rothfuss went to hearings that supported moving the high school that served the monument from Shoshone, California, to Beatty, Nevada. The daily journey for students made it difficult to recruit families with school-age children. Not only did changing the school's location save thirty miles a day in travel, but Beatty High School also offered a full complement of extracurricular activities as well as a considerably larger student body than the thirty students in the Shoshone school's upper seven grades. The park staff's morale rose visibly when high school–age children started attending the Beatty school, assisting in the recruiting of new staff. Rothfuss also built his own workforce over time, assembling what he later called a "highly motivated staff that was pleased" to serve at Death Valley.[40]

Facilities at Death Valley posed another serious challenge. In the National Park Service, remedying poor facilities required a place on the monument's priority list. To achieve this end, any superintendent needed to establish facilities development as a leading goal, convey that objective to the regional office, and then typically wait a number of years until funding appeared. At Death Valley, Rothfuss recognized that the limited support of the regional office increased the predicament's complexity. The problems at the monument were so dire that they demanded a swift remedy. Stovepipe Wells, perhaps the most decrepit lodging facility in the national park system, became the test case. To accelerate perception of the need, Rothfuss pulled out an old report from a safety engineer at Sequoia who observed that the Stovepipe Wells facilities were dilapidated. Rothfuss suggested that the area was such a potential deathtrap that Death Valley personnel should burn the buildings and replant the area in cactus. The dramatic assessment catapulted Stovepipe Wells to the front of the funding queue, and within the next few years, the National Park Service spent more than five million dollars on property improvements. During that time, Death Valley was the top priority in the nation for a special fund to rehabilitate concession facilities, improving another substandard part of the monument's physical plant.[41]

The increase in staff morale and improvement in the monument's facilities paralleled a sweeping cultural shift that further altered Death Valley's position within the National Park Service. The *Cappaert* decision and the Mining in the Parks Act made national park–caliber resource protection possible at the monument, removing much of the stigma that had dogged Death Valley. Americans no longer regarded their deserts exclusively as wastelands. Many had learned to appreciate the stark beauty and unusual landforms of desert regions, especially after the Glen Canyon Dam buried canyonlands in southern Utah, and a generation of forceful writers, from Joseph Wood Krutch to Edward Abbey, extolled desertland beauty. The "most weird, wonderful, magical place on earth—there is nothing else like it anywhere" is how Abbey described the stark terrain of southeastern Utah that would become Canyonlands National Park in 1964. Seven years later, a national monument similar to Death Valley, Arches (also in Utah), become a national park.[42]

So it was that Death Valley's struggle for park status became an integral component of a larger debate about the future of California's desert lands. Technological innovations made the desert even more accessible, and enthusiasts of off-road
vehicles and others continued to roam with wild abandon, often destroying fragile ecosystems and endangering desert plant communities. Powerful environmental organizations sought remedies. They brought along the remains of the bipartisan conservation coalition in Congress, recently fractured by the rise of Ronald
Reagan and the end of liberal Republicanism it portended. James Watt's tenure as
secretary of the interior provided a rallying point for this coalition, which found
in the desert a way to reverse the Reagan administration's antienvironmentalism.
Asserting that Death Valley and Joshua Tree National Monuments were endangered to the point of destruction by population growth and callous misuse, they
sought a legislative remedy.[43]

Such a perspective placed Death Valley directly in the path of opposing but
converging trends. Even while the US economy faltered in the 1970s, congressional support for environmental protection remained constant. At the same
time, new movements that fervently opposed such goals came forward as part of a
backlash against the changes in US society and the global economy. Throughout
the 1970s and 1980s, legislation pushed federal land-management agencies toward
greater cooperation. After the Wilderness Act of 1964 and the Endangered Species
Act of 1973, which mandated review processes that agencies undertook separately,
the 1976 Federal Land Policy and Management Act (FLPMA) required interagency
cooperation. Although initially the old interbureau rivalries persisted, leading to
countless efforts to reinvent practices that peer agencies had long utilized, the
combination of the burdens of compliance in financial cost and work hours led
agencies to consider each other's practices and to promote cooperation. At the
same time, the principal opportunities to derive a living in the desert changed
from irrigated agriculture and ranching to recreation and tourism. Yet many who
felt that the era's trends disenfranchised their life choices avidly worked to limit
the reach of federal environmentalism and the legislative package that underpinned it. The desire to preserve the eastern Mojave Desert and transform Death
Valley from national monument to national park became the site of a new generation of environmental battles.

Following the guidelines of the 1976 Federal Land Policy and Management
Act, which required federal agencies to manage "the public lands and their various resource values so that they are utilized in the combination that will best meet
the present and future needs of the American people" (PL 94-579), the Bureau
of Land Management unveiled the *California Desert Plan.* Its proposal governed
twelve million acres of the eastern Mojave, making it the largest effort at regional

planning ever attempted in the United States. It divided these acres into different management districts or "zones": two million acres were designated as wilderness study areas, and the remaining ten million acres were classified for "intensive," "moderate," or "limited" development. In a manner that would not have seemed possible before the FLPMA, the Bureau of Land Management took charge of its lands and made difficult administrative decisions that pointed to clear goals. The *California Desert Plan* introduced a higher level of management to the California desert.[44]

The plan also articulated the differences between environmental and development positions. Conservationists were not thrilled with the BLM plan, objecting to what they believed were its tepid objectives. Developers and their supporters were incensed at what they saw as a locking up of valuable resources, and several sued the government. As a result, the bureau conceded a number of conditions, including the resumption of the famed Barstow-to–Las Vegas motorcycle race.

The National Park Service watched as the BLM found itself under assault. Agency director James M. Ridenour, President George H. W. Bush's appointee, worked to keep his agency out of the fray. An outspoken opponent of "thinning the blood," the practice of adding national park areas of lesser national significance, Ridenour expressed little interest in the addition of land affected by heavy multiple-use recreation. As a compromise and de facto protection against what he called the "heavier footprint" of the BLM, Ridenour supported expansion and national park status for Joshua Tree and Death Valley National Monuments.[45]

The BLM's concessions to developmental forces prompted a powerful response from the energized environmental community. During Watt's tenure as secretary of the interior, this constituency was easily outraged and typically mustered wide support. The "deserts as dumps" model seemed a relic of an earlier time, and although no one thought of the Mojave as one of the "last best places," as articulated in the 1980s environmental phrase to describe areas worth preserving, desert spaces had acquired their own powerful set of enthusiasts. A broad array of environmental groups beseeched Senator Alan Cranston, who became incensed at the BLM's proposal and planned legislation to trump it. In 1985 Cranston sent Kathy Files, his chief of staff, to Death Valley to tour areas that his proposed legislation would add to the monument. Patty Hedges of the Wilderness Society accompanied Files, and many environmental groups joined to support Cranston's idea. In 1986 Cranston introduced Senate Bill 2061, an attempt to create comprehensive protection for the eastern Mojave. Under this bill, called the California Desert Protection Act (CDPA), Death Valley National Monument would become Death Valley National Park, and its boundaries would expand by more than one million acres.[46]

Death Valley National Monument held a complicated position during the battle for the CDPA. It provided environmental advocates with a powerful tool: any land that Congress added to Death Valley enjoyed national park system protection and became de facto "sacred space." Securing national park status for Death Valley National Monument also improved the chances for protection of the Mojave Desert in general. Any BLM land that the government could transfer to the national park system enjoyed not only the protection of national park–area designation, but the tacit support of much of the public as well.

Questions of wilderness designation complicated the struggle for the CDPA. Under the Roadless Area Review and Evaluation process in the 1970s that resulted from the Wilderness Act of 1964, the government recommended almost two million acres of Death Valley for wilderness designation. Cranston's original bill affirmed the wilderness recommendation, a legislative decision that ensured fierce opposition from development forces. By the mid-1980s, wilderness was a loaded concept, the single protection strategy that most incensed antienvironmental groups. In 1991 Congress updated the wilderness recommendations in the CDPA to reflect the new climate. Throughout the CDPA process, park opponents such as Representative James Hansen (R-UT), a vehement opponent of the very concept of public land, focused on wilderness designation as a primary reason to fight the CDPA. Although Death Valley superintendent Edwin Rothfuss attempted to mollify the congressman, the very idea of wilderness made western representatives such as Hansen apoplectic.[47]

The National Park Service actively supported national park status for Death Valley for strategic as well as administrative and political purposes. After the 1979 passage of the Alaskan National Interest Lands Conservation Act, the park system's future seemed to head north. Alaska contained the largest and most spectacular remaining tracts of public lands, but building a nationwide constituency with a program to preserve Alaska proved difficult. Traditional national parks became increasingly unattainable in the lower forty-eight states. After the establishment of the last three—Guadalupe Mountains, Redwoods, and North Cascades—in the late 1960s, finding even medium-size tracts of spectacular scenic lands under federal administration in the continental United States that were not already controlled and strongly defended by the US Forest Service was unlikely.[48] The greatest contiguous federal holdings were in the deserts, making the effort in the eastern Mojave crucial to agency aspirations to continue to expand its profile in the lower forty-eight states.

At the local level, national park status resolved a number of issues for Death Valley National Monument. Increasing visitation, management concerns, and regional development outside the monument impinged on the proposed national park. Death Valley managed its considerable internal threats with aplomb, but it had little control over growth outside its boundaries. The more stringent protection and greater reverence that national park status offered were considerable attractions to monument officials. A larger land base would provide a considerable buffer to the most heavily used features of Death Valley, while the opportunity to control visitation inside the monument as well as the ecological circumstances of the larger region also offered advantages to management. National park status had been an oft-considered goal at Death Valley since the monument's establishment. The CDPA provided the first genuine opportunity to achieve this objective.

Strong congressional support for national parks persisted throughout the Reagan era, but the CDPA did not fare well. Despite Cranston's efforts, the initial version of the CDPA failed to emerge from the Senate committee reviewing it. Cranston reintroduced his bill in various forms during subsequent congressional sessions. During 1991 the House of Representatives passed a version of the CDPA, HR 2929. Its Senate companion bill, SB 21, failed to reach the Senate floor. Senator John Seymour (R-CA) followed the Republican Party's antigovernment platform, creating a procedural problem that buried the bill in committee. In 1992 a change in California's US Senate representation gave the stalled project hope. Seymour lost his seat to former San Francisco mayor Dianne Feinstein, a Democrat and desert partisan. In the same election, Barbara Boxer, another Democrat, replaced Alan Cranston, who departed the Senate in poor health after becoming embroiled in a savings-and-loan scandal in the late 1980s. Feinstein, whose political relationship with Cranston began in the early 1970s, quickly picked up the CDPA and became an active proponent of protecting California's deserts and enlarging Death Valley National Monument. However, Republicans continued to control the Senate, stalling action on the CDPA.[49]

After two more years of political maneuvering and nearly nine years after Cranston's first bill, in 1994 Congress finally enacted the California Desert Protection Act (PL 103-433). Although Senator Malcolm Wallop (R-WY) filibustered the bill, Feinstein obtained sufficient Republican support to ensure its enactment. Passed just before the congressional elections of 1994, when voters swept into office the "Contract with America" Republican Congress, the bill was a conventional conservation bill. What made it unique was the quantity of land involved—by any federal land-management standard, 4 million acres was considerable—and the fact that the land was in the desert. The sheer quantity of land created possibilities that had never before existed. The act tripled national park and wilderness acreage in the southern and eastern parts of California, to more than 9 million acres. The total was almost as large as the states of Massachusetts, Connecticut, and Rhode Island combined. National Park Service holdings increased by more than 3 million acres; Death Valley added 1.2 million acres and became a national park, as did Joshua Tree, which grew by 234,000 acres. After the CDPA, Death Valley National Park joined the park system at 3,336,000 acres, by itself nearly twice the size of Delaware. The resulting national park was truly massive; describing the new boundaries required sixteen typed pages. The CDPA also established an entirely new unit of the national park system: the 1.6 million-acre Mojave National Preserve, an area formerly managed by the Bureau of Land Management as the East Mojave National Scenic Area. In addition, the CDPA designated sixty-nine new wilderness areas on lands administered by the bureau. Congress designated approximately 95 percent of the expanded Death Valley National Park as wilderness, as well as half of Mojave National Preserve and Joshua Tree National Park.[50]

The bill's passage, a response to the growth of the postwar era and the end of the de facto preservation that had long been an advantage of remote location, created a new order in the California desert. As technological innovation made the desert accessible and millions of people moved closer to it, its comprehensive preservation became a necessity. The nine years that elapsed between the CDPA's initial proposal and the final bill indicated the degree of difficulty involved in the process, but the bill's passage, especially by a Republican-controlled Senate, spoke volumes about the ongoing public commitment to the preservation of the national natural legacy. Even the desert now belonged in the pantheon of the American spectacular.

With the creation of Death Valley National Park, the National Park Service gained more land and more complicated management obligations. De facto preservation ceased to be a viable alternative, compelling new strategies within the former monument as well as on the new lands. The National Park Service confronted traditional organizational issues such as resource management and wilderness protection and a new one in the fact of enormous regional growth. The Mojave Desert was becoming a very full place.

The CDPA also created an even greater need for interagency cooperation in the Death Valley area. The ascent to national park status, the creation of the Mojave National Preserve, and the reassignment of Bureau of Land Management acreage to the national park system helped foster joint planning and management. The requirement to manage lands for wilderness, long anathema to some in the recreational user community, brought different agencies further together. Because of the new legislation, the agencies operated in each other's spheres, and the BLM and the National Park Service reached accommodation about long-term planning in the eastern Mojave.[51]

The interagency planning effort that resulted became a model for federal land management in the twenty-first century. As a result of the CDPA, the government assembled an interagency planning team to orchestrate the subsequent twenty years in the desert. Planners utilized the desert as a pilot project of the National Performance Review for ecosystem management and planning. The Mojave Desert became, in the words of then vice president Al Gore, an "innovative management laboratory," where scientists and managers could plan and implement long-term ecosystem management.[52] An extended process created a blueprint for managing the region in the early twenty-first century and proved the fundamental necessity of interagency cooperation that has continued ever since.

Tom Wilson with Timbisha Shoshone basketry, sometime in the 1930s. One consequence of the National Park Service using fire to control the invasive tamarisk trees at Eagle Borax was the incineration of the Wilson-Billson camp and its archaeological record. (Courtesy National Park Service, Death Valley National Park)

Although the indigenous peoples of Death Valley have lived in the region for millennia, it took a lengthy struggle with the National Park Service and the federal government to secure their rights to a portion of their homeland. (Courtesy National Park Service, Death Valley National Park)

The pursuit of the valley's mineral riches was one of the key ways by which this arid landscape entered the nineteenth-century American economy and cultural imagination. Gold Hill Mill, Warm Spring Canyon road, Death Valley Junction, Inyo County, California. (Courtesy Library of Congress, Prints and Photographs Division, HAER, reproduction number CA-292-8)

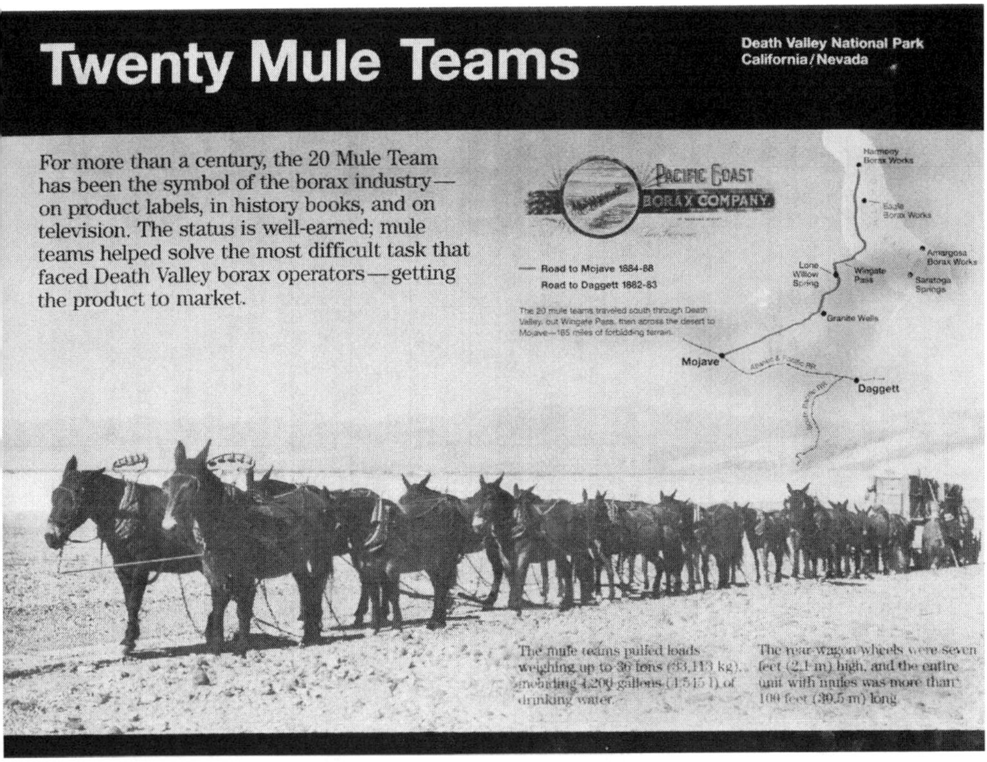

Twenty Mule Teams

For more than a century, the 20 Mule Team has been the symbol of the borax industry— on product labels, in history books, and on television. The status is well-earned; mule teams helped solve the most difficult task that faced Death Valley borax operators—getting the product to market.

PACIFIC COAST
BORAX COMPANY

— Road to Mojave 1884-88
Road to Daggett 1882-83

The 20 mule teams traveled south through Death Valley, out Wingate Pass, then across the desert to Mojave—185 miles of forbidding terrain.

Harmony Borax Works
Eagle Borax Works
Amargosa Borax Works
Lone Willow Spring
Wingate Pass
Saratoga Springs
Granite Wells
Mojave
Daggett

The mule teams pulled loads weighing up to 30 tons (83,113 kg), including 1,200 gallons (4,515 l) of drinking water.

The rear wagon wheels were seven feet (2.1 m) high, and the entire unit with mules was more than 100 feet (30.5 m) long.

Moving heavy loads of borax from the rich veins in the valley to distant markets over rough roads led to the invention of these twenty-mule wagons, which became symbols of the industry. Interpretive sign at Harmony Borax Works, Death Valley Junction, Inyo County, California. (Courtesy Library of Congress, Prints and Photographs Division, HAER CAL, reproduction number 14-DVNM, 4-1)

The growth of tourism in Death Valley prior to its becoming a national monument is reflected in this attractive brochure for the inn and hotel, essential amenities for the traveler. (Courtesy Death Valley lodging brochure, Maps and Ephemera Collection, Special Collections, Honnold/Mudd Library of the Claremont Colleges, Claremont, California)

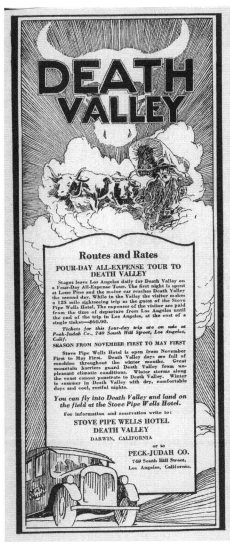

To bring tourists to Death Valley, dubbed "California's Playground," the Peck-Judah Company offered regular bus transportation to the desert site from Los Angeles. (Courtesy Death Valley tour brochure, Maps and Ephemera Collection, Special Collections, Honnold/Mudd Library of the Claremont Colleges, Claremont, California)

This eccentric Moorish castle is the creation of two idiosyncratic souls, Death Valley
Scotty, a prospector, raconteur, and con man, and Albert Johnson, a wealthy Chicago
businessman who did not mind getting conned. Together, they conceived of this sprawling home for Johnson and his family, where Scotty also lived. It became part of the
national park in 1970. (Courtesy Library of Congress, Prints and Photographs Division,
HABS CAL, reproduction number 14-DVNM, 1-3)

To identify to visitors that they were entering the national park, the National Park Service situated signs such as this one to demarcate its management boundary and the beginning of the tourist experience. Entrance sign on Highway 374, Beatty Road. (Courtesy Library of Congress, Prints and Photographs Division, HAER CAL, reproduction number 14-DVNM, 3-11)

Funding through the Civilian Conservation Corps brought hundreds of young men to Death Valley in the 1930s, to build roads, trails, lodges, and other amenities; their construction work and personal experiences were transformative. (Courtesy National Park Service, Death Valley National Park)

Automobile tourism, as reflected in the hardened roadbed, early on became the prime way by which visitors arrived at and experienced Death Valley. Ubehebe Crater Road, near the intersection with State Route 267. (Courtesy Library of Congress, Prints and Photographs Division, HAER CAL, reproduction number 14-DVNM, 3-8)

As a result of the Endangered Species Act (1973) and the listing of the Devil's Hole pupfish, an ice-age relic, as deserving federal protection, this site was made a part of the national monument. (Courtesy National Park Service, Death Valley National Park)

The scale of the valley and its geological formations dwarfs the human experience, part of Death Valley's great appeal (and some of its danger). (Courtesy National Park Service Digital Image Archives)

The massive dunes, smooth and rippled, shift with the winds that sweep across Death Valley and are emblematic of the natural forces that make and remake this malleable terrain. (Courtesy National Park Service Digital Image Archives)

CHAPTER 4

Native Americans and the Park

Death Valley National Monument was established in the heart of the homeland of the Panamint Shoshones, whose descendants later were called "Timbisha." Federal officials drew up the monument's boundaries with scant regard for the region's prior inhabitants and with even less recognition of their historic status and position. The United States had long given priority to the claims of miners and anyone else who understood the nation's land laws ahead of those of the people who had historically lived in the area. These legal codes placed the Timbisha in a peculiar jeopardy. The Bureau of Indian Affairs (BIA) had never given the Timbisha formal status as a tribe, and thus they lacked direct access to the meager advantages the government could have provided. The tribe did not have legal standing, either, which would have granted it access to the US federal court system. Caught in limbo at the monument's founding, the Timbisha had little control over the land on which their lives had long depended.

In this regard, they shared much with other Native Americans who lived inside or adjacent to national parks. Until the 1970s, such disregard was a typical part of national park–area creation, a process in which the agency created landscapes devoid of people, best described in 1963's Leopold Report as "vignettes of primitive America." To reflect the values of nineteenth-century romanticism, national parks became landscapes from which the government had removed people, indigenous or otherwise. This primeval America, a vestige of a world before the European entry, erased Indians from that landscape of meaning; they did not signify. This exclusive formulation of the role of national parks began with the founding of Yellowstone National Park in 1872 and continued for at least the next one hundred years.[1]

Native peoples were absent from these lands only in a figurative sense; often they remained in or near national park areas, treated as symbolic representations of a distant past and divested of all but mythic status. If resident Native Americans wanted to play the part of mythic Indians and dance and perform ceremonies for visitors, they were welcome in the national parks. But if they deviated from that purely symbolic role and became a real presence, the National Park Service treated them as a people who did not much matter to the agency's operations or concern.[2]

In so responding, the NPS perfectly mirrored the desires and values of middle- and upper-middle-class white Americans. Mainstream America had little place for Indians except as a manifestation of a defeated past. Where federal land received special designation, someone—often Native American but occasionally Anglo-American—was likely to be displaced. In the western national parks and across Alaska, the instances of such treatment are numerous. Resident populations were also prevalent in the eastern national parks, those bought with congressional dollars while filled with people who presented an image or a history the National Park Service did not yet appreciate or value. The result was a pattern that served one set of goals but proved a harsh reality for prior residents of national park areas. As the United States designed national parks to fulfill the combination of educational and nationalistic functions that the early and mid-twentieth century demanded, the federal government enforced a policy of exclusion that wrote Native Americans and other longtime residents out of these lands' narratives. Instances of callous treatment and removal of Native peoples were so common that, in retrospect, some have come to regard the National Park Service's treatment of them as the agency's original sin.[3]

The removal of Native peoples and the manipulation of their land claims resulted from the convergence of a number of trends. Congress usually established national park areas from federal lands, creating an inherent contradiction. Federal land belonged to the people of the United States. Yet the lands selected for national parks often belonged to Native peoples, many of whom the government had moved only recently; that said, federal ownership of these terrains trumped any prior claim. As the treatment of Spanish and Mexican land grants after the 1848 Treaty of Guadalupe Hidalgo revealed, US law alone defined the legal status of what had become American land. Law provided justification for behavior that might not otherwise have withstood scrutiny. At the same time, the nation reached for a broad cultural identity, and "nature," as codified in the national parks, provided it. This oft-lethal combination of legal principle and national identity framed around "empty" wilderness devastated Native Americans, not least the Timbisha, who had made their home in what became Death Valley National Monument long before Europeans arrived in the New World.

The Timbisha's creation story tells of their people's emergence on earth at Ube-hebe Crater, when Coyote, who carried them, put down his basket and slept. While he rested, the people crept out of the basket and scattered around Death Valley. Part of a larger group of Western Shoshones referred to as the Panamint Shoshones, the Timbisha descended from prehistoric Native Americans who wintered on Death Valley's floor and spent summers in the Panamint Mountains to the west. These Panamint Shoshones were a small westerly arm of the main Shoshone people. They were neighbors to Southern Paiute to the south, Kawaisu to the south and west, and Northern Paiute to the north and west, providing a rich, interconnected world of desert dwellers.[4]

Small populations made relationships among the different groups in greater Death Valley an essential component of survival. The Timbisha Shoshones inhabited several districts in Death Valley and the surrounding mountain ranges. During historic times, no more than 100 to 150 individuals lived in this area of roughly five hundred square miles. The boundaries between the Shoshones and neighboring groups such as the Paiute or Kawaisu were flexible. Even linguistic difference did not halt social interaction. Neighboring Kawaisu, Northern Paiute, and Southern Paiute all participated in this wider social and economic circle. Fluctuation in available food required families to go outside their immediate areas to gather or hunt; a lack of permanent ownership of hunting-and-gathering areas facilitated this practice, emphasizing cooperation. Individual families often attended fall festivals outside their own district. These kinds of social ties extended beyond the immediate Death Valley area. Intermarriage among the different peoples was common, strengthening kinship networks.[5]

Death Valley's environment played a key role in shaping Timbisha culture. The sparse desert, broken up by several groups of high mountains, afforded a variety of habitation zones and food sources. The Shoshone economy depended on subsistence from nature; piñon nuts from mountain trees and mesquite pods gathered in the valleys provided important food sources that were supplemented by hunting small animals, particularly rabbits, and some larger game such as bighorn sheep and deer. Eventually, the Shoshones farmed in small gardens around the various valley springs. This sparse economy compelled groups of families to maintain close connections while dispersed for part of the year throughout several hundred square miles of territory.

A seasonal cycle of migration predicated the economy of the Western Shoshones, a crucial factor and one that ever after complicated their relations with the Anglo-American world. Individual families or a small group of relatives traveled separately from the rest of the group during most of the year. In winter, when cooler temperatures and occasional moisture made resources comparatively plentiful, larger numbers camped together in villages. Dependable food and water supplies helped determine the location of such communities. Cooperative economic efforts were rare, but when they occurred, they usually involved hunting. Communal rabbit hunts were quite frequent, whereas antelope hunts took place less often. Typically, these larger operations included several villages. Families also gathered during the fall to collect pine nuts and hold festivals, at which the Shoshones conducted ceremonies, socialized, and gambled. The pine nuts harvested at the fall gatherings might last as little as a month, ensuring that the tribal population needed to replenish the stores by other means.

Although the economy placed limits on cooperation between villages, those groups in the Death Valley area tended to associate more with some villages than others. According to ethnographer Julian Steward, these groupings of villages, known as "districts," shared collective names and evinced enough unity that Steward labeled them as "bands," a higher level of social organization by anthropological standards. A "chief" with limited power led each district. Indicating the loose nature of affiliation and the lack of power in the hierarchy, the Shoshone word for chief translated as "big talker" or sometimes "talker." Leaders typically functioned as facilitators, deriving power from their service to the group. They coordinated the fall festivals and hunts, activities of considerable practical and ceremonial significance, and also handled the equivalent of foreign relations involving different villages. According to Steward, these were significant positions, not temporary roles; as such, they had social value, and leaders typically passed them to their male relatives.[6]

Furnace Creek was an important center of Timbisha Shoshone life. Historical accounts indicated a substantial settlement with deep roots in Death Valley, albeit without a consensus about exactly who lived there and when they arrived. One of archaeologist Julian Steward's informants told of several families that lived in the area for many generations. Another informant said there was no Shoshone settlement until Bill Boland arrived in 1883. Still other information suggested that Bill Boland's father lived at Furnace Creek in 1852, and the Bolands maintained that Furnace Creek was their home. Steward's research confirmed that Shoshone settlements were present at Furnace Creek since contact with the Euro-American world. The Timbisha articulated this position in 1970s, when negotiations over Native American rights in Death Valley began. In a letter to the federal government, Timbisha representatives contended that Shoshone peoples had occupied Death Valley since "time immemorial."[7]

Furnace Creek offered ample evidence of ongoing Shoshone habitation. When Anglo-Americans arrived in 1849, they found a considerable Shoshone presence, albeit very few people at that precise moment. A party of '49ers encountered what they described as a "big Indian camp," although only one Shoshone remained to meet the newcomers. The Shoshones were a consistent presence, and nearly every passerby remarked upon them. An 1857 US surveyor-general map showed Shoshone huts at Furnace Creek. During a visit to Furnace Creek in 1858, one traveler observed a rancheria of more than one hundred people, with twenty or thirty structures, standing at the mouth of Furnace Creek. An 1861 summer party found no Shoshones along the creek. One observer rightly noted that at that time of year, the Shoshones were most likely at their summer camp in the high mountains on the other side of the valley, living on stores of pine nuts and dried rabbit. Wildrose Canyon or Johnson Canyon, areas where several valley families passed the summer, provided the most likely summer locales. A number of people from the Panamint group intermittently lived near what would become Darwin, a mining town in the Panamint Mountains founded in 1875. The pattern of seasonal occupation confounded whites. A party of prospectors in 1886 discovered a deserted Indian settlement at Furnace Creek, but by 1890, the Panamint group constituted nearly the entire population of the Furnace Creek village, and traditional hunting and gardening took place throughout the decade. By that time, the Boland and Wilson families both lived in Death Valley on a permanent basis.[8]

At the same time, Anglo-American economic endeavors provided new employment opportunities for the Timbisha. In 1860 a Shoshone led a party of whites into Surprise Canyon, just south of Hall Canyon. Indian oral histories told of Native American groups in the Panamint Mountains and Panamint Valley to the east of Death Valley cutting wood for the charcoal ovens at Wildrose Canyon in the 1870s. Shoshone people lived around Telescope Peak in February 1873 and in the Panamint Mountains around 1875. Beginning in 1881, mining operations at Eagle Borax in southern Death Valley and, in 1883, at Harmony Borax near Furnace Creek employed area Shoshones. Although these operations each lasted only a few years, they set the stage for the growing importance of wage work for Indians from the settlement and elsewhere in Death Valley. Haying and irrigation at the Greenland Ranch became important seasonal sources of wages in the 1890s. The opportunities were so plentiful that Indians from the south end of the valley also worked there on occasion.[9]

By the beginning of the twentieth century, Shoshone people had become well ensconced throughout Death Valley and its surroundings. Even after Anglo-Americans settled the area permanently in 1883, the Shoshones maintained their traditional social structure. Some mined or allowed others to mine their claims, while others worked for the Furnace Creek borax operations and further north at Harmony. Still other Shoshones grew crops or planted orchards, selling the surplus. They also worked for wages as guides or on ranches. Some women cleaned in boomtowns such as Rhyolite, bringing additional wages home. Even before 1933, when the National Park Service became part of the local community, the Death Valley Shoshones had begun to alter their historic ways of subsistence.

Soon after 1900, the Bureau of Indian Affairs became involved with the Death Valley Shoshones for the first time. A 1906 survey of California Indians by BIA special agent Charles Kelsey listed two families in the Panamint Valley by name, Panamint Tom and his cousin Panamint Joe, antecedents of the modern Timbisha. Kelsey noted nine families comprising forty members who lived in Death Valley, but provided no names or additional details. Part of a state of California effort to account for the large numbers of unenrolled Indians—those not registered in any tribe recognized by the government—Kelsey's work paved the way for an allotment of land from the public domain in 1908 for Hungry Bill, Panamint Tom's brother, in the Panamint Mountains. In 1911, in response to the survey, the federal government established the Bishop Indian Agency at Bishop, California. Despite the 160-mile distance and the very difficult country to traverse, the Death Valley Shoshones fell under the Bishop Agency's jurisdiction. The distance impeded the relationship, and within a few years, the Bishop Indian Agency focused its energy on closer tribal groups. Despite the shift in emphasis, the Death Valley Shoshones remained a responsibility of the Bishop BIA staff. They were on BIA census rolls from 1916 until 1940. After 1926 the BIA closed the Bishop Agency and transferred jurisdiction of the Sierra Nevada region first to the Walker River Agency and then back to its original home in the Carson Agency.[10]

Before 1900 federal Indian agencies began their often-misguided attempts to help Native peoples while at the same time providing an avenue for assimilation into US society. By the turn of the twentieth century, federal Indian agencies sought to rehabilitate their reputations. Many dispensed with their predatory nineteenth-century traits and had become paternalistic but comparatively benign institutions. These federal organizations still retained powerful influence over Indians, for they controlled the livelihood of their charges. Most agencies expected Indians to conform to the dictates of the federal agent; in return, the agency offered services. The landless Indians who lived within agency jurisdiction posed the greatest difficulty, especially if they were far from the Indian agency headquarters. In some cases, agencies helped secure land for their remote charges, but this was an infrequent circumstance.[11]

The Death Valley Shoshones were among those who lived at considerable remove from BIA facilities and therefore received little assistance. Only Hungry Bill appears to have directly benefited from the agency's assistance, but his relationship required an interminable amount of time to develop. An initial General Land Office ruling in 1907 granted Hungry Bill a homestead claim in Johnson Canyon in the Panamints; on review the agency reversed the award decision, ruling that as a Native American, Hungry Bill was ineligible to homestead. The

Carson Indian Agency again filed the claim, and in 1908, the Bureau of Indian Affairs approved the allotment, issuing a permanent patent in 1927. The agency also deeded a winter village settlement at Hall Canyon on the west side of the Panamint Mountains to a Shoshone named George Hanson. He and his family cultivated alfalfa and fruit and raised goats on the property. In 1923 a flash flood destroyed the irrigation system, and Hanson asked the government for relief. The BIA could not help; under the law, Hanson did not own the property, making him ineligible for government assistance. In 1928, as part of an effort to adjudicate Shoshone land claims, Congress set aside a tract for the Death Valley Shoshones. A portion of the tract was deeded to Hanson, allowing for federal help in rebuilding his irrigation works. In only one other case, an allotment given in 1936 to Robert Thompson, son of Panamint Tom, did a Death Valley Shoshone receive title to land.[12]

Federal educational programs also offered little to the Death Valley Shoshones. Educating Indians had long been a primary BIA focus, and officials sought to place Death Valley children in school. After 1910 some Death Valley Indian children attended the Carson City Indian School, which offered a curriculum that reached tenth grade and emphasized vocational skills. The first group arrived in 1911, and Death Valley children continued to attend until 1918. Throughout the era, BIA officials sought more pupils for the school. In 1915 Carson School superintendent Frederick Snyder contacted the Shoshones at Lida, seeking to enroll their children. Many parents did not want their children that far from home, and the desert's great size made it possible to keep them out of the reach of boarding-school officials. Some children attended public school in Darwin and Beatty as early as 1915, and BIA officials recognized the merit in this change. In 1918 BIA commissioner Cato Sells urged the Bishop Agency to place all Death Valley Shoshone children in public schools and pay tuition for them; in 1920 E. B. Merritt, the assistant commissioner, directed the agent to "consider them under his jurisdiction" and to enroll them in public schools.[13]

BIA regulations entitled off-reservation Indian children to public school at federal expense, resulting in a struggle between the Death Valley Shoshones and the federal government. Tuition posed a considerable expense to the BIA. In 1920 seven Shoshone families with sixteen school-age children lived at Furnace Creek; the federal government would have to pay Inyo County, California, if they attended local school. To resolve this situation, the Bishop agent tried to coerce the Furnace Creek families with school-age children to move to Owens Valley to attend Indian schools. Cost saving was clearly a motivating factor. The families refused, establishing an important precedent. If they did not leave, they could protect their land claim to the area. In addition, the group did not want to be under government jurisdiction, choosing to continue to work at Furnace Creek. The Bureau of Indian Affairs eventually relented, paying tuition for Furnace Creek children to attend public school starting in 1922.

Death Valley Shoshone resistance in this case yielded important dividends. In 1925 and 1926, a school with room for fifteen pupils opened at Furnace Creek. Teachers also taught adult Indians there after hours. Between 1926 and 1932, interruptions in public school funding resulted from shortages of federal appropriations and conflicts with the public school districts and other factors. With the advent of the New Deal and the ascension of John Collier to commissioner of Indian affairs, funding became more consistent. Officials referred to the school at Death Valley as the "Death Valley Special School," although it was under control of the Ryan District. Other Shoshones from Death Valley continued to attend public schools at Darwin and Beatty, and in the 1920s, at least a few lived at the Carson and Sherman boarding schools. After 1931 six Death Valley Shoshones consistently attended Carson, and at least a few attended Sherman. Six more Indian children attended public school in Furnace Creek.[14] Even without a land base, by staying in their home place, the Death Valley Shoshones received one of the primary benefits offered by the BIA.

By 1933, when Death Valley National Monument was established, the Death Valley Shoshones had considerable experience in dealing with agents of the federal government. But they had never encountered the National Park Service and had little reason to be hopeful about the new administrators. Tribal elder Pauline Esteves recalled:

> They all wore uniforms and the people were kind of intimidated because they were used to hearing about uniforms, cavalry and that kind of stuff, so beware of the uniforms. Here they are with these people wearing uniforms and taking charge and walking all over the place. They felt [that] since there was just a very small number of people living here, [we] could never confront them. So, they said we will just be wary of them, stay our distance, and just don't upset them because we know that the outcome is not going to be very good.[15]

The Death Valley Shoshones had other reasons to fear these newcomers. The new monument stretched across their homeland, covering nearly every area where the Shoshones lived and subsisted. The presidential proclamation had not included small areas of private land such as Hungry Bill's allotment and non-Indian holdings at Furnace Creek and other places in the monument boundaries. The National Park Service acquiesced on the allotment of Panamint Tom's home in Warm Springs Canyon to his son, Robert Thompson, but in general, the agency set out to administer the new monument with little thought to its prior inhabitants, their history or culture, habits or needs.[16]

In this respect, the Shoshones in Death Valley fared no differently from most Native American groups who encountered the National Park Service. Even before Congress established the agency, the federal government itself had removed Native peoples from park landscapes and even denied them historic rights to hunt and fish within national park boundaries. In the 1930s, the National Park Service's mission, preserving spectacular and important places and presenting them as emblems of national greatness, generally ignored Native Americans. From the Grand Canyon to Glacier National Park, Native peoples found their historic uses of lands within national parks circumscribed and their options limited. The National Park Service usually even rebuffed legally recognized tribes' efforts to use the national park lands for historic purposes. The small group of Shoshones in Death Valley, not recognized as a tribe by the federal government in the 1930s, stood little chance of gaining the rapidly expanding National Park Service's attention.[17]

Even before the National Park Service's arrival, the population of Death Valley Shoshones became more concentrated. Families were still living at a number of the traditional locations throughout the 1930s, but they gravitated to specific enclaves because of outside pressures and specific economic opportunities. By 1940 the Shoshones occupied only a few sites, principally Furnace Creek, while Wildrose Canyon in the Panamints still served as a summer settlement. The National Park Service added to the pressure to coalesce, gradually restricting hunting rights and further concentrating the Shoshone population. Monument staff also revised regulations to curtail the raising and selling of horses and burros, a long-standing Indian livelihood. As Indians had fewer options, they stayed closer together, finding in community solace and sustenance. As a result, the winter population of the Furnace Creek settlement increased substantially in the 1930s, reaching as many as sixty people. Residents came from a variety of families throughout Death Valley, instead of just from families with roots in the immediate area. Employment at the Pacific Coast Borax Company's Furnace Creek operation provided another important reason for the concentration. Its jobs replaced subsistence activities, and the Indian village stood on land claimed by the company. Indian men worked in area mines. When the hotel opened, the women followed into company employ.[18]

The Great Depression inaugurated an era of even harder times at Death Valley, placing the Shoshones at great disadvantage. State and county governments tended to treat the group as an unwarranted burden. In this difficult era, the National Park Service and the BIA came to the defense of the Shoshones. In

1936 federal observers noted that the Indians were in a crisis. Still suffering from the Depression, Inyo County was reluctant to add new people to its relief rolls. Although Indians formally became US citizens in 1924, they were not taxed as were non-Indian citizens, and county officials simply did not want to support people who did not contribute to county coffers. Inyo County officials and the Pacific Coast Borax Company, which feared that the Indian presence would have a negative impact on hotel visitors, sought removal of the Death Valley Shoshones from Furnace Creek. Death Valley superintendent T. R. Goodwin and Alida Bowler, the BIA superintendent at Carson Agency, Nevada, opposed the proposal, thinking that removal would be improper as well as difficult. Bowler and Goodwin recognized Furnace Creek as traditional territory for the Death Valley Shoshones. Bowler argued that even if the Indians were removed to another location, within a year most would drift back to their traditional home and way of living, wintering in Death Valley or adjacent valleys and then moving into the Panamint or other mountain ranges during the summer. Bowler and Goodwin considered a forty-acre Indian village at Furnace Creek as the possible site for a permanent home for the Shoshones.[19]

Goodwin's and Bowler's perspectives reflected significant changes in federal thinking about Indian people as embodied in the Indian Reorganization Act (IRA) of 1934 and in John Collier's principled leadership of the BIA. Effectively, the combination of law and policy emancipated Native Americans, albeit under the BIA's watchful eye. For the Death Valley Shoshones, this change meant that government agencies that long denigrated their pursuits and ways of thinking now became advocates of their cause. Although the Indians appreciated such efforts, they rightly remained wary.[20]

Bowler and Goodwin spearheaded a drive that made great strides in changing this wariness. Shortly after the monument's establishment, the National Park Service and the Bureau of Indian Affairs expressed concern about the abysmal living conditions and the poor health of the Shoshones. After Inyo County denied relief funding, the two agencies cooperated to alleviate the dire conditions. Federal officials insisted that the county upgrade educational services and construct a schoolhouse. They made arrangements for the NPS to distribute relief supplies that the BIA Carson Agency would supply to Shoshone people in the valley and sought to have a self-supporting Indian colony set up in Death Valley, modeled on the successful colony in Yosemite National Park. When Goodwin arranged for a physician to examine local children, the doctor discovered that many suffered from malnutrition.[21]

Calls for removal of the Shoshones from Death Valley particularly perturbed National Park Service officials. Colonel John R. White, the superintendent of Sequoia National Park who ran Death Valley from afar, insisted that the Indians "cannot or should not be moved away from their home." As was common during the New Deal, he used Emergency Conservation Work programs to help alleviate the Indians' deteriorating living conditions.[22] In White's estimation, the Death Valley Shoshones lived in "hovels," a condition that federal dollars and inter-agency cooperation could easily alleviate. White's perspective had become widely held after the start of the New Deal in 1933. In a number of national parks, CCC or ECW programs constructed new housing for Indians who lived and worked on parklands.[23] Such effort was indicative of an important change in perception, as the National Park Service began to take more ready account of Native peoples inside its boundaries.

The NPS needed the BIA to improve the situation of the Death Valley Sho-shones, and Alida Bowler emerged as the Indians' strongest advocate within that agency. She carried their case to national leadership, circumventing opposition from her immediate superiors. In 1936 Fred H. Daiker, assistant Indian commis-sioner, told Bowler that the bureau did not have any funds for the Death Valley Shoshones. Their off-reservation status and location within a national monument removed them from bureau responsibility, he insisted. Instead, Daiker thought a New Deal rehabilitation grant provided the best possibility for relief. The Sho-shones might be able to establish official status as a community of half-blood Indians, which would permit them to organize under the Indian Reorganization Act and attain some measure of the protection it offered. No one acted on Dai-ker's premise at that time, although in 1937, George Hanson and his family at Indian Ranch voted eight to zero to accept the Indian Reorganization Act. The family did not follow up with a constitution or other required organizational mechanism, making the vote a largely empty gesture.[24]

More substantive was the federal rehabilitation grant that the Death Valley Shoshones accepted, which provided funds for constructing nine houses in the colony. The "Trust Agreement for Rehabilitation Grant to Unorganized Tribe" provided sixty-five hundred dollars from the Emergency Relief Appropriation Act of 1935, an award that contained a rider: the monument supervisor had to deter-mine whether the Indians who received houses possessed the capability to repay all or part of the construction costs. In addition, the Death Valley Shoshones promised to maintain and operate the water system built with grant money. Con-struction of the houses began in 1937.[25]

The construction documents became the catalyst for a formal interagency agreement. On May 23, 1936, BIA commissioner Collier and acting National Park Service director Arthur E. Demaray signed a memorandum of understanding that agreed in principle to the establishment of an Indian colony in Death Valley National Monument. Under its terms, the Indian agency purchased five thou-sand dollars' worth of building materials and delivered them to the monument.

The National Park Service supplied building plans for houses and outbuildings for the Indian families, supervised construction of buildings, and provided most of the labor. Both agencies anticipated that Pacific Coast Borax would donate land for the project as a way of ensuring the proximity of its employees, but the company balked. Eventually, the National Park Service provided a site, just a short distance from the main road through the monument. The BIA selected the families who received houses, subject to the approval of the National Park Service, and the agency was entitled to charge for upkeep and maintenance. The National Park Service also promised to provide employment whenever it could.[26]

Locating the new village required additional finesse. The existing Indian settlement had been north of Furnace Creek Ranch on Pacific Coast Borax Company land. The company eventually refused to allow the colony to remain on its holdings, moving the people on four separate occasions. When the National Park Service selected the colony's location, it did not consult the Death Valley Shoshone. This changed after negotiations, leading the agency to houses on a forty-acre tract of National Park Service land south of Furnace Creek Ranch. The Shoshones still were not pleased. They found this new location less desirable, distant from the school and from the mesquite grove that was one of the reasons for the settlement's original location. Yet under the circumstances, they had to accept what the government offered. Once Pacific Coast Borax determined that it would not allow the Indians to continue to stay north of the ranch, their options were limited.[27]

The federal government moved the Indians before completing construction. The tribe "didn't think it was right because people were being moved" without their consent, Pauline Esteves remembered, "and there wasn't even a home built there already for them to move in to, so they had to live in little tents on their own." None of these temporary dwellings had plumbing, sanitation, or even running water. "Water was piped down," Pauline Esteves recalled. "They had to build their own little places for bathrooms and [there was] just a spigot out there to haul their water from." To stay cool in the summer, Grace Goad remembered, "We would put gunnysacks up, a whole bunch of them and put water on them. When the wind blows, it's nice and cool." Even worse, the bricks that the Shoshones expected to receive never materialized. Instead, the National Park Service built their homes from adobe.[28]

Between 1938 and 1940, the National Park Service and the BIA attempted to clarify the status of the Death Valley Shoshones. The key question was whether these people qualified as "ward" Indians, entitled to all of the BIA benefits and services. If they did not, officials wondered if existing regulations could legally transform them into wards. Since the Dawes Act of 1887, ward status depended primarily on membership in a tribe with a reservation or ownership of other trust property such as an allotment. After the Indian Reorganization Act of 1934, declaration of status as a person of one-half Indian blood or more also allowed people to qualify. Ward status had advantages; it made the designees the responsibility of the US government. Federal officials technically considered nonward Indians dependents of local government.[29]

The transfer of the forty-acre tract at Furnace Creek village to the Shoshones seemed to be the best solution. Goodwin and Bowler recognized that without a land base, the Death Valley Shoshone were trapped in a netherworld of federal regulations. The Indians lived on federal land, but were the responsibility of the very distant and not very accommodating Inyo County government. The National Park Service entered the village project with Bowler's assurance that Collier could help make the area into a reservation. When officials recognized that such an option would cede control of land in the monument's heart, the National Park Service reversed its stand, a decision that inaugurated more than fifty years of tension between the monument and the Shoshones, who were effectively trapped between these two Interior Department agencies.

Worse, the entrapment of the Shoshones encouraged the local county government to dispense with any obligation to them. Inyo County had always been poor. Sparsely populated, large in area, and devoid of a rich economic base, it struggled through the Great Depression in the manner of many rural counties across the West. It had few resources to offer, and the little it had, county officials intended to save for their own. Bowler applied consistent pressure to persuade Inyo County to assist Death Valley Indians, but found that county officials insisted that even nonreservation Indians were the sole responsibility of the federal government.[30]

At every turn, Bowler found her efforts stymied by the Death Valley Indians' atypical legal status. In 1938 the BIA Washington office once again informed the Carson Agency that the Death Valley Shoshone were ineligible for federal relief funds. Exasperated, Bowler asked Commissioner Collier if his agency could declare the colony a reservation so that the BIA could assert jurisdiction. Bowler met with the village residents and helped prepare a petition to Collier seeking the establishment of the forty-acre tract as a reservation. The group had complied with the terms of the Indian Reorganization Act by forming a council; a reservation was the next step to the autonomy the Indians sought and that Collier intended to provide to Native Americans. Twenty-one adults, including most of the inhabitants of the village and Tom Wilson and his wife, who at the time were living in southern Death Valley, signed the petition. Representatives for the Thompson, Shoshone, Kennedy, Patterson, and Boland families also participated.[31]

Legal constraints hampered the chances of creating a reservation inside Death

Valley, however. Only Congress could create an Indian reservation, and during the New Deal, other needs took precedence. Nor was there any guarantee that the National Park Service would support legislation that took even a small amount of its land. The 1938 agreement granted the Death Valley Shoshones right of occupancy. The only administrative authority on which the government could base a reservation proclamation, the Indian Reorganization Act, did not apply to national park system lands. With the reservation's prospect in serious doubt, Goodwin championed the Indians' cause. He encouraged the National Park Service to acknowledge the urgent need for a reservation and recommended that the two agencies jointly suggest legislation that would transfer title of the forty-acre Furnace Creek tract to the BIA. Such a transfer would permit the BIA to grant title to the Indians without a legislative measure. Goodwin pointed out that precedent for an action of this nature existed at Death Valley. The agency had already granted Robert Thompson title to his father's lands. The NPS declined, but Goodwin remained undeterred. If he could not help the Shoshones get land, he could at least agitate for better conditions. By November 1939, he reported that the circumstances of the Indians had improved: "By use of Indian funds and CCC labor we have taken them off the Borax Company lands and placed them in a most interesting Village, to which all tourists seem to gravitate." Goodwin even proposed expanding the village project into a tourist attraction, a suggestion the National Park Service ignored.[32]

Once located on National Park Service land inside the monument, the Shoshones found themselves working with another agency, whose local officials were sympathetic but whose higher administrators were not. Goodwin served as an important advocate for the Shoshones in National Park Service discussions, but like Bowler, his position and the inarguable fact that what he proposed contravened larger agency objectives such as land acquisition and exclusive control of national park areas limited his influence on policy.

By 1940 efforts to create a reservation inside Death Valley National Monument had collapsed. There was little precedent for taking national park land for such purposes, and while National Park Service officials expressed differing opinions about the proposal, no consensus on its efficacy materialized. Agency officials and their BIA counterparts tried to resolve the issue, and each agency managed to convince itself that the other did not favor a permanent reservation. After a meeting with BIA officials in Washington, an NPS memo indicated the agency thought that Collier did not favor a reservation. BIA officials believed that they had approved the forty-acre village based on Bowler's assurances that the National Park Service could convert the land to a reservation. Assistant BIA commissioner Daiker told Bowler in November 1939 that he thought the National Park Service would not support legislation; even if it did, he averred, congressional approval was uncertain.[33]

The BIA's response to its perception that the National Park Service did not favor a reservation was to attempt a return to the Indian Reorganization Act as a legal basis for transferring land to the Death Valley Shoshone. An October 1939 BIA memorandum ordered the bureau's Indian Organization section to "take the necessary step for the enrollment of this band of Shoshone." Daiker instructed the Carson Agency to recognize members of the group as persons of one-half Indian blood under Section 19 of the Indian Reorganization Act. Recognition provided ward status, Daiker opined, although without a reservation, the Shoshones could not incorporate and receive the act's full benefits.[34]

The issue remained tangled. Frank Parcher, acting superintendent of the BIA's Carson School, questioned whether the Indian Service could expend its funds for Indians who did not possess a reservation. The Department of the Treasury previously had defined "ward" Indians as those who lived on government land, a premise that stemmed from a 1925 comptroller general's opinion that no guardian-ward relationship existed between the federal government and Indians without a reservation, trust land, or a treaty relationship. The extension of citizenship to Indians in 1924 made many governmental agencies and large parts of the public less sympathetic to special measures for Native American welfare, a sentiment reflected in the comptroller's opinion. Parcher prompted discussion in Washington, where officials wondered whether the comptroller's opinion superseded the Indian Reorganization Act. At the time, clearly established policy recognized people with at least one full-blooded Indian parent as eligible for services under Section 19. Many officials thought that passage of the IRA after the comptroller's decision modified the basis for ward status. Throughout the 1930s, the federal government treated such people as federal charges and allowed them to receive benefits. In July 1940, the BIA said that only recognition under Section 19 might be necessary for benefits under the IRA and that the Death Valley Shoshones were "entitled to the benefits and privileges as wards of the government without regard to their blood status." Under that ruling, BIA offices could treat the Indians as wards of the government and extend aid to them.[35]

Despite the debate, IRA recognition did not follow, and the status of the Shoshones did not change. The Death Valley village simply remained a site where the National Park Service allowed Indians to live by agreement with the BIA. Bowler left the Carson Agency in 1940, but that office continued to administer the village and assist individual members of the Indian group. Death Valley Shoshone children remained in the BIA boarding school, renamed the Stewart Indian School, in Carson City, Nevada; a few stayed in the local school. The BIA created work programs for the people in Death Valley. In 1939 a second rehabilitation grant provided five hundred dollars for a community laundry, which the government intended to counteract decreasing employment at the monument and borax company. Between 1939 and 1942, a branch of the Wai Pa Shone trading post, an Indian cooperative in Nevada that marketed Indian crafts, operated in Death Valley. Community members had an easily accessible outlet for their crafts. A community service worker lived at the village in the winter of 1939, paid by the BIA and the trading-post cooperative. Although neither she nor the Shoshones thought the laundry and the trading post were good ideas, the woman continued to help run the operations. When funds for the community service worker evaporated the following year, one of the Shoshone women took over the trading post. A BIA physician regularly provided health care through 1941.[36] The National Park Service was quite proud of its accomplishments at the village. In spite of its unusual legal status, the Death Valley Indian village resembled a reservation.

Conditions for Native Americans did not improve during World War II and worsened when hostilities ceased. Despite the war's emphasis on expanding freedoms abroad, and the beginning of the extension of civil rights to African Americans in its aftermath, conservatives in power used the idea of freedom as a way to divest government of its legal responsibilities for Native Americans. Their most egregious effort was a policy called "termination," which attempted to sever the relationship between Native Americans and their land and simultaneously end direct federal responsibility for them. Initially called "liquidation," termination gained momentum in 1953 with a resolution by the US House of Representatives that called for an end to federal responsibility for Native Americans. The rationale, argued by BIA commissioner Dillon S. Myer, the architect of Japanese internment during World War II, declared that tribal status held Indians back socially, economically, and politically; cutting federal ties would permit progress. Opponents such as the noted Indian advocate Felix Cohen charged that the policy was mere racism designed to defraud Indians of the limited assets that remained to them.[37]

Termination echoed earlier policies such as assimilation, the effort between 1880 and 1920 to divest Indian people of their cultural distinctions, language, and history. But this postwar project was more insidious still. Under termination's auspices, the federal government took an active role in ending tribal governance, dividing tribal lands and generally erasing the presence of traditional Indian tribal and community structure.[38] It was as if the BIA, after failing to meet the needs of its charges for more than a century, decided to simply erase them from history.

Termination caused dramatic changes in BIA policy toward the Death Valley Shoshones. As it implemented the policy, the bureau distanced itself from non-reservation Indians. The lack of formal land rights prevented an attempt to legally disband the group, but that was small consolation for the Shoshones. The village remained on National Park Service land, an unusual situation that allowed the BIA further to disengage from supporting its residents. The Indians did not respond, and members did not seek to force the BIA to recognize their rights. From the 1950s until the early 1980s, the Bureau of Indian Affairs largely ignored or forgot the Death Valley Shoshones.[39]

The National Park Service's policy toward Native Americans within monument boundaries was hardly more enlightened during the 1950s. Although local agency officials had supported the Death Valley Shoshones, such enthusiasm was not sufficient to counteract overall national trends. Nor was the National Park Service particularly enthusiastic about Native American rights; the agency retained many of the cultural traits of its founding generation, few of whom expressed more than token sympathy for Native Americans. With the ascent of Conrad L. Wirth to the directorship in 1951, the National Park Service had a builder at its helm. The Mission 66 program provided resources for capital development, taking much of the agency's energy and making it loath to challenge Congress or even Department of the Interior policy. As did the BIA, the National Park Service experienced pressure to reexamine its relationship with Native Americans in Death Valley and elsewhere.[40]

At Death Valley, the National Park Service acquiesced to a version of termination. As occurred elsewhere in the park system, some agency officials sought to capitalize on the climate to remove Indians from the monument. On October 31, 1956, Region Four director Lawrence Merriam recommended changes in policy for the Death Valley Indian village. Merriam challenged the validity of the 1936 Memorandum of Agreement that established the community. A new policy, dated May 9, 1957, obviated the 1936 agreement by asserting that the Shoshones were not wards of the state. The new policy, "Death Valley Indian Village Housing Policy," made only the occupants present in the village houses and their descendants eligible for housing under five-year renewable special-use permits. Under its terms, when a house became vacant, the agency was to tear it down. The policy initiated a rental charge of eight dollars per month and also imposed agency-crafted civic conditions regulating behavior. If residents engaged in disruptive conduct, the document warned, the National Park Service could evict them from their homes.[41]

For the Death Valley Shoshones, this policy was a direct threat to their very existence at Furnace Creek. Although the policy appeared for the first time to permit the demolition of houses, the Shoshones had experienced prior removal of their dwellings. Johnny Kennedy had come home from World War II to find his house demolished; federal workers had also destroyed Johnny Boland's house. Even more, in a reprise of the earlier BIA effort to move the people, the National Park Service wanted to move the Death Valley Shoshones to Lone Pine, almost one hundred miles by road from their existing homes. "We said 'we're not from over there, that's not within our territory,'" Pauline Esteves insisted. "It would be wrong for us to move anywhere and so we stayed on."[42]

By its strict adherence to statute, the National Park Service helped disinvest the Death Valley Shoshones. The 1936 agreement with the BIA provided the Indians with a sound land base, albeit in a convoluted arrangement. The BIA's withdrawal of support for the Indians meant that the National Park Service had no partner, a circumstance that terminated the original cooperative arrangement. The Indians remained in Death Valley, but without federal status even as wards. The federal government had transformed them from Indians with special protection to people inside a national park area with a prior claim to land but without legal sanction for their continued presence. The NPS had no entity with which to create a new arrangement, nor is it clear that the agency would have agreed to any more formal arrangement than the 1936 agreement had codified. Nor could the agency simply transfer land to another entity, as Congress had to approve any such maneuver. The agency could only exercise administrative jurisdiction. Without an agreement, five-year renewable permits made the most sense. They retained administrative control at the local level, where the National Park Service showed its greatest sympathy for the Shoshones in Death Valley.

Such transitory authority for their persistence in the heart of their homeland offended the Death Valley Shoshones and made them insecure about their status. The land was theirs, they thought, but they could stay on it only with permission of the National Park Service; even more degrading, they had to renew that status every five years. Worse, they were required to pay rent on their houses. "A lot of people weren't going to pay, then one paid and so the rest of us had to pay, otherwise we had to leave if we didn't pay," Grace Goad recalled. In Shoshone eyes, she added, "That superintendent [Fred Binnewies] wasn't worth a darn."[43]

The National Park Service retained final authority over the village, inevitably leading to conflict with the Shoshones, whose rent payments remained erratic. In some instances, monument workers tore down adobes officials classified as dilapidated. The National Park Service regarded such structures as eyesores and hazards; the people who resided in them saw them as home, no matter what their condition. In at least one case, a Shoshone family who left for a higher elevation in the summer returned a few months later to find their dwelling removed.[44] The new arrangement made the Death Valley Shoshones fearful.

Eventually, the new policy realized the Indians' worst fears, as it evolved into an attempt to remove the Indian village altogether. In April 1958, rent on the Indian houses had been in arrears for two years, resulting in a lack of funds for maintenance of the buildings and surrounding property. The conditions at the site had become appalling. "Laundry facilities, flush toilets, showers, etc. have all fallen into a complete state of disrepair, and sanitary facilities consist of very poor pit toilets," one NPS observer noted. "Several of the unoccupied houses have partially collapsed and are beyond repair." As Pacific Borax's business changed, employment opportunities diminished for the Shoshones, leaving most on some kind of government assistance. As a result, the National Park Service adopted a new stance designed to gradually eliminate housing in the village. Agency officials framed it as an effort to help the Indians; without employment options, the village held little promise, agency officials argued. Yet this strategy, codified in regulation in May 1963, also reflected a growing disdain for Native Americans within the monument, a throwback to an older attitude about national parks that were supposed to be devoid of human habitation. In the following decade, the relationship between the Death Valley Shoshones and the National Park Service worsened. The National Park Service attempted to collect the monthly eight-dollar rental fee, but failed, leading to frustration that had long-term ramifications. As late as 1967, when the monument attempted to provide electricity for the Indian village, the National Park Service abandoned the plan because agency officials would not support the project unless the inhabitants were prepared to pay monthly electric bills.[45]

Facing continued obstacles to their presence in Death Valley, the Indians recognized that proving their claim to land was an essential step in controlling their destiny as a people. The lack of a land base and permanent legal status made it difficult to qualify for federal largesse. In the changing climate toward Native Americans that followed 1970, the Shoshones strengthened their circumstances. In September 1973, Indian village residents submitted articles of association to the Bureau of Indian Affairs under the name Death Valley Timbisha Shoshone Band, but the bureau failed to approve the application. At about the same time, as a response to Indian demands for improved civil rights stemming from the cultural climate of the 1960s, a new federal policy abolished termination and replaced it with "self-determination." This revised philosophy encouraged Indians to control their individual and collective destinies. Self-determination took away the BIA's absolute control of Indian life, led to attempts to reclaim land, and fashioned a more clear and autonomous place in US society for Native Americans. Even with the new attitude toward autonomy, Native Americans remained wary of the federal government and the nation.[46]

At Death Valley, the newly organized Timbisha looked for ways to stay in the Indian village. They enlisted Indian support groups that had emerged in the aftermath of the 1969 occupation of Alcatraz and the 1973 standoff at Wounded Knee, South Dakota, when Indian activists held off Federal Bureau of Investigation agents near the site of the 1890 massacre. In February 1975, an Indian task force meeting inaugurated efforts to resolve the complicated status of the village and its inhabitants within the monument. George Foreman, a representative of California Indian Legal Services, detailed Timbisha complaints. Foremost was the lack of electricity, improper sanitation, and tenant status, endured in lieu of legal title to the land or ownership of their houses. According to Foreman, the National Park Service allowed the Timbisha to live in the village, but agency policy refused them basic rights of existence: they were not allowed to gather firewood, construct improvements to their homes, or modify the land in any way.[47]

The Timbisha could point to a long list of National Park Service shortcomings. The housing situation drew most of their ire. The three Death Valley superintendents between 1960 and 1972—John Aubuchon, John W. Stratton, and Robert J. Murphy—simply ignored the 1957 policy as a result "of its human and political insensitivity," and the Timbisha wanted the written documents to reflect new national realities. "Aubuchon, he was one of the good ones," Grace Goad remembered of this superintendent's relationship with the Timbisha. Nor had the monument offered employment to the Timbisha. Before the mid-1970s, only Charley Shoshone and Ross Bowen had secured work, both in the monument's maintenance department. At the task force meeting, attorney Bruce Greene from the Native American Rights Fund outlined the historical and fiduciary relationship between the federal government and Native Americans. He noted the longstanding attempts to include the Timbisha in the monument's workings, the efforts before 1945 to improve their living conditions, and legal precedent, which together outlined the National Park Service's moral and legal obligations to assist as soon as possible. There was no justification for the agency to relegate Native Americans living in Death Valley to economic purgatory, Greene exclaimed.[48]

The National Park Service defended its actions, with officials reiterating claims offered in previous meetings with the Indians: Federal regulations limited agency authority. The National Park Service did not have the authority to unilaterally grant land to the Timbisha. Neither the executive branch nor the Department of the Interior could change the boundaries of a national monument without a congressional decree. The National Park Service had a specific mission, and it was prepared to help—as long as that help did not interfere with the agency's overall goals and its authorizing legislation.[49]

The Timbisha and the National Park Service sought common ground. Timbisha attorneys asked if the agency would permit moving the Indian village to a new location and allow new construction if the BIA would fund the work. National Park Service representatives agreed to the possibility, within the framework of traditional agency authority. Superintendent James B. Thompson suggested the National Park Service could be of more help if the community reached a consensus about its needs. If the Timbisha presented the National Park Service with a clear set of goals and objectives, Thompson averred, the agency would do its best to help.[50]

Self-determination and the ongoing frustration of the Timbisha led to further efforts to attain title to land in Death Valley. In 1976, under the terms of the Indian Reorganization Act of 1934, the Timbisha filed a petition seeking formal recognition as a community of half-blood Indians. This was more than a little unusual; the designation of half-blood was archaic by the 1970s, but the Timbisha had been seeking legal recourse for almost forty years. Even though the government had deemed them ineligible for this half-blood designation in the 1930s, in 1977 Congress judged the Timbisha eligible for that status. Formal designation provided exactly what the Timbisha had always sought: a legal way to access federal resources.[51]

Soon after, federal services to the band resumed, and new ones were offered. The BIA's Home Improvement Program provided funds for the purchase of six mobile homes. The Indian Health Service agreed to provide financing and planning for water and sewage systems for the Death Valley village. The National Park Service encouraged the development, and before 1977 ended the band added eight trailer sites along the eastern side of the village and significantly improved the water system.[52]

Timbisha success did not improve the poor relationship with the National Park Service. Rightly or wrongly, the Timbisha regarded the National Park Service with wariness; the band still considered the 1957 policy that condoned removal as an assault on their very existence. During December 1977, the Owens Valley Indian Housing Authority complained to Secretary of the Interior Cecil Andrus that NPS policy still endorsed gradual elimination of Indian housing at Furnace Creek. Even if the agency did not intend to implement the 1957 order, the existence of the policy remained offensive. Others sympathized. In January 1978, California Indian Legal Services admonished the agency for adhering to the "outdated, if not illegal," 1957 policy.[53]

The NPS's general demeanor toward Native Americans was beginning to change, especially after the 1978 passage of the American Indian Religious Freedom Act, guaranteeing Native Americans the right to use federal lands, including national park areas, for religious ceremonies. The next year, Congress passed the Archaeological Resources Protection Act, considered the first major piece of archaeological resources preservation since the Antiquities Act of 1906, which added another layer of federal protection for Indian remains and cultural resources.[54]

Death Valley followed suit. In 1978 the National Park Service agreed to extend its water and sewage systems into the Indian village and began to collect refuse.

At the same time, the Indian Health Service and the National Park Service cooperated to provide funds to purchase additional trailers to replace the village's
dilapidated housing stock. Government regulations required the Timbisha to
have good credit to secure loans for the new mobile homes. Only a handful qualified; even those who did found that their new trailers still were on National Park
Service land, ensuring that the long-standing tension continued. To bridge the
gap, the agency paid closer attention to the cultural needs of the Timbisha. In
June 1979, in conjunction with efforts to attain federal tribal status, park staff and
the Timbisha met to determine the level of traditional religious practice in the village. Park officials reported being surprised to find that the Timbisha engaged in
little religious activity, a relative measure that may have reflected agency expectations rather than Timbisha practices.[55] Yet such moves helped open communications with the Timbisha and began to remove the taint of the 1957 policy.

Despite the improved atmosphere, housing remained a core issue and the
source of many of Death Valley's ongoing problems. Conditions in the village
were abysmal. Superintendent Donald Spaulding, who succeeded Thompson in
1976, described them as "deplorable." Over the next couple of years, newspapers
began to publicize the poor housing conditions. In October 1981, NPS landscape
architect David Geissinger described the abominable conditions in the Indian
village in his development planning report on the monument. He concluded that
the need for BIA construction funds stood in the way of solving the problems at
the Indian village and encouraged the National Park Service to assent to a permanent village.[56] As the Timbisha gained control of their fate, Geissinger's approach,
which made the National Park Service into a good neighbor while safeguarding
monument values, had much merit.

The Timbisha persisted in their strategy of simply staying on their lands, having learned that their presence provided the best claim to them. "Some of my
elders, especially three women, stayed here all winter, all summer. They would
move close by, but only for a little while, and they would come back again," Pauline Esteves recalled. "And they would say 'we'd better not stay away too long or
they're going to tear down our little houses and then what are we going to live in?
That would be one way they could get rid of us.'"[57]

When the Timbisha received formal status as a tribal government in 1982, they
finally attained the legal sanction that gave them greater control of their destiny.
On January 4, 1983, after a long process of lobbying, the Timbisha became a federally recognized tribe. The BIA technical report supporting the recognition concluded that the modern Death Valley Timbisha Shoshone band was the direct
descendant of Panamint Shoshone groups that inhabited Death Valley when
Anglo-Americans arrived in 1849. Ethnographic research determined that virtu-
ally all of the 199 members could establish their ancestry conclusively as Shoshone

people from the Death Valley area. The group continuously inhabited the area and functioned as a political unit throughout the historic period. Traditional leaders survived as late as the 1940s, it concluded, and the Timbisha retained considerable cultural distinction from surrounding non-Indian populations.[58]

The National Park Service quickly dealt with the newly energized entity with formal standing. In meetings throughout early 1983, the agency addressed living-condition issues in the Indian village. In June a capstone meeting that addressed Timbisha concerns inspired a National Park Service planning effort. Utility upgrades for the village and housing improvement headed the list. A special study of alternatives for land status, community demography, and needs for improvement of living conditions required a special study. The monument had to address such issues before it could proceed with its *General Management Plan.* The agency explored ways to include the Timbisha in the actual planning and development of the *GMP.*[59]

The National Park Service's willingness to include the Timbisha in planning suggested important changes in their relationship. Although sympathy for the Shoshones had permeated the monument since the 1930s, the agency never felt compelled to address Timbisha issues. The legislation creating the tribal government allowed the Timbisha to receive trust land for their reservation, and tribal leaders regarded a permanent land base of their own as the answer to the problems they faced. Potential conflict arose over the question of the size of trust land. The Timbisha anticipated a large homeland. The National Park Service and Department of the Interior recognized that if such a vision came to fruition, it would likely include not only all of Death Valley National Monument, but much of the Bureau of Land Management domain in the eastern Mojave Desert as well. Although such a vast transfer was an unlikely result of gaining tribal status, it clouded the perspective of the groups and led to a new wariness.[60]

From the National Park Service's perspective, the Timbisha required considerable assistance. As an isolated and young population (more than half its members were less than thirty years old), the Timbisha were "impoverished, unskilled, isolated from employment opportunities, [and] unsophisticated about modern political behavior and institutions," one National Park Service observer noted early in 1983. The Indian village, in this assessment, had failed as an income-producing attraction, and its residents were in dire need of direct assistance. The National Park Service very much wanted conditions in the Timbisha village to improve, and officials were willing to help. The National Park Service had only one stipulation: that the Timbisha conform to agency policy in running the village. This became an enormous cultural issue to surmount, with the National Park Service in essence demanding control of the Indians' internal affairs in its effort to protect monument values.[61]

Ownership of monument land was the sticking point. The agency had long labored to establish the premise that national park lands were inviolable. A generation of statute defended the principle, although rarely against claims of Indian sovereignty, and the agency reflexively defended this principle. Throughout the country, National Park Service officials worked hard to eliminate inholdings, tracts of private land surrounded by national park areas. In the previous decade, the National Park Service had cleaned up much of the mining land in Death Valley. From the agency view, a reservation in the monument, while ultimately a tenable solution to the Timbisha question, amounted to a step backward. It created a new inholding over which the agency could exercise only minimal control.

The Timbisha, by contrast, remained adamant about a formal reservation. Much of their misery, they believed, stemmed directly from being landless throughout the twentieth century. The tribe had gone to great lengths to remain in Death Valley and had made even greater efforts to attain formal tribal status as a prerequisite for the assembly of a permanent land base. In Death Valley, trust lands for a reservation could come only from the monument's holdings. In 1983 the Timbisha could not persuade the National Park Service to support the creation of independent trust lands within monument boundaries, but the agency recognized that a valid claim to the village existed. At the same time, the monument granted another in the long line of five-year renewable-use permits, continuing the status quo that had been the source of so much mistrust even it as reflected a sincere effort to resolve the complex situation.[62]

Park officials clearly understood that the Timbisha intended to pursue a permanent land base. The tribe sought not only the existing forty-acre parcel, but also an adjacent forty acres, which would provide enough shaded area to protect their trailers and would keep its members away from public view. The Timbisha band had mostly lived in Furnace Creek from November to June; they hoped to become year-round residents in permanent housing instead of trailers. They sought a second parcel of land near Fish Lake Valley, California, where some of the group spent their summers.[63] Possession of both parcels guaranteed that the Timbisha could continue their historic patterns of seasonal movement.

Infrastructure in the village posed an ongoing problem. The existing utility system serviced only part of the Timbisha community. The first houses that received electricity were mobile homes on National Park Service land; Pauline Esteves estimated that the Timbisha first turned on their lights in 1978. In June 1983, National Park Service, BIA, and Timbisha representatives met to find a way to provide electricity to the rest of the village. The National Park Service made an important concession in support of this goal. Officials agreed to permit aboveground transmission lines instead of requiring the preferred underground placement. The difference in cost, from fifty thousand dollars (which was not available) to seven thousand dollars, made the project possible.[64] Even though the power lines were distant from the monument's main visited areas, they had the potential to establish a precedent that concerned agency officials.

Other issues stood in the way of a final agreement. The Timbisha resented paying for utility services provided to the village. If it was indeed their land, the community argued, then the resources were theirs as well, and the National Park Service was asking them to pay for what belonged to them. Some Timbisha refused to pay monthly fees for water service, claiming that because their presence preceded the monument, its water belonged to them. During 1985 most village residents refused to pay the monthly agency utility bills for trash pickup. The National Park Service threatened to stop providing service. To resolve the problem, the tribal council agreed to pay utility bills in a January 1988 memorandum of agreement. Payment was not always forthcoming. In 1990 a portion of the past-due sum was turned over to the Internal Revenue Service for collection. In January 1992, the Timbisha owed more than thirteen thousand dollars in utility payments.[65]

The five-year-permit system also remained a point of contention for the Timbisha. "They resent," one observer noted, "asking the National Park Service for permission to do almost anything." The Timbisha regarded the National Park Service as an adversary and assumed that their requests would be routinely denied, yet they lived in the village under the authority of NPS special-use permits. In October 1985, on the advice of an attorney, village residents refused to renew their permits, in effect residing in the monument without legal authority. This decision was controversial and provocative, but addressed the primary issue from the Timbisha perspective: their right to be in Death Valley. In the end, their protest opened the way to an accord.

Timbisha objectives were clear: they wanted a land transfer to create a permanent reservation. The National Park Service proposed a long-term lease, from twenty-five to ninety-nine years, which agency officials suggested would make the tribe eligible for federal funding. Tribal representatives disagreed, and throughout the late 1980s and early 1990s, the Timbisha and the National Park Service struggled to reach an accommodation. The agency offered a series of alternatives that included five-year renewable permits, long-term leases, support for the establishment of a bona fide reservation, or relocating the Timbisha outside the monument. The agency's administrative authority allowed it to implement any alternative except establishment of a reservation. Congress had to vote on a reservation. In the end, the National Park Service wanted to preserve its land base; the Timbisha sought to acquire land. The division between them seemed irreconcilable.

The California Desert Protection Act of 1994 (PL 103-433) became the catalyst for the resolution of the Timbisha land question. The very legislation that enlarged and upgraded Death Valley to national park status also included the stipulation that the Timbisha would receive a share of the National Park Service's benefits. Section 705(b) of the CDPA directed the secretary of the interior to identify lands suitable for a Timbisha reservation, "located within the Tribe's aboriginal homeland area within and outside the boundaries of Death Valley National Monument and the Death Valley National Park."[66] The legislation also required the National Park Service to create employment opportunities for Timbisha people. The price of national park status for Death Valley was the creation of a Timbisha homeland.

But securing the final resolution proved more difficult than anticipated. In the first post-CDPA meeting, "a cast of thousands" filled the auditorium at the park, Death Valley National Park chief of resources management Linda Greene remembered. The initiation of the secretary of the interior's study of the Timbisha question attempted to attain a high level of participation from all the constituencies involved in the question. The media were out in force; also represented were the Timbisha people, other Native groups, national conservation and environmental organizations, and many other constituencies. The level of participation reflected the magnitude of the questions at stake. With such attendance, it seemed that dialogue, however difficult, would bring resolution.[67]

It did not, at least not immediately. In 1995 the Timbisha met with federal officials and presented their proposal for 850,000 acres of reservation land. The large size of the proposal was exactly what the National Park Service and other land managers had feared. At the same time, the Timbisha discovered a proposal put forward by the CR Briggs Mine. The project, two miles from the national park, planned a cyanide heap-leach gold mine, the most environmentally destructive kind of mining, in the Timbisha homeland. Feeling that the mine owners and government agencies had not adequately advised them of the proposal, the Timbisha people asked Secretary of the Interior Bruce Babbitt to halt mining. The Department of the Interior did not take action on either Timbisha request. Despite powerful statutory provisions for a Timbisha homeland in Death Valley, in March 1996, after extensive planning efforts, Babbitt announced that his department would no longer consider the question of trust lands within Death Valley National Park. The Timbisha believed that the National Park Service had written them out of the park.[68]

Recognizing the vulnerability of federal agencies to negative publicity, the Timbisha mounted a campaign to bring their plight to public attention. They proceeded on the homeland and mining issues simultaneously, proposing what became known as the Timbisha Shoshone Death Valley Land Restoration Project. They also asserted that the gold mine illegally received a permit to operate because the Bureau of Land Management, which administered the land leased for the mine, had not engaged in adequate consultation and review. The Timbisha sued the BLM. The tribe also helped form a group, the Alliance to Protect Native Rights in National Parks, to bring more national attention to their situation. Between 1996 and 1999, the Timbisha consistently applied pressure to draw attention to their claim. In 1996 the band asked President Bill Clinton to stop the National Park Service from further studying the mine issue. It also sued Inyo County, California, where the mine was located, arguing that the proposal did not meet California's environmental regulations. The lawsuit proved unsuccessful, but it began to alter the negotiating climate.[69]

National Park Service regional director John Reynolds had always been deeply interested in the situation, and the NPS Indian Liaison Office, headed by Pat Parker, became involved. New Death Valley superintendent Richard Martin supported the process, throwing his energy into finding a solution. The National Park Service again returned to the table, willing to cede a land base to the Timbisha. By 1999 the issue of securing land for the Timbisha approached resolution: an environmental impact statement (EIS) for the Northern and Eastern Mojave Planning Effort was in preparation, and the Department of the Interior and the Timbisha held hearings in Pasadena and throughout eastern California on the jointly developed plan. Although the final proposal did not yield the 850,000 acres the Timbisha originally sought, its nearly 8,000 acres of trust land and 1,000 acres of shared-use land were an important concession by the National Park Service. In April 2000, the National Park Service unveiled a comprehensive plan to establish a permanent homeland in the *Draft Legislative Environmental Impact Statement.*[70]

The *DLEIS* recommended transferring 7,500 acres in trust to the Timbisha Shoshone Tribe as a permanent reservation. That acreage included 314 acres at Furnace Creek that would be excluded from Death Valley National Park. The BLM managed the remaining 7,200 acres at Death Valley Junction and Centennial, California, and at Scotty's Junction and Lida, Nevada. The report also acknowledged Timbisha ceremonial practices and provided for access to and traditional use of sacred areas. This included a recommendation to designate part of western Death Valley National Park as the Timbisha Shoshone Natural and Cultural Preservation Area. Inside this proposed area, the National Park Service authorized low-impact, environmentally sustainable traditional tribal uses, activities, and practices. The Timbisha, National Park Service, and BLM viewed the designation as a way to recognize common interests. Examples of traditional tribal uses, practices, and activities included seasonal Timbisha camping and gathering of piñon nuts and other plants for medicinal purposes. The taking of park wildlife remained prohibited.[71]

On November 1, 2000, President Clinton signed the Timbisha Homeland Act, ending nearly seventy years of Timbisha dispossession. The government implemented the CDPA, and the Timbisha had what they most desired, a land base that was theirs alone. On January 20, 2001, a celebration in the Timbisha village acknowledged the long struggle for land. Pauline Esteves presented attorney Peter Taylor with a handmade stone tomahawk, and Steven Haberfeld of the Indian Dispute Resolution Service received arrows. A number of women sang traditional Shoshone songs, and a barbecue fed the revelers. After hours of dancing, the party broke up, and the Timbisha went back to sleep in their same homes—but on their own land.[72]

The relationship between the Timbisha and the National Park Service continued to evolve. Many in the NPS believed that the agreement was reached because "the right time in history" finally arrived, that a "new level of consciousness had been reached," in the words of resource management chief Linda Greene. The combination of Timbisha persistence, the tenets of the California Desert Protection Act, and the willingness to compromise to attain larger objectives made a solution possible. The National Park Service attained new sensitivity to Native concerns, but after nearly seventy years of mistrust, the gulf remained. "I think that was their plan, that one day we would all vanish," Esteves observed. Instead, the Timbisha stayed and, by staying, asserted their rights. The National Park Service learned to give grudging respect to these hardy people in their midst, and the Timbisha slowly began to trust the agency. "In some cases, we still have to keep reminding them on the different things that we are working on, but they seem pretty receptive," Esteves remarked. "I think that in time they will come around."[73]

CHAPTER 5

Managing Death Valley

Throughout its history, Death Valley National Monument, and its successor, Death Valley National Park, has struggled within the national park system. The unique characteristics of desert management required greater creativity and broader thinking than those needed at most national parks. An oft-crippling lack of financial and human resources for Death Valley and the parallel absence of respect for desert features in the National Park Service limited the site's development. "It is a fair assessment to say that this park has been neglected," observed park superintendent J. T. Reynolds, echoing a long line of Death Valley superintendents.[1] Three generations of park personnel battled the interrelated quandaries that arose from these deficits, and their collective persistence, professionalism, and commitment were largely responsible for the successful management at Death Valley.

Among the most knotty of the late-twentieth-century concerns was recreation. National Park Service could not anticipate, for instance, the transformation of outdoor recreation technology. The advent of air-conditioned automobiles, the increased popularity of lightweight trucks and later sport utility vehicles, and the development of other backcountry technologies, such as ultralight camping equipment, combined to give visitors new freedom in the desert. Beginning in the 1970s, visitors could reach more of Death Valley's vast backcountry, where the National Park Service had long relied on limited access for de facto preservation. The monument's staff suddenly had to provide expanded services to visitors with a wider array of interests covering a broader terrain. The need for use permits so that the agency could monitor backcountry use became apparent as the number of backcountry travelers grew dramatically, but Death Valley initially failed to implement such a regulatory system. A new management structure became essential, and backcountry patrols began, followed by daily trail and hiking reports.

That Death Valley was no longer as remote and isolated from the traveling public as it had been also meant that by the 1970s, it experienced many of the particular problems of US society as a whole, notably a spike in criminal activity. As use of national park areas increased, incidents of crime of all kinds multiplied. After the Stoneman Meadows riot in Yosemite National Park on July 4, 1970, when the agency had to call in the National Guard to evict illegal campers in the meadows, the National Park Service found itself policing the public in ways it had never anticipated.[2] Death Valley became central to that transformation, for the desert had long been a haven for those who sought to avoid the watchful eye of law enforcement agencies.

Even before the events at Stoneman Meadows, Death Valley had experienced a horrific portent of the future of its newfound responsibilities. In September 1969, nearly a month after the murders of actress Sharon Tate and six others and the subsequent killings of Leno and Rosemary LaBianca, someone set a thirty-five-thousand-dollar Michigan Articulating Loader on fire near the racetrack in the western portion of the monument. A National Park Service crew put the fire out, and this instance of malicious vandalism quickly turned into a hunt for some of the most heinous criminals of the era. A group of marauders in a red Toyota 4x4 and dune buggies appeared to be the likely culprits. Park staff set out to investigate, bringing in California Highway Patrol (CHP) officers and county sheriffs. On October 10, an interagency team raided the old Barker Ranch, arresting ten young women and two men. Two days later, they returned to retrieve evidence and captured four more people. Among them was the mastermind of more than a dozen murders, a self-proclaimed prophet with a convoluted and lethal philosophy—Charles Manson.[3]

Inyo County residents had noted the presence of Mansonites for as much as a year before, and there had been a number of incidents with these erratic young people when, on a number of occasions, members of the Manson family came in contact with local law enforcement. But it was the fiery destruction of the Michigan Articulating Loader that sharpened the focus of regional authorities. A California Highway Patrol officer posted at Death Valley and National Park Service ranger Dick Powell conducted the first raid on the Barker Ranch. Subsequent raids that led to Manson's capture included a cross-agency range of heavily armed officers.[4] This collaborative relationship would prove essential in the years to come in good part because Manson's capture illustrated the extent to which the Mojave Desert had become part of coastal Southern California. No longer did this remote landscape provide refuge simply because it was large, forbidding, and dry. Nor did its size insulate the monument from the perils of urban life.

After Stoneman Meadows and the Manson case, Death Valley, like the rest of the national park system, intensified the law enforcement functions of the ranger division, shifting a considerable amount of resources toward a different kind of management.

A major example of why this shift in fiscal and human resources occurred was the May 1990 discovery by park rangers of a major methamphetamine laboratory in the monument's southern extent. The perpetrators, members of an outlaw motorcycle gang, chose the location for its remoteness, and their operation was tied into illegal air traffic in drugs. The bust was the largest of its kind in Southern California to that time, and it revealed a network of illegal operations and airstrips inside the monument and across the adjacent desert. Eight people were arrested and convicted; law officers seized three airplanes.[5]

The dismantling of the massive methamphetamine operation elevated drug interdiction to a major concern. Death Valley had addressed the question of drug transportation since the late 1960s, but the location of a laboratory in the monument represented an elevated level of threat. The new circumstances promoted cooperation with other law enforcement agencies, including US Customs, and the monument was able to secure new resources to support drug interdiction. In 1991 Death Valley received seventy-seven thousand dollars in special drug interdiction funds and added a GS-9 staff ranger at headquarters, followed by the replacement of a seasonal with a GS-7 ranger at the South District in 1992. The drug enforcement ranger, as the position came to be known, cooperated with regional law enforcement agencies. In 1992 seven military ground missions and ten aircraft missions announced that the monument's law enforcement had taken a considerably more aggressive approach toward drug interdiction.[6]

The emphasis on law enforcement and drug interdiction came in an increasingly complicated management climate. The passage of the National Environmental Policy Act (NEPA) in 1970 compelled the National Park Service, and other federal agencies, to adopt new statutory obligations. Among these were a series of comprehensive environmental regulations that included the writing of an environmental impact statement or environmental assessment for undertakings such as the construction of new roads or buildings or for any wholesale changes in patterns of use of existing structures. The Endangered Species Act forced monument administrators to consider the fate of each of Death Valley's many plant and animal species during the planning phase of any development project.[7]

The need for documentation to support these new activities led to high-quality technical and scientific information necessary to comply with new environmental regulations. Federal statute required a general management plan as well as a range of other studies for the monument. In 1976 the Death Valley staff compiled *Management Options for Natural and Cultural Resources, Death Valley*

National Monument: Environmental Assessment, which explored the monument from a number of angles not covered in early National Park Service publications. Research became a focus of the agency in the 1970s, prompting projects such as *Historic Resource Study: A History of Mining in Death Valley,* the definitive history of mining in the monument, written by Linda W. Greene and John A. Latschar.[8] In addition, Death Valley's biological diversity enticed numerous university and privately funded research projects.

With these new tools, Death Valley faced the combined issues of compliance and visitor onslaught head-on. Once again, despite developments throughout the 1970s—a seemingly sufficient number of campsites, patrols of remote stretches of road, and an increase in staff to ensure visitors to Scotty's Castle enjoyed a positive interpretive experience—agency efforts proved insufficient. In the post-NEPA climate, more people came to the desert to live and vacation every year, and the demands on the monument fully exceeded the resources that the National Park Service provided. Visitor management became the most visible manifestation of the National Park Service's dilemma at Death Valley National Monument.

Death Valley also had other uses, and the monument was subject to requests for an array of special permits. Since the 1920s, the desert became a much-sought-after location for films. With Southern California's dominant role in the film industry, the use of Death Valley made economic as well as visual sense. Although the most famous movie shot in Death Valley was George Lucas's 1977 *Star Wars,* an astonishing array of films—including *Greed,* a 1925 silent film; *King Solomon's Mines* (1950); *Spartacus* (1960); *Zabriskie Point* (1970); and *Helter Skelter* (1976)— were filmed in whole or in part in the region. When such activities occurred inside National Park Service boundaries, special permits were required, and Death Valley staff invested countless hours of staff time in management of these activities. The immense popularity of *Star Wars* and Lucas's return to Death Valley for two subsequent films in the series guaranteed ongoing managerial support.[9]

Another dimension of the staff's obligations resulted from the desert's heat. Automobile manufacturers began using Death Valley as a testing ground to determine a newly designed vehicle's capabilities in hot weather. This too required special permits, which the monument willingly provided. At the same time, it also produced a number of remarkable instances of industrial espionage. Jim Dunne, a freelance photographer who became a senior editor at *Popular Mechanics* magazine, became the most intrepid of the espionage photographers. In 1974, in search of a Chevrolet Corvette prototype he suspected the company was testing in the national monument, Dunne hired a helicopter and a pilot to search for it. When he found the car, he had the pilot block the road with the helicopter. The photographer took his pictures, returned to the helicopter, and earned a fat paycheck for his efforts.[10]

Death Valley also provided a remarkable setting for endeavors to test the endurance of the human body. Even for highly trained athletes, such activity is extremely dangerous; the conditions in the monument are so harsh that a single mistake could be fatal. The military initiated such endeavors, one of the first of which was a July 1959 trek for 250 marines from Camp Pendleton, California. The military planned a two-week, 175-mile march from Death Valley to Mount Whitney, starting 225 feet below sea level about 10 miles from the monument and ending at the peak's 14,496-foot summit. In August 1966, two newsmen, Cliff McAdams and Gordon Ritzman, completed a 136-mile trek across Death Valley.[11] Such occurrences were curiosities in the 1960s, because the cult of physical fitness had not yet spread over the nation.

By the 1980s, extreme sports had become a growing obsession with a widening part of the population. Iron Man triathlons, in which participants swam, ran, and bicycled extraordinary distances, attracted first a hard-core cadre of participants and later the *ABC's Wide World of Sports* audience. A plethora of new events proliferated, including the Hi-Tec Badwater Ultramarathon, a 135-mile footrace that started in 1987. It begins at Badwater and finishes on Mount Whitney. Considered one of the most physically difficult challenges, the Badwater Ultramarathon codified the activities extreme sports pioneers undertook in Death Valley. Even the winners suffered immensely. "It was the worst experience of my life," insisted thirty-two-year-old Gabriel Flores, who won the race in 1998. The runners are responsible for their own support, leaving the monument in the position of providing backup, but no ranger and no park administrator could ever feel entirely certain that participants would not require their assistance.[12]

Special permits and the management of their constituencies remained a constant issue, especially as the monument worked to stay in compliance with National Park Service policies. During the late 1970s and the 1980s, resource management became a primary focus at Death Valley. In part, this transition began with rulings such as the *Cappaert* case and new legislation, including the Mining in the Parks Act. It was inspired by system-wide changes in priorities such as confirmed in the General Authorities Act of 1970 and reaffirmed eight years later in the Redwood National Park Expansion Act; "though distinct in character," as the General Authorities Act asserted, the parks "are united in their inter-related purposes and resources into one national park system as a cumulative expression of a single national heritage." The NPS could no longer distinguish between its parks and their assets, a fact that had troubled Death Valley's early history with the system.

Another new factor in resource management was the emergence of planners as important policy managers in the National Park Service. The ways in which monument administrators understood and implemented revised federal statutes contributed to new visions of management. At Death Valley, superintendents presumed that national park status would eventually occur, but no timetable existed. Planning took on an anticipatory tone, as administrators considered their choices in conjunction with the chance that Death Valley would become a national park in the near future. Planning as a management tool also diversified during this period. Especially after 1980, the National Park Service adopted a philosophy of "planning to protect" to meet the complicated demands of modern preservation amid booming visitation.

Planning culminated in a general management plan and environmental impact statement that the National Park Service approved in 1989.[13] The monument completed the long, arduous process of compliance with NEPA, and Death Valley had a tool for management more comprehensive and better designed than any in its history. In the almost two decades since the passage of NEPA, Death Valley had spent considerable effort to try to meet the standards of the new law. Despite the ongoing shortage of resources and personnel and the still dismal maintenance and housing situation, Death Valley finally had a plan that compared to the best in the park system.

The 1989 plan was bold, simultaneously redesigning the monument's overall management structure and emphasizing four major areas long of concern at Death Valley. The division of the monument into management zones designated all but 3 percent of the monument as a natural area. The plan divided the remainder among small special-use, historic, and park-development areas. This division allowed the monument to isolate the remaining mining sites to 2,057 acres, with the goal of phasing out all but 1,159 acres of active claims. Facilities and services had never met expectations, and the plan offered a strategy to meet current standards. Planned improvements included the replacement of obsolete facilities, especially the maintenance areas at Cow Creek and Wildrose and relocation of Emigrant's facilities to Stovepipe Wells. Recognizing that safety hazards still abounded, most particularly old mining shafts and equipment left behind when extractive operations ceased, the plan sought to secure tunnels and shafts and educate visitors about the dangers of abandoned mining equipment. In keeping with the new emphasis on resource protection in the National Park Service, the plan presented a comprehensive approach to minimizing the impact on resources that followed the 1983 *Natural and Cultural Resources Management Plan*. Improving the visitor experience was the final goal, and to meet it the park argued that it must renovate campgrounds, create peak-use overflow camping sites, develop reception centers at monument entrances, upgrade and construct new wayside exhibits, and improve roads.[14] Visionary in its reach, the new plan envisioned Death Valley as equal in status to any other major national park area.

National Park Service administrators also regarded declining air quality and visibility as major issues for Death Valley. Air quality became a significant issue in western national parks after 1970. Declining air quality, a result of outside pollution from Southern California and power plants scattered across the Southwest, befouled visitor experiences. Research conducted between 1975 and 1977 indicated a connection between oxidant air pollution—the results of combustion—and the decline of plant vitality, most notably desert holly. In response to such problems and to adhere to the dictates of the California Desert Protection Act of 1994, the National Park Service, Bureau of Land Management, and US Fish and Wildlife Service banded together to create a new interagency management plan for more than 7.7 million acres. Designed to provide a twenty-year blueprint to attempt to manage growth in the eastern California deserts, federal planners designed the *Interagency Desert Management Plan: Northern and Eastern Mojave.* It contained detailed plans for the new Mojave National Preserve and Death Valley National Park and for BLM lands. The desert management plan amended the existing *Death Valley General Management Plan* of 1989, allowed for the management of new Death Valley wilderness that stemmed from the passage of the California Desert Protection Act, created the first general management plan for Mojave National Preserve, and crafted management decisions for BLM wilderness areas that amended the *California Desert Conservation Area Plan* of 1980. Planners addressed issues such as access to public lands; infrastructure; habitat management, including that of the threatened desert tortoise and other sensitive species; wilderness management; and wild horse, burro, and alien and exotic plant and animal species management. Other themes included the proposed expansion of Fort Irwin, visitor information facilities, recreation, mining, and utility corridors. In 1995 the parties formed an interagency multidisciplinary planning team to create the plan.

Following federal procedures, the planning process included public hearings throughout the desert region. The public participated in workshops and open houses during three different stages: the scoping sessions, when participants identified issues; after the development of alternatives; and during the review period for the draft and final documents. The first set of workshops was held in September 1995, in Las Vegas, Nevada, and in Baker, Barstow, Furnace Creek, Independence, Lone Pine, Needles, Pasadena, Ridgecrest, and San Bernardino, California.[15]

This massive planning effort attracted attention from proponents and detractors of a managed desert. Some advocates of all-terrain vehicles chafed at proposed restrictions, while organizations such as the Sierra Club thought that the proposals did not protect natural resources sufficiently. The National Park Service found itself trapped between constituencies, unable to please either opponents or supporters. While the particular protections of national park lands minimized their problems with opponents, the entire planning process elicited comment from a range of sources. The plethora of issues, from desert-tortoise protection to the off-road race from Barstow to Las Vegas, meant that in every comment period, myriad voices would be heard. At the same time, the National Park Service had to hold true to its values. "A park like Death Valley is a last stand for protecting resources," Reynolds observed.[16]

Although Death Valley National Monument was created to preserve the desert, the presidential proclamation that brought it into existence paid little heed to the cultural properties inside its boundaries. This de facto designation of a natural area diminished the significance of cultural activities such as mining. At the time, the National Park Service system generally treated national parks and monuments based on what agency officials perceived to be the most important set of qualities each possessed. Despite the marvelous historic and prehistoric character of Death Valley, natural issues dominated the first generation of management. From 1933 until passage of the National Historic Preservation Act (NHPA) in 1966, the preservation of historic resources at Death Valley was an afterthought.

Death Valley's cultural resources were vast and varied, but it took many years for the agency to be able to begin to identify, categorize, and manage the variety of prehistoric and ethnohistorical cultural resources inside the monument. Death Valley contained more than fifteen hundred individual resource sites, including house circles, rock shelters and shelter rocks, campsites, quarries, hunting blinds, rock art, and other types of remains. Many of these were evident to naturalists and surveyors in the 1930s. Many more were uncovered as the monument implemented its programs on remote lands inside the boundaries.[17]

Before 1966 archaeological reconnaissance and stabilization dominated the activities that the National Park Service later classified as cultural resource management (CRM). Throughout the 1930s and 1940s, seasonal park naturalists mapped fossil beds and tracks in Death Valley areas such as Tin Mountain, Copper Canyon, Saratoga Springs, and Titus Canyon. After such fossil discoveries, the agency tried to minimize damage from unregulated visitation. During the first thirty years of the monument's history, finding the time and financial resources for even such baseline research always proved to be difficult. Death Valley personnel constantly fell short as they tried to manage the growing number of cultural sites with a minuscule workforce. The drain on available labor during World War II intensified the problems of resource management, as military obligations took much of the National Park Service into uniform. The Civilian Conservation Corps had engaged in nascent cultural resource activity by collecting and cataloging materials.[18] Throughout the war, the remaining monument staff continued these practices.

The New Deal initiated a transformation in the National Park Service's approach to archaeology that continued after the war. Federal funds, mostly for salvage work, permitted the growth of a nascent cultural resource management infrastructure. The emphasis that Frank Pinkley, superintendent of southwestern national monuments, placed on archaeology before 1940 created a cadre of specialists who remained with the agency or returned to it after World War II. The discipline's increasing professionalization also enhanced its growing significance to the park system. Archaeologists gradually took leadership positions in the National Park Service, carving out additional responsibilities for their profession. By the early 1950s, archaeologists considered themselves scientists who utilized scientific techniques to discern the past. The combination of these factors turned archaeology into the primary cultural resource function in most of the park system throughout the 1950s and 1960s.[19]

Yet the National Park Service emphasis on the archaeological ruins and artifacts of southwestern culture did little for Death Valley. Since the monument's cultural resources did not match the model the agency followed, the Southwestern National Monument Group devoted few resources to Death Valley's programs. The agency funded very little fieldwork, and the monument failed to receive resources to protect cultural resources and present them to the public. Despite recognition of the need for a museum to display Death Valley's collections, ongoing budgetary factors precluded construction. In one telling instance, park naturalist L. Floyd Keller plaintively wrote that Death Valley could afford a slide projector only because of the "abbreviated tour of duty of the Seasonal Naturalist." The lack of resources forced him to use a personal camera for monument activities.[20]

In the 1950s, archaeology's renewed importance in the nation's universities sparked efforts to explore and protect Death Valley's cultural resources. A host of private and university-sponsored projects aimed at surveying the area's vast archaeological deposits came to the monument. A team of University of Southern California scientists, working in cooperation with National Park Service archaeologist Louis Caywood, mapped and cataloged some of Death Valley's known cultural sites, concentrating on areas such as Mesquite Spring, Daylight Pass, and Manly Terrace. A University of California archaeological survey completed surface excavations of caves north of Furnace Creek in 1951, illustrating the need for proactive management of cultural sites to protect them from unauthorized collecting. Historically, the monument had depended for protection on the size of the desert and the general lack of knowledge about its resources. To minimize trails to such locations, agency archaeologists typically restricted inspections of sites to one annual visit.[21] This did not constitute adequate protection.

Between the early 1950s and the 1966 passage of the NHPA, the National Park Service relied on contract work to accomplish research goals in Death Valley. This approach was a mixed blessing, for it enabled the agency to conserve some of its limited resources, but it left the scientific agenda in the hands of university researchers. This practice also diminished the National Park Service's input into park archaeology and its control over the study of the monument's archaeology.

The limitations of National Park Service funding and staff levels also compelled the agency to depend on contractors to restore cultural sites. Before 1966 private sources funded the few restoration projects that took place, with the monument's longtime patrons and landowners inside its boundaries typically taking the lead. In 1953, for example, the Pacific Coast Borax Company spent more than one thousand dollars to restore Harmony Borax Works. Contracted labor crews encircled the site with a wrought-iron fence and repaired or replaced its dilapidated features. Company officials hoped that the fence would dissuade relic hunters who periodically raided the site. In time, those same officials hoped, Harmony Works might become a museum highlighting borax mining in Death Valley, and they were pleased when that year Pacific Coast Borax moved a historic building from Twenty-Mule-Team Canyon to Furnace Creek Ranch. The company had used the building as its headquarters and base of field operations during the age of borax mining and concluded that the building would be more valuable to the public if it was relocated to a more accessible location and retrofitted with safer entrances and furnishings consistent with its late-nineteenth-century history. Their efforts resulted in a well-equipped showplace—the Borax Museum—that opened in November 1954. Short on labor and funding, the National Park Service eagerly supported Pacific Coast Borax's effort.[22]

Pacific Coast Borax's renovation of its old headquarters offered a complicated picture of the monument's protocultural resource management. Although the company valued the property, most visitors regarded it as something other than a historic artifact. The National Park Service's mission included the preservation of nationally significant historic resources, but Congress typically did not provide enough resources to fulfill that mission. The circumstances led to a conflating of different kinds of objectives—the National Park Service's need for historic ambience and Pacific Coast Borax's desire to preserve and promote its past.

The monument's planning process underscored as well the secondary role of cultural resources. Death Valley's extensive 1960 *Master Plan* illustrated the National Park Service's spotty knowledge of the archaeological landscape it stewarded. Because of this lack of baseline data, the plan made few provisions for cultural resource management. Instead, it served as a catalog of existing issues at the monument, detailing many significant cultural resources. It also advocated an acceleration of natural resource and archaeological research projects. Such limited strategies reflected the lack of structure for this kind of management across the national park system, the relative lack of significance accorded historic resources in general, and the constraints of managing a large national monument without adequate resources.[23] Cultural resources at Death Valley were caught in a trap that limited their significance to the National Park Service even as the demands of their management exponentially expanded. Without resources, the agency could not possibly fill the gap.

Only a statutory imperative could alter this fraught situation, and with the passage of the National Historic Preservation Act, a new era began for cultural resource management. The law created a legislative requirement to assess and monitor cultural resources. It required the National Park Service to identify and evaluate prehistoric and historic sites and ruins and determine their potential eligibility for inclusion in the National Register of Historic Places. The NHPA also expanded the National Register of Historic Places to encompass places of local, state, and regional significance. Supplying matching federal funds to state and local governments to conduct surveys and develop preservation plans for specific projects made compliance feasible. The act simultaneously created the Advisory Council on Historic Preservation and established procedures to provide a level of protection to sites that might face impacts from federally funded projects. With the National Park Service's creation of the Office of Archaeology and Historic Preservation in 1967, historic preservation finally reached administrative parity with archaeology.[24]

Executive Order 11593 in 1971 further accentuated the National Park Service emphasis on historic preservation. Labeled an order for the "Protection and Enhancement of the Cultural Environment," this attempt to clarify the NHPA charged federal agencies with the responsibility to survey all lands in their jurisdiction and nominate suitable properties to the National Register of Historic Places. It required the secretary of the interior to advise other federal agencies in matters pertaining to the identification and evaluation of historic properties. The order required federal agencies to assess any activity on federal land or that used federal funds, and then to evaluate and record its potential impact on cultural resources. Along with the NHPA, the 1971 executive order gave the National Park Service a clear mandate to identify and manage the cultural resources under its care in prescribed ways. Longtime NPS regional historian Gordon Chappell described Executive Order 11593 as a "kick in the pants" for the National Park Service.[25]

Death Valley National Monument's size and its hundreds, even thousands, of potentially eligible sites presented monument staff with a daunting task, such as the question of historical significance that dogged the evaluation process. Some in the National Park Service regarded Death Valley's historical features as insignificant in a national context, and the monument's planning process reflected that perspective. The controversial 1971 *Historical Resources Management Plan* continued that theme, disparaging some of the monument's historical resources. The project's team leader, Ross Holland, described Leadfield's historical significance as slight, remarking that nothing about the former mining town warranted time or funding for its preservation. Yet Holland's report generated significant criticism from those who cared about the monument's cultural resources. The "idea of compliance initially was to get F. Ross Holland [and] give him six months to run around looking at all of the parks in California, Nevada, and Arizona, and come up with a list of the historic resources," Gordon Chappell recalled. "Well, you can figure how many of those he could look at in six months."[26]

Committed personnel found ways of countering Holland's assertions, a reactive mode that achieved important results. In the early 1970s, Death Valley staff placed National Register of Historic Places nominations atop their priority list. National Register nominations had the advantage of codifying the significance of selected properties and, if listed, would grant them de facto national significance. For a monument battling the agency's negative evaluations of its resources' importance, the nomination process allowed it to expend limited funds to its advantage. That had been the plan. In reality, the effort to secure National Register status for cultural resources at Death Valley fell far short of its goals. Many nominations were undertaken, few were completed, and even fewer were submitted to the State Historic Preservation Office. Responsible for this failure was a decided lack of personnel, resources, and expertise.

Despite these many difficulties, Death Valley began the arduous process of complying with the statute when in 1974 it nominated its first entry to the National Register: the former mining town of Skidoo. The site was an excellent candidate for a national historic district. A typical frontier mining town, at its peak it had boasted a population of more than five hundred and contained stores, saloons, stables, and crude residential dwellings. Various mill facilities, which varied from one-man operations to complex company structures, surrounded the town. Near Skidoo, a fifteen-stamp mill spread down one of the hills, and small wooden and sheet-metal structures dotted the area at the top of the mill. When he first visited in the mid-1970s, historian Gordon Chappell "was surprised to find the Skidoo Mill basically still standing. Winds and vandals had ripped a lot of the corrugated metal off of it but the framework was still largely intact. On the lower floor, somebody had attached a cable to some of the machinery and tried to drag it out the side wall. And they had done a fair amount of damage." The remains of water vats were scattered about, and a loading chute, made of decaying wood timbers, perched above the vats. Concrete pads marked the former locations of mining shacks and offices. Mine shafts and test pits littered the surrounding area.[27]

Skidoo was a considerable historic asset. The town possessed impressive interpretive qualities; it permitted easy access to visitors and interpretation in ways matched by only a few other mining sites. A comprehensive example of how mining operated between 1875 and 1930, it was one of the few sites that illustrated the process of large-scale mining of narrow ore veins. The surface mill structures represented the era's practices and provided an excellent example of the gravity-fed system by which equipment separated gold from its ore. The area also contained examples of where workers had mined the ore veins to the surface, and visitors could view the mine workings along these veins above the ground. Skidoo made it possible to tell the story of mining after the initial wave of nineteenth-century borax extraction.

Skidoo clearly met the criteria for inclusion on the National Register, yet it highlighted the complicated nature of managing cultural resources at Death Valley. The federal government owned the land on which the town stood, but before the 1976 passage of the Mining in the Parks Act, that acreage remained subject to mineral entry. At least thirty-two unpatented mining claims and part of two patented ones lay within the boundaries of the proposed National Historic District. These patented lands and unpatented claims were beyond the agency's reach. Worse yet, lax national law, particularly the Mining Act of 1872, allowed individuals to easily perfect mining claims on federal land. As a result, claims in and around Skidoo posed a threat. The stamp mill was privately owned, adding another layer of complication to the already difficult circumstances. The relationships between landowners and the National Park Service were at best frosty, and the agency faced the prospect of being unable to use the new statute to protect an important historic resource inside monument boundaries.[28]

Seeking the preservation of Skidoo was a risk the National Park Service had to take, and with good reason. When regional historical architect Robert M. Cox inspected the structures in 1977, he described their condition as desperate. Emergency stabilization work on the buildings was essential, but the National Park Service required permission from a host of claim holders before it could start work. At the same time, the agency needed a mechanism for including the remains of the community within the monument. Barring a court ruling that invalidated mining claims to the property, the agency could only expend funds to buy the site or hope for the unlikely prospect of a donation.[29]

The sentiment in the National Park Service for an aggressive move at Skidoo came not from Death Valley, but from the regional office. Thomas Mulhern, chief of the region's newly formed Division of Park Historic Preservation, and regional historian Chappell argued that the National Park Service should try to acquire the part of the claim where the mill stood. Neither in use nor necessary for extant mining, the property needed significant protective care. Passage of the Mining in the Parks Act in 1976 bolstered the agency's case. Acquisition granted necessary legal authority and the justification for funding to stabilize the structure. The idea was more popular at the regional office than at the monument. "More than one superintendent viewed such a project as merely another headache he didn't need," Chappell noted, "and so they dragged their feet, and dragged their feet, and dragged their feet."[30]

While that attempt faltered, the National Park Service pursued a number of strategies to secure the Death Valley properties. Some negotiations with private owners continued for more than a decade. As late as the early 1990s, the agency contested a number of mining claims in the Skidoo Historic District. Using the criteria established in the Mining in the Parks Act, the agency charged that claimants failed to develop the property even to the minimal requirements of the Mining Act of 1872. This tactic had been successful in other cases inside the monument and it seemed the best strategy to achieve National Park Service goals. So, in 1992, the National Park Service informed claim owners Carl Dresselhaus and Virginia Troeger that their mill's deterioration posed a potential risk to public safety. The letter included a tacit offer to accept the land as a gift, with a pledge for National Park Service restoration and maintenance of the structures. After this gentle push, Dresselhaus and Troeger reversed their previous position and worked with the agency to resolve the issue. They formally donated Skidoo in December 1992, but the elapsed time led to further deterioration. "By the time we got the property, the mill building had collapsed around the stamps," Chappell recalled. The National Park Service promptly requested emergency stabilization funding for the following fiscal year. As it waited for money, it documented the collapse of the upper third of the main structure, a tremendous cultural resource loss. It continued to monitor the condition of the rest of the property, developing a preliminary historic structure report in 1998. Stabilization efforts have continued ever since, but even so Chappell lamented what had already been lost: "All we have . . . is a ruin."[31]

The variety of new legislation introduced throughout the 1970s played a major role in cultural resource management in the National Park Service and by extension in Death Valley. One of these was the Archaeological Resource Protection Act (ARPA) of 1979, which offered the National Park Service an important tool in one of its oldest battles, the struggle with pot hunting. Since early in the twentieth century, pot hunters had been the scourge of the archaeological community, and their depredations were what sparked the passage of the Antiquities Act (1906); with this precedent and new authorities embodied in ARPA, the National Park Service attained an added enforcement mechanism to sanction illegal archaeological harvesting.[32]

At Death Valley, pot hunting had been an ongoing issue. Not only did the monument contain pre-Columbian artifacts, but the rich fabric of the region's mining history also yielded many valuable finds that the malicious and the unknowing thought to claim for themselves. The National Park Service worked assiduously to prevent such looting, training enforcement and curatorial staff in ARPA regulations and practices. Beginning in the 1980s, the monument handled ARPA cases during most years; as with many other park obligations, the mandate expanded with the establishment of the national park in 1994.[33]

By the early twenty-first century, illegal taking from national parks had reached epic proportions. Death Valley became a focus in 2001, when two men, Frank Embrey and David Peeler, were observed taking artifacts from inside the monument. A few weeks later, law enforcement officers associated with a joint federal task force dubbed Operation Indian Rocks raided five locations in Nevada and seized more than six thousand artifacts. The investigation revealed that an organized gang had been raiding federal sites in the desert for as much as a decade, and as it continued, more than fifty archaeological sites were assessed for damage; another series of raids netted forty-six hundred more artifacts. Tough indictments followed.[34]

Pot hunting continued because the park has never had sufficient resources to halt such predatory raiding. "We do not have enough Law Enforcement Officers to adequately patrol the park on a daily basis nor do we have the cultural staff to monitor sites the way that they should be," Kelly Turner noted. "One archeologist in this park is not enough . . . and the locals know it. Occasionally we get lucky and one of our law enforcement officers catches someone but the heavy-duty looters know where to go and how to avoid the officers or other park staff."[35]

The demands of Section 106 and Section 110 of the National Historic Preservation Act, as amended in 1980, required that the National Park Service undertake specific steps when certain activities within the monument boundaries took place. Such compliance demanded considerable resources and constant attention. A combination of the need to make management more efficient and a desire to reflect the importance of cultural resources led to significant changes in management strategy throughout the agency.

In October 1984, Death Valley National Monument established a Resources Management Division that combined the functions and staff of the Mining Division and the resource management functions and staff previously under the Resources Management Division of Visitor Services. The shift in essence merged two very different monument responsibilities. It combined the management of the complex mining arrangements within the monument that it inherited with the passage of the Mining in the Parks Act and the hands-on care that characterized cultural and natural resource management. This readjustment of administrative boundaries was atypical, for few parks faced a similar configuration of issues.

At the same time, consolidating compliance functions in a resource management division mirrored accepted practice in the National Park Service.[36]

Still, organizing the new Resources Management Division at Death Valley required innovative leadership. That's because Death Valley's historical emphasis on natural resources had slighted cultural resource management. Trained personnel were few in number, and cultural resources received only intermittent funding. One person served as a cultural resource specialist, and a curator staffed Scotty's Castle. Furnace Creek added a museum technician who previously had worked for the Death Valley Natural History Association. Gaps in staffing remained, which became a concern with the establishment of the new division. In May 1985, the monument converted a new resource technician position to one responsible for cultural resources. Compliance demanded even more personnel, and the National Park Service added a cultural resource management specialist. The amount of work justified additional support, but the monument's resources were limited. With compliance perennially looming, cultural resource management gained in stature. Statutory obligations helped explain the needs of CRM in a competitive environment. The National Register nomination program continued as the agency addressed other mandates. During the first year, monument personnel completed fifteen additional nominations.[37]

The new resource management division retained the cultural resource management responsibilities of its predecessors. Despite an inadequate budget, the division made significant advances at a number of Death Valley properties. After a visitor died at the Keane Wonder Mine in June 1983, the agency spent $150,000 on barricading open mining shafts with nets made of steel cable and stabilized the remains of the forty-seven-hundred-foot gravity-powered aerial tramway on which gold ore was lowered sixteen hundred feet to the mill. The monument sealed additional hazardous open shafts with removable steel cable nets at Skidoo, Del Norte, and several other locations.[38]

Cabin homes and campsites from earlier mining efforts abounded, and old and dilapidated camps and abandoned mines posed ongoing safety threats to visitors. Under the terms of the Surface Mining Control and Reclamation Act of 1977, the Abandoned Mine Reclamation Fund was established in the US Department of the Treasury. Funds were collected from active mining operations to pay for reclamation. A decade of effort to establish the program culminated in a budget initiative that provided NPS project funding for a service-wide competitive program to reclaim degraded lands and waters and to mitigate safety problems at abandoned mining sites in the national park system. At Death Valley, with its abundance of old mines and a perennial lack of resources, the program created an opportunity to improve visitor safety. A 1996 US Geological Survey report identified 115 hazardous sites in Death Valley, which allowed the park to secure resources to mitigate some of these dangers: in 2001, for instance, the park completed 350 closures at a cost of $500,000, with mitigation of as many as 4,800 openings at 243 mine sites in the park. By 2012, with the help of $4.8 million from the 2009 American Recovery and Reinvestment Act, Death Valley targeted many of its thousands of mine hazards; notable among these safety fixes were the closing of 200 shaft openings and the stabilization of the Keane Wonder Mine Tramway.[39]

The creation of the Timbisha homeland also had a strong impact on cultural resource management at Death Valley National Park. CRM specialists have served as liaison officers to the Timbisha Indians, working with tribal chairpersons to ensure Native American involvement in planning and development. The establishment of the preservation areas also mandated new modes of cooperation and higher levels of responsibility and accountability. Even though the ethnographic landscape became a primary CRM consideration, cooperation that drove the process remained elusive. In one instance, after the establishment of the homeland, the Timbisha, the park, and Xanterra, the park's concessioner, strove to create design guidelines for development in the Timbisha village and on other tribal parcels. The goal was to attain architectural consistency, not to impose uniform requirements. The criteria aimed for low-profile structures that blended into the landscape, but the plan did not prescribe a cultural style. Billy Garrett, an architect in the Denver Service Center known for his sensitivity to tribal history and culture, designed the plan. In the end, the Timbisha decided against it. Even though they recognized the process as reasonable, they decided the program was too bureaucratic. The process of building bridges was "not that easy," Linda Greene observed. "Real rapport will take time."[40]

Yet the absence of a full complement of cultural resource professionals exacerbated the park's cultural management strategies generally, and until the National Park Service could find additional fiscal and human resources, a situation that has depended on the park's fluctuating budgets, their efforts have achieved mixed success.

A similar outcome characterizes their ability to manage the park's many natural resources. Its mission is straightforward—to protect the physical environment from overuse, manage flora and fauna to preserve native species, and exclude exotic species to ensure the landscape's long-term ecological health.[41] Yet achieving those laudable goals has been complicated by the initial priority granted to infrastructural development for the fledgling national monument. Even as infrastructural development proceeded, however, the National Park Service faced a quandary with which it had little experience. A dependable water supply was essential for the monument, but the presidential proclamation that established Death Valley did not grant the National Park Service clear water rights. Miners, ranchers, and other inhabitants already claimed nearly every available drop, and the agency, arriving late in the region, received only the lowest-priority right. Securing a dependable water supply became essential; it underpinned not only National Park Service planning activities, but the ability to manage monument resources as well.

Nevares Springs, near Cow Creek, became a primary acquisition target. Adolphus Nevares, a Hispanic married to a Death Valley Shoshone woman, moved to the region before 1900. He owned 320 acres that controlled this critical water source, with his water coming from a spring that kept his acreage green throughout the year. Nevares grew alfalfa, melons, and some vegetables, but after he tired of farming in the early 1930s, he rented the plot to a man who intended to raise pigs. White and Goodwin instantly recognized the danger of a pig farm inside Death Valley. Not only were pigs one of the most fecund species, but they produced incredible quantities of waste, daily ate the equivalent of 25 percent of their body weight, left an overpowering aroma, and portended increased truck traffic as producers hauled them and their needed supplies to and from market. Even more threatening, if the pigs escaped, they were likely to reproduce wildly, becoming another feral species inside Death Valley, much like the burros that by the 1930s traveled the monument in herds. Some monument officials speculated that Nevares floated the rumor about the pig operation to force the National Park Service to purchase his rights. Unsubstantiated or not, the prospect compelled the agency to actively pursue purchasing his springs.[42]

The acquisition of Nevares Springs proved a major challenge to the National Park Service. Nevares was a cagey negotiator, and he offered options to several mining interests as well as to the pig farmer. Some of the options carried fifty-thousand-dollar price tags, well beyond what the National Park Service could afford. White and Goodwin thought that Nevares was bluffing, hoping to force the agency to meet his demands. As 1935 ended, White offered Nevares a six-month option in an attempt to secure time to obtain funds from Congress. While the agency sought to determine how much to offer, Nevares prepared for a legal battle. Like many in the West, he held decidedly antigovernment views and feared the application of federal power. The threat of the doctrine of eminent domain or some similar legal means to take his land made Nevares wary of National Park Service intentions.[43]

The Washington, DC, office of the National Park Service viewed the acquisition of Nevares's spring with trepidation and excitement. Acting director Hillory A. Tolson allowed that although the agency needed the tract for its water supply at Death Valley, expenditures for such acquisitions were not likely. The agency could not find a legal justification to give Nevares even the one thousand dollars that White proposed to secure the option, since its ability to follow through on the contingency depended on congressional approval of additional funds. With efforts for federal money apparently stymied, White looked outside the agency. He solicited the Sierra Club and other conservation groups in the hope of securing funding for a lengthy option, but received little support. Blocked, White and Goodwin explored appropriating the water by developing a ground source above the Nevares property, precisely the kind of action that had started so many western water fights in the nineteenth century.[44]

This tactic had statutory precedent. White and Goodwin based their approach on the western water doctrine of prior appropriation, codified in 1922 by the US Supreme Court in *Wyoming v. California*. The decision legally affirmed the principle of "first in time, first in right," while granting useful applications of water priority for ongoing use. The agency interpreted Nevares's use of water as an unimproved use, one not sufficient to meet the standard established in the prior-appropriation doctrine. If National Park Service lawyers could convince the courts that Nevares had simply taken the water without effort to build, retain, or otherwise divert its flow, the agency might be able to establish a new and superseding right by building its own waterworks at a point before Nevares diverted his water. The federal government could have easily designated Emergency Conservation Work dollars for such a purpose. Such an inflammatory tactic might have succeeded. It certainly would have been expensive, not only in dollars, but in legal precedent and negative public relations as well. If the National Park Service developed a priority right, a court battle would have followed. Nevares would have claimed that the National Park Service engaged in what later generations called a "taking," necessitating not only adjudication but likely a legislative remedy as well. The National Park Service characteristically avoided litigation and, as a result, dropped the proposed strategy.[45]

Acquiring Nevares's property remained a priority for the monument, and the National Park Service avidly pursued the purchase. Despite ongoing communications between Death Valley and the national office, National Park Service directors from Arno B. Cammerer to Conrad L. Wirth could not secure congressional approval to meet Nevares's financial demands. Throughout his more than twenty years in the area, White urged the agency to act. Cow Creek water could make Death Valley "blossom like the rose or its desert equivalent," he contended in one memorable letter, and savvy strategist that he was, the superintendent understood the value of establishing agency primacy in the desert. The National Park Service needed control of water resources inside the monument, but funds to buy the Nevares property were not forthcoming.[46]

The acquisition process proceeded slowly, requiring almost a generation to reach fruition. During 1938 the National Park Service offered Nevares $17,500 for his Cow Creek holdings, an amount Nevares considered appallingly low. At the same time, agency specialists continued to seek ways to avoid having to purchase the property at Nevares's price. The water from the springs at Cow Creek flowed in clearly visible channels beyond Nevares's land. The agency secured rights to the surplus water and constructed a series of intakes along the streambeds that exited Nevares's property. Using six-inch pipe, the National Park Service diverted above- and belowground surplus waters to a point five hundred feet from the Nevares property line, into a collection tank known as the Cow Creek Utility Area. A hydroelectric generator at the storage facility powered a system that took the excess water to a swimming pool and also irrigated National Park Service facilities. Nevares regarded construction of this water system as an escalation of hostilities, and in 1939, he attempted to thwart the monument's efforts. He diverted the majority of his water to new grape vineyards or to a gravel sink field, where he could spill excess water, depriving the National Park Service of the surplus. Nevares continued these actions until early 1940, when the National Park Service sought an injunction against taking water that California water law assigned to the agency. Before the end of the year, the agency and the landowner were involved in litigation.[47]

Ultimately, the agency was able to circumvent Nevares. A temporary restraining order in August 1940 prevented Nevares from wasting water, one of the cardinal sins of desert living. The ruling came from a local court and illustrated the degree to which Nevares's action violated regional norms. No matter how the local court felt about federal authority, it had to stop the abject waste of water. The injunction ordered the cessation of wasteful diversion and allowed monument representatives to enter Nevares's property to redirect the main flow of water back into Cow Creek. Nevares defied the order, telling White and Goodwin he intended to ignore the court's decision and use the water on his land as he saw fit.[48]

Despite such intransigence, the National Park Service continued to try to mollify Nevares. The monument's water supply remained tenuous between 1941 and 1948, as Nevares diverted water on occasion and at other times let it flow as surplus. Exasperated, Death Valley officials considered ways to build a stronger relationship with the man who had become their most significant local adversary. Goodwin even hired Nevares as a gardener in 1942 in an attempt to sway him, but little changed. On July 21, 1948, National Park Service director Newton B. Drury again initiated negotiations to purchase the Nevares tract. Nevares held firm at his original asking price of fifty thousand dollars. The National Park Service refused this sum, but the parties continued to negotiate. Finally, after more than a decade of frustration, the agency opted for condemnation, the least-popular method of federal land acquisition.[49]

Authorized under the power of eminent domain, the condemnation process allowed governments to supersede owners' objections by paying fair market value for private property if the purchase furthered the public good. In Death Valley, the federal government's petition claimed that Nevares's improvements were insufficient under the standards of the General Mining Act. It asked for a legal designation of the claim as "abandoned." Before filing the papers, the National Park Service made Nevares a final offer of twenty thousand dollars; he refused it. On September 15, 1950, the National Park Service filed a writ of condemnation and declaration of taking in federal court. Judge C. E. Beaumont decided the case on February 13, 1952, awarding Cow Creek to the National Park Service for forty thousand dollars. Nevares did not get his asking price, but the ruling handsomely rewarded him for the lost property. Even at this relatively high cost, the National Park Service secured its future at Cow Creek by obtaining the water that it saw as so vital to management of Death Valley's natural resources.[50]

Securing Nevares's water rights was a crucial step in securing water supplies for Death Valley National Monument, but the struggle did not end with this particular victory. At the close of the twentieth century, for example, new threats to the site's water quantity and quality emerged from outside its boundaries. Consider how Death Valley became embroiled in the regional water politics created by the explosive growth of Las Vegas, more than 150 miles away. As Las Vegas's population grew, it drew more water from common desert sources, forcing every other adjacent entity to scramble to maintain its share. Death Valley was the sink, the last place to which water flowed, leaving it vulnerable to development elsewhere. The spillover from growth reached the once sleepy community of Pahrump, an unincorporated community about 60 miles east of Furnace Creek, which evolved from a small town into the only urban area in Nye County, Nevada. Its rapid expansion from less than ten thousand people to as many as thirty thousand during the 1990s demanded more water, creating uphill momentum from Death Valley to Pahrump to Las Vegas.[51]

The pressure to rewrite the rules of desert water began with Patricia Mulroy, general manager of the Las Vegas Valley Water District. Mulroy understood that the era of dam building was over. Future increases in delivered water would come from redistribution of existing sources rather than the creation of new water projects. At the same time, she strongly promoted water conservation, recognizing that the increase in desert populations produced greater demand and that only extreme care would allow the existing system to continue to function. In any circumstances, reallocation was difficult, an alteration of the status quo sure to enrage even its beneficiaries. Her aggressive pursuit of water seemed to many an assault on rural life from the most upstart city of all.[52]

The Las Vegas Valley Water District fired a salvo in 1989 designed to do more than simply get the attention of the many autonomous rural water districts in the Mojave Desert. Mulroy's claimed 805,000 acre-feet of water in twenty-six valleys across Nevada, some as much as 250 miles from Las Vegas. Her requests included enormous amounts from the large regional aquifers that supported springs in Death Valley. Despite Mulroy's promise that she would not "wipe out" rural Nevada, the people of the desert regarded the water grab as social genocide. When the water district began the costly studies that would lead to an environmental impact statement, the National Park Service immediately recognized a threat to Devils Hole and the pupfish protected by the *Cappaert* decision. "We and the [National Park Service] in Fort Collins pay real close attention to what the Southern Nevada Water Authority is doing," observed Terry Fisk, a Death Valley hydrologist. "But slowing down growth in Nevada to protect Death Valley is probably beyond the scope of what we can accomplish here."[53]

Mulroy's tactics precipitated a change in the national monument's standing among desert populations. The National Park Service had long been unpopular in parts of the rural West because its critics believed it locked up land that they thought could be put to more productive use. Its status as a federal agency also engendered animosity in an increasingly antigovernment rural West, home to the Sagebrush Rebellion of the 1970s and early 1980s and the so-called Wise Use movement that succeeded it. Yet when a big city came in search of desert waters, rural residents suddenly regarded Death Valley National Monument as a much-needed ally; the federal influence that rural residents usually disdained became an important weapon in the battle to preserve their shared water resources.

Although Las Vegas later shifted its tactics to acquire Colorado River water, thereby eliminating one major threat to Death Valley, the park's managers watched with trepidation as, closer to home, the little town of Pahrump grew exponentially. Unlike Beatty at the northern entrance to Death Valley, a community that had been stagnant for nearly a century and had lost a number of its few jobs as a result of a major mine closure in the late 1990s, Pahrump's growth attracted its own individualistic constituency. By 1997 the town added three casinos to the one already there, and it became home to a strongly antigovernment constituency that resented not only federal authority but also state and even on occasion county government.[54]

With a sign outside of town that read "Welcome to the New Old West," Pahrump's growth posed a complex threat to Death Valley's water sources. The community remained unincorporated, and its governmental institutions came late to the resource battles that typically drive conflict in the Intermountain West. Pahrump struggled to find enough water, in some circumstances drawing from regional groundwater supplies. In a town that disdained governance, many wells were not registered. Its users drew water at alarming rates with little regard for the "first in time, first in right" doctrine that had long governed western water.

Before its bankruptcy in 2001, a planned golf course and resort near Pahrump epitomized the problem, but it was only one of a number of entities with designs on the monument's water.[55]

A decade later, water-pumping pressures in the valley had not moderated, quite the reverse. With "an estimated 11,000 domestic wells—more than any other groundwater basin in Nevada," the Nevada Department of Water Resources advised that groundwater pumping in the Pahrump Valley "has exceeded its perennial yield (19,000 acre feet) for over 50 years." With the community's anticipated population growth, the National Park Service anticipated that this ongoing overdevelopment of groundwater might "decrease the discharge to Saratoga Springs and the Amargosa River," which drains into Death Valley. This would have immediate downstream consequences, for "Saratoga Springs is one of the largest springs discharge areas in Death Valley NP, and home to the Saratoga Springs pupfish."[56]

Another part of the Death Valley groundwater flow system, the Amargosa River, provided a different set of dilemmas. Beginning ten miles north of Beatty at Springdale, the river winds its way beneath the surface toward the Amargosa Valley and disappears into Death Valley. Also known as Alkali Creek, the river contributes to the springs at Ash Meadows that support the Devils Hole pupfish. A source for agricultural water since the early twentieth century, which culminated with the Cappaert operation, the springs had been stressed by human activity long before the 1990s. "Devils Hole has been the canary in the mine shaft," then superintendent J. T. Reynolds observed. By 2001 development threatened the water table, and as the final stop along the water source, the monument once again faced the prospect of losing a share of its water to upstream development. "We need to understand that since we are down gradient, we better know what's happening above gradient and how it is affecting us."[57]

Increased mining and commercial activity around the monument's periphery and the continuing threat that high-level nuclear waste would be stored at nearby Yucca Mountain provided another troublesome dimension to the area's water quality and supply. The Nevada Test Site, home to more than 127 aboveground atomic and nuclear tests and the more than 350 belowground tests conducted before cessation in 1993, created a radical change in the region's biology and posed a significant threat to regional water quality.[58] Even worse, it again encouraged the public to think of the desert as a wasteland. This sentiment contributed to the highly political decision in 1987 to site the nation's high-level nuclear waste at Yucca Mountain.

Long before Death Valley attained national park status, the National Park Service recognized the need for intensive research and monitoring to document baseline conditions and the possible impact of pumping water for Yucca Mountain.

The Nevada Test Site had been dangerous; Atomic Energy Agency scientists and their successors in subsequent agencies had known that testing contaminated water beneath the test site, assiduously working to conceal that information. Later research showed that contaminated water spread, posing health and safety issues in the Amargosa Valley and for Death Valley. Yucca Mountain increased the risk and inspired even greater fear; not only was the siting uncharted territory, but advocates had also exhausted their credibility with the public as a result of earlier prevarication. Such an enormous project posed a heightened level of concern for the monument. Since its de facto designation as the nation's only high-level nuclear waste repository, it served as an ominous reminder of the limits of Death Valley's ability to control its destiny. Yucca Mountain posed the threat of its enormous need for water along with the prospect of contamination of a scarce resource in an accident. Although the project remained mired in political controversy throughout the 1990s, President George W. Bush signed the nuclear waste repository project into law in 2002, creating a genuine long-term issue for Death Valley. "We're just trying to stay in the fight," observed Death Valley superintendent J. T. Reynolds. "We just have to make sure that we get our opinion and our suggestions in the mix when decisions are made, and if there is any way in which we can stop certain things that are decreasing the quality of water or air . . . we have to do that."[59]

Then there were the burros. As early as 1934, agency officials had recognized that feral burros abounded inside the monument, especially in areas where they could find water. A majority likely were pack animals and their descendants. Because many mining claims proved unproductive, some owners simply let their burros go; other animals ran off from prospectors. Burros adapted easily to the region's extremes of weather, climate, and topography and variations in quantity and quality of diet. The absence of predators and prolific breeding resulted in rapid population increases. In 1938 more than fifteen hundred burros roamed Death Valley National Monument. Their impact was significant: burros, which eat an estimated three tons of browse, forbs, and grasses, successfully competed with indigenous bighorn sheep and other animals for food and water. The burros habitually fouled water holes with their waste and roamed the desert in family groups, eating sparse vegetation and driving off other species.[60]

The National Park Service initiated a policy of burro removal in Death Valley under the mandate of resource management in the 1930s. The action reflected the agency's goal of protecting native plants and animals, first articulated in a 1916 paper by Joseph Bird Grinnell and Tracy Storer. A 1921 resolution from the American Association for the Advancement of Science raised this goal to the level of canon. In 1924 burro reduction began at the Grand Canyon. The national park eliminated twelve hundred animals by direct reduction, the agency's euphemism for shooting burros, during the program's first five years. By the time Goodwin considered direct reduction at Death Valley, the agency had considerable precedent for the decision. Burro removal at the monument began in earnest in 1939. During World War II, burro reduction slowed because of a lack of agency personnel, but the end of the war again accelerated its pace. Between 1939 and 1948, the National Park Service eradicated more than one thousand burros at Death Valley. As the 1950s approached, the monument had institutionalized burro shoots.[61]

Even in the 1940s, the US public considered burro removal controversial. Goodwin observed that many area residents opposed direct reduction. They considered burros an important part of Death Valley's history and aesthetic appeal, a visual testament to the importance of mining in the region's history. Some residents just plain liked the animals, and they especially protested the shootings. After 1950 burros became one of the earliest recipients of California's growing emphasis on environmental protection. As Californians expanded into the desert in large numbers, even the most rapacious recognized the powerful imprint of humanity. The corresponding sense of loss not only led to protection for burros, but also added another dimension to the appreciation for deserts.[62] Monument policy and local and regional interests again collided, this time in a manner that had the potential to create genuine resistance to agency goals.

Despite such opposition, the National Park Service continued its burro-reduction actions. In the early 1950s, hunters discovered that wild burros in California's deserts made fine targets for sport hunting. State wildlife laws did not protect the animals, federal restrictions applied only within national park areas, and the burros were plentiful. The slaughter angered the public, and in 1953, the California Legislature made killing burros illegal on state lands. Burro protection became part of the state Department of Agriculture's Fish and Game Code, and in 1957, the California Legislature supported the designation of burros as a protected species. The state established a major burro sanctuary in the Death Valley, Saline Valley, and Panamint Valley region.[63]

The creation of the burro sanctuary proved problematic for the National Park Service. Because the Golden State was a hotbed of environmentalism, its interest groups routinely criticized state administrators' failures to maintain an effective boundary or a well-defined management program for the burro sanctuary. Political disputes followed, as the burros multiplied, adding to the monument population. Estimates put the California wild burro population in 1958 at between two and five thousand animals, higher than it had been a decade earlier, numbers that began to devastate the landscape and undercut bighorn sheep populations.

California's burro law offered a remedy. It permitted a live-capture program to relieve pressure on available forage. The state Department of Agriculture established criteria to determine the number of feral burros that teams could capture and remove under a permit system. Assessments from state officials working for the California Department of Fish and Game and federal representatives from the Bureau of Land Management, US Fish and Wildlife Service, and National Park Service formed the basis for the number. Federal and state land managers hoped that unlimited permits to capture live burros would keep animal populations under control.[64]

Because burros freely traveled between jurisdictions and were Sacramento's responsibility while on state lands, National Park Service officials worried about their jurisdiction over burros within monument boundaries. Were they state property? California determined that they were, as it categorized them as game animals, subject to state jurisdiction wherever found. Gordon Fredine of the National Park Service pointed out a clear exception: in places where the State of California had ceded jurisdiction, such as Death Valley National Monument, burros and other species fell under federal jurisdiction. The National Park Service could pursue direct reduction on those acres because its responsibilities were separate and defined in federal statute: whenever an exotic species jeopardized the welfare of a native species, National Park Service policy dictated effective control of the exotic.[65]

The difference in the agencies' responsibilities remained at the core of the National Park Service's argument. Agency authority relied on federal statute to fulfill its missions. By the late 1950s, the agency had established a forty-year history of independence of all state authority except by specific agreement. If burros on federal lands were subject to California's authority, bighorn sheep, bears, or any other species might also be subject to state laws. Under such circumstances, a hunter could conceivably request a permit from a state to hunt within national park boundaries despite National Park Service regulations expressly prohibiting hunting. Such an issue threatened much more than Death Valley National Monument; it challenged the entire concept of protected areas such as national parks.

As the 1950s ended, feral burros remained a major issue for Death Valley. Throughout the decade, the National Park Service treated burros as if federal law and national park regulations governed their management. Other federal agencies gratefully followed the National Park Service's lead. Well into the 1960s, the agency and the BLM worked to eliminate burros. Public outcries and increased scientific interest compelled the agencies to devise new approaches even as they continued existing management practices. With the exception of the live-capture program, federal and state authorities largely confined burro management to direct reduction.

To deepen the agency's understanding of burro ecology, Lowell Sumner, an NPS scientist, organized a research team to conduct population, concentration, and food studies. The researchers discovered that burros were prevalent in the Panamint Mountains on the monument's west side, but bighorn sheep were not. Although the appearance of burros always ensured a shrinking number of desert bighorns, Sumner reported that in Death Valley, springs that burros used heavily showed no evidence of use by bighorn sheep. This important clue helped shape new agency policy. After publication of Sumner's work, the agency closely examined the relationship between burros and bighorns. Despite the fact that many regarded Sumner's assessment as counterintuitive, if bighorn sheep and burros truly did not use the same springs in Death Valley, the urgency of their removal diminished.[66]

Sumner's report gave the National Park Service room to maneuver. The agency needed to remove burros because they were an exotic species, not native to the area, but the animals had a strong constituency. Advocates felt they belonged not only in the desert, but as historic characters in the monument's drama as well. Sumner's report allowed the National Park Service to avoid direct conflict with this vocal and increasingly powerful constituency.

Even as efforts at developing new strategies took shape, the National Park Service continued to remove burros from Death Valley National Monument. A two-pronged approach that included capture and removal as well as direct reduction yielded surprising results. By 1967 the National Park Service and BLM removed 3,570 burros—1,790 by live trapping and 1,780 by direct reduction. In the changing cultural climate of the late 1960s, shooting burros became harder to justify to a more interested and emotional public. In 1968, because of public outcries, Death Valley National Monument halted its direct-reduction program.

The end of the National Park Service's direct-reduction program pushed agencies in the region closer to one another, but this also added a layer of frustration; the NPS now faced countless expensive and time-consuming collaborative efforts for what many in the National Park Service regarded as an internal issue. Despite those sentiments, cooperation remained the only viable strategy, and the agency formally recognized that managing native species inside the monument demanded the involvement of other government entities.

On July 6, 1970, the National Park Service and the California Department of Fish and Game signed a memorandum of understanding that defined burro jurisdiction. Under its terms, federal and state representatives agreed to consult with each other before initiating fish and wildlife research projects. They also agreed to coordinate natural resource management when implementing any plan, program, or regulation that affected the distribution, numbers, species, or public use of fish and wildlife on National Park Service land. A technical study committee, composed of biologists, wildlife managers, and other professionals from the involved

agencies, formed to study regional fish and wildlife problems and to develop recommendations for long-range programs. Since burros consumed much of Death
Valley's energy and resources, monument superintendent Robert J. Murphy made
a management plan for the species the monument's top priority.[67]

In this context, Death Valley National Monument implemented a new feral
burro–management plan in November 1970. Under its provisions, live trapping became the principal method of burro removal. The National Park Service resorted to direct reduction only to remove isolated populations or where
traps interfered with or jeopardized bighorn desert sheep populations. To limit
the ingress of burros, and in cooperation with other state and federal agencies, it
established a five- to ten-mile buffer zone around the monument's perimeter. The
California State Fish and Game Department and the California Department of
Agriculture, BLM, and Department of Defense Naval Weapons Center at China
Lake participated in the program.[68]

At the same time, public sentiment in support of burros intensified, and a
change in law indirectly hamstrung the National Park Service's cooperative
efforts. The passage of the Wild and Free Roaming Horse and Burro Act in 1971
laid out new federal standards for animal management. It required all federal
agencies except the National Park Service to protect wild horses and burros. A
combination of sentiment that envisioned the burros as a charismatic species, a
growing environmental movement, and an increasing disdain for federal management contributed to the provision's makeup. The National Park Service's particular mission, best articulated in the Leopold Report's definition of national parks
as "vignettes of primitive America," exempted it from the provisions of the act,
but the law affected the actions of each of the agency's partners in transbound-
ary management. None of the other agencies could pursue aggressive reduction,
and many were tentative even about live capture and removal. The National Park
Service could remove as many burros as it cared to, but without fences to enclose
the monument and lacking close supervision of its boundaries, its actions were
meaningless. The acknowledgment of the National Park Service's unique management obligations did little to resolve the question of the burros' presence inside
Death Valley National Monument.[69]

To assess the impact of burros on the monument and devise a series of alternatives for removal, the National Park Service undertook an environmental impact
statement, one of the NEPA requirements. The combination of public input and
extensive management choices in the EIS diffused the tension inherent in the process. In September 1977, the National Park Service's draft EIS provided twenty
alternatives for removal of the burros. These included complete or partial removal
of the herds, trapping, shooting, sterilization, relocation, and carcass disposal.
The interim burro plan of the BLM's Bakersfield District served as a model for

Death Valley. The National Park Service drew up a cooperative agreement regarding burro management with the BLM and the US Navy at the China Lake Naval Weapons Center. A 1981 burro census estimated that thousands of animals still remained within the monument. After twenty-eight helicopter flights, the census counted more than 1,000 burros in the Butte Valley–Anvil Spring Canyon area alone and nearly 700 in the Cottonwood-Marble Canyon area. Natural resource managers estimated that the burro population increased more than 10 percent annually, upping the ante for immediate action.[70]

At the beginning of the 1980s, the National Park Service again reevaluated its burro policy. A live-capture program had proved successful at Grand Canyon National Park. Despite the exorbitant cost of nearly one thousand dollars per live capture, the program dramatically decreased the number of burros in the park. By July 1981, the Grand Canyon's burro population had dropped to an estimated dozen. At the same time, the BLM also demonstrated success in burro management. At the end of 1981, the BLM removed 385 burros from its lands and placed them through its Adopt-a-Burro program. However, this strategy was as expensive as the Grand Canyon program, and the BLM lacked the resources to continue. Facing similar fiscal restraints, the National Park Service needed a way to appease the public supporters of burros and to find groups to pay for such a program. When Edwin Rothfuss became superintendent of Death Valley in 1982, regional director Howard Chapman told him that implementing the burro-removal plan was the monument's top priority.[71]

Under Rothfuss, Death Valley embarked on an expensive and ambitious removal plan designed to satisfy the public and eliminate burros from the monument. The three-phase plan approached the question of burro resolution from an analytical perspective. During the three-year first phase, National Park Service personnel trapped burros and turned them over to animal protection groups for placement. After that the plan allowed animal protection groups one year to remove as many of the remaining animals as possible. Following the live-removal period, the National Park Service planned to again implement direct reduction. The National Park Service, BLM, and four animal rights groups signed the agreement on July 2, 1982, and the three-year roundup began in October 1983. The National Park Service and BLM constructed a live-capture corral near Ridgecrest, California, and brought in wranglers and helicopters to chase and remove burros. When the roundup ended in April 1986, crews had removed nearly 6,000 burros from the monument at a cost of $1.7 million. Animal protection groups agreed to arrange for the adoption of all captured burros. Their adoption program succeeded in relocating only 60 percent of the total, for the large number of captured animals taxed the resources of the advocacy community. During the second phase of the plan, from the fall of 1986 to the winter of 1987, protection groups removed an additional 230 burros and announced that they had completed their work. Direct reduction resumed on July 1, 1987.[72]

The burro-management strategy of the 1980s served as a model for national park and monument managers throughout the country, but with the 1994 California Desert Protection Act, which considerably expanded the area in which the National Park Service managed feral burros, burro management had to begin anew—this time on lands where the animals were firmly entrenched. The agency set out to assess the burro question in a regional context, and in early 1995, the superintendents of Death Valley National Park and the Mojave National Preserve completed an interim management policy that addressed the questions of burros on the former BLM lands. A 1998 draft EIS established a limit of 297 burros in Death Valley National Park and 130 in the Mojave National Preserve. The National Park Service estimated that it had to remove at least 110 burros from Death Valley National Park and 1,100 burros in the Mojave National Preserve to reach the new herd limits.[73]

Burros remained a long-term threat to native species, and the park pursued a strategy of long-term elimination. In the park's strategic plan that covered the period until 2005, the stated goal was the 100 percent reduction of the exotic feral burro population by September 30, 2005. The initial goals were bold. Strategies for capture included helicopter-assisted roundups and water-trapping corrals, with programs to relocate burros outside the park in a variety of adoption settings. The National Park Service often found itself in the position of spending valuable resource management dollars to secure the approval of outside constituencies. If this strategy produced less than optimal results—by 2009 an estimated 400 to 500 burros continued to range across the park, and its rangers continued to cull those feral animals that migrated in from off-site—it helped maintain Death Valley's standing with a large portion of the US public.[74]

Exotic animals such as burros remain a vivid symbol of the land's declining health, but that was less true of their flora counterparts, and as such exotic plant species, or invasives, drew less attention from government agencies and environmental groups.[75] Although the agency actively protected native plant species inside park boundaries, it tolerated exotics in some circumstances. This forbearance occurred when exotics were particularly beautiful or useful for shade or some other purpose. In other cases, the National Park Service introduced exotics as landscaping, sometimes leading to infestations that threatened native plants.

At Death Valley National Monument, two kinds of tamarisk—salt cedar and athel—became primary examples of exotic plant infestation. A wispy, gray-green tree native of Mediterranean countries in southern Europe and the Middle East, salt cedar tamarisk arrived in the United States early in the nineteenth century, reaching California as ornamental foliage around 1850. When it escaped cultivation, salt cedar spread rapidly, replacing native species in the typical pattern of Old World plants in the New World. Common along desert watercourses, salt cedar sometimes took over streambeds and other wet spots, creating thickets that stretched for miles. The leafy canopy that produced shade resulted from an incredible thirst for water. The plant reached deep into the soil, creating a comprehensive and wide-reaching root system that sucked every drop of moisture in the vicinity. A single large tamarisk consumed as much as two hundred gallons of water each day, making a stand of tamarisk a tremendous drain on water supplies.[76]

During the 1930s, the National Park Service introduced more of the exotic plants in its landscaping. The agency detailed landscape architect John Bergen to provide shade to the buildings under construction for the National Park Service and Civilian Conservation Corps workers who made Death Valley their home, and he arranged the planting of various species. In one instance, workers planted date palms around the patios and residences of the superintendent and chief engineer. CCC crews surrounded other areas with acacia or paloverde. Around the park village and along the drainage leading away from the village, Bergen planted two hundred cuttings of athel tamarisk. In June 1934, he pronounced the experiment a success, with 90 percent of his transplants thriving. The tree, which reached as high as twenty feet, provided ideal shade for National Park Service homes. It grew rapidly in the desert, showing resilience against drought and flood and little of the vulnerability of other species to Death Valley's great heat. Bergen's treatment of the plant as an ornamental and the subsequent cultivation contributed greatly to the spread of athel tamarisk in Death Valley.[77]

A basic misunderstanding of the plant's origin hampered National Park Service efforts to devise an eradication process. Agency correspondence during the 1940s often referred to salt cedar as a native species, and as such it merited agency protection. A special report commissioned by the regional National Park Service office in 1947 finally concluded that Death Valley should pursue the plant's eradication. The "disproportionate abundance" of tamarisk made the plant undesirable, even if the agency might consider it an indigenous species. The prolific growth of tamarisk and its impact on people and water sources finally compelled agency action.[78]

It did not act fast enough, and could not because of budgetary constraints. In 1962 the monument's master plan included an extensive list of native and nonnative plant species and their locations. Researchers found athel tamarisk at Cow Creek, Emigrant Ranger Station, Furnace Creek, Grapevine Ranger Station, Saratoga Springs, Scotty's Castle, Stovepipe Wells, and Warm Springs—nearly every place where agency personnel worked or lived. Each location possessed abundant water by the desert region's standards, ensuring that the plant could thrive. Tamarisk seemed to be taking over parts of Death Valley.[79]

Not until the 1970s and 1980s did the removal of athel and salt cedar tamarisk become a major part of every resource management effort at Death Valley National Monument. And the key to its eradication plans was the introduction of herbicides. The National Park Service began with Silvex, but when this herbicide proved ineffective, it turned to Tordon, which produced better results. Much like coping with burros, tamarisk removal required considerable resources and attention and compelled interagency cooperation. In 1993 agency removal efforts targeted the Amargosa River drainage, the Stovepipe dune field, and other wetland areas. At the same time, BLM fire crews burned or used chain saws to attack salt cedar tamarisk plants on adjacent acreage. Such cooperation highlighted the level of threat such plants posed. No agency could address it without working with its neighbors, an ongoing effort as tamarisk continues to appear and reappear in the park and the surrounding desert.[80]

Passage of the California Desert Protection Act and the change to national park status further altered natural resource management at Death Valley National Park, leading to regional planning efforts for desert recreational lands. In 1995 the Northern and Eastern Mojave Planning Effort, which involved the National Park Service, BLM, and US Fish and Wildlife Service, began. The effort simultaneously attempted to plan the future of the desert and create the appropriate compliance documents, most important an environmental impact statement for Death Valley. Beginning in 1995, the National Park Service held more than forty public meetings. The result, a draft EIS/*General Management Plan,* became public in September 1998. A revised draft followed in September 2000, with a final plan published in 2001.[81]

The new plan treated the park's natural resources as part of a larger bioregion. Juxtaposing the National Park Service mission with the demands of desert recreational users, the agency fashioned a sometimes-controversial resource management agenda. In the most general terms, the National Park Service proposed to carry out its statutory obligations as it promoted visitor service, providing it a legally defensible position when it came to the implementation of policy. This provided the agency with more than sufficient justification to continue existing policies on even the newest parklands. With protecting native desert plants as a primary agency mission, the National Park Service could continue its policies of exotic removal from not only the area once reserved in the national monument, but also the entire CDPA addition of more than one million acres, further accentuating one fundamental difference between national parks and other federal lands.

The same might be said of the agency's related enforcement of all existing endangered- and threatened-species policies, with special attention for Devils Hole and other sensitive habitats, protection that requires continual updating; in mid-2012, for instance, a new species of scorpion was discovered in a remote area of the park, a find that further intensifies the park's long-standing commitment to wilderness preservation.[82]

At the same time, the wilderness designation that accompanied the CDPA required a new degree of administrative dexterity from park managers. Wilderness had been a thorny issue for National Park Service officials because it limited management discretion. At Death Valley National Park, the agency faced an enormous administrative burden. Because most of the park was now designated wilderness, that notation altered the way supervising personnel managed existing parklands. The development of such management techniques occurred under guidelines established by the Northern and Eastern Mojave Planning Effort, which included the development of a consistent management policy for Department of the Interior wilderness areas in the California desert. Adhering to the act and the policy directives gave the National Park Service a prescription for management, describing the appropriate agency responses to a wide variety of situations. As the twenty-first century approached, much planning remained before the park truly integrated wilderness into its resource management planning: Death Valley was to manage and protect resources to enhance public understanding and appreciation of park wilderness, and it assigned itself the task of restoring disturbed lands.[83]

By the completion of the 2001 *General Management Plan,* Death Valley National Park had recognized that conventional natural resource management— the wildlife and plant management that had been characteristic of the National Park Service throughout its history—no longer sufficed. The combination of new influences on the region, the growth of population, and a host of other factors forced the park to conceive of innovative ways to protect everything from viewsheds to water as well as natural and cultural resources. It has unpacked new tools, such as geographic information systems, to aid its management of the sprawling landscape. This technology is proving to be indispensable in helping the park develop a baseline for monitoring and maintaining its wilderness character and for ensuring that these wildlands remained, as a 2012 study of Death Valley put it, "natural, untrammeled, undeveloped." Balancing these aesthetic demands with "opportunities for solitude or a primitive and unconfined type of recreation" and mapping out the uses that encroached on these back-to-nature experiences— from increased visitation, dust-spewing off-road vehicles, and sonic-booming military-jet flyovers—have led park administrators to embrace the concept of the desert as a place of scarcity. Doing so has allowed the park to fashion its vision of twenty-first-century resource management as minimalist; whenever and wherever, it would leave as light a footprint as possible. Yet this strategy also underscores an important realization and vital concession: managing Death Valley National Park never has been nor ever will be simple.[84]

CHAPTER 6

Death Valley in the Twenty-First Century

At the dawn of the twenty-first century, Death Valley National Park's prospects had improved, for it had addressed many of the issues that had vexed its managers since 1933. Between the 1980s and late 1990s, Death Valley had completed the transition to national park status, added an enormous wilderness area, and standardized procedures and practices at a new and higher level than before. The park had already synchronized its management with the 1991 Vail Agenda, the redefinition of National Park Service objectives that stemmed from the agency's seventy-fifth-anniversary conference and its powerful emphasis on resource management as the lead management goal for the park system.[1]

Death Valley had also addressed long-term issues such as burro management, and the regional planning process proceeded apace, promising the kind of integrated management of the desert that park staff had craved for more than fifty years. The Timbisha Shoshone were on the verge of attaining their long-term goal—land designated as their homeland in perpetuity—a reality that had led to strife within the Department of the Interior and between it, the park, and the tribe. Even the unbelievable backlog of maintenance issues that the park faced was being addressed. In the three decades following 1980, Death Valley had improved its ability to protect its resources and serve its visitors.

That said, the new century also presented an array of new challenges at the park level and in the National Park Service as a whole. In 1995, to meet the objectives of Vice President Al Gore's call to reinvent government, a major component of which was to reduce the size of the federal government, National Park Service director Roger Kennedy made a tactical decision to change the agency's hierarchy. He froze all positions in the parks, forced the central offices to absorb the cuts in staffing and funding, and then moved surplus people into the park-level positions. Kennedy designed this strategy to reduce staffing by 30 percent and save thirty million dollars.[2]

Kennedy's decision redistributed authority, power, and resources throughout the National Park Service. It purposely eviscerated the regional offices, long the mainstay of management, oversight, and specialized expertise, leaving few managers who could hold park-level management accountable. The changes left each regional director with a minimal staff in cultural and natural resources, one person representing the rangers, one in administration, and very few others. The National Park Service moved interpretation, maintenance, and all other professionals into park-support offices. This change created two regional offices where the agency previously had only one, but the two offered less support and assistance than their predecessors, and the oversight long housed in the regional offices simply disappeared. Clusters of parks, based loosely on geographical similarities, determined regional priorities for research, preventive and rehabilitative maintenance, and most other budget functions previously handled by regional office staff. Parks were supposed to work closely together and share their expertise.[3]

By most accounts, the reorganization upended the standard practices of the agency, but did not replace them with a viable operating system. When the regional offices disappeared, people moved into leadership positions in parks for which they had no expertise or previous experience. Some parks found themselves with assistant superintendents, the operations chief of the park, who had never served in a park and had little conception of how parks functioned. Many experienced people took "early out" retirement options, sometimes with large incentive packages. Often the ones who left had precisely the expertise that the agency needed, leaving not only a gap in institutional memory but also diminished capacity. "The 1995 reorganization was a waste of money, people, and lives," observed longtime National Park Service historian and superintendent Melody Webb in one of the most strident attacks on the reinvention process.[4]

Even more daunting was a change in the distribution of responsibilities that accompanied the restructuring. As part of the reorganization, a nationwide programmatic agreement shifted compliance to park superintendents instead of regional offices. The complicated legal nature of most of compliance mandates required at least some centralized authority. The process demanded an even larger share of scarce park resources. The specialists sent from the regional offices to the parks were supposed to pick up such obligations, but they also had to learn the day-to-day responsibilities of their new postings. In the end, Kennedy's reorganization, designed to streamline agency functions, saddled the parks with new obligations without providing adequate resources to manage them.

The solutions to the issues created by the new structure were few. Ever since its 1916 founding, the National Park Service has aggressively courted the public. Its focus on visitor services had been a central part of this outreach, but with the agency's budget slashed, and its staff sharply reduced, something had to give. Even governmental review agencies saw the paradox of the transformation. In 1995 a General Accounting Office report on the national park system suggested that doing more with less had never yielded optimal results for the park system, calling into question the strategy that national circumstances forced on the agency. The National Park Service, the report recommended, should reduce services or seek more comprehensive partnerships with private entities.

The impact of the reorganization on Death Valley National Park was greater than at many other parks. Death Valley had always suffered from a lack of resources and from the National Park Service's inability to provide adequate staff, dollars, and material to meet the park's needs. The transfer to national park status in 1994 heaped new obligations atop existing ones, and the reorganization of 1995, which stripped Death Valley of its access to regional office expertise, followed directly on the heels of the national park proclamation. The kind of management partnerships that the National Park Service engaged in elsewhere, such as at the Presidio in San Francisco and at Tallgrass Prairie National Preserve in Kansas, was not easily found in the desert. Death Valley had long been a version of Sisyphus's ordeal, except that at this park, when staff pushed the rock uphill, the hill just rose higher.

This arduous situation faced park superintendent J. T. Reynolds when he succeeded Richard H. Martin on January 2001. A thirty-year NPS veteran with experience in almost every kind of national park setting, Reynolds had most recently served as deputy superintendent at the Grand Canyon. When he moved to Death Valley, he recognized the challenges he inherited: "I knew that this park needed some improvements. The maintenance facility had been neglected and some of the rundown cultural resources needed a lot of care." Fortunately, Reynolds enjoyed these kinds of challenges, observing, "That's what got us to Death Valley."

The park's maintenance facility posed the first challenge. A backlog of more than five billion dollars in maintenance needs throughout the system had overcome the National Park Service, and no place was more decrepit than the Civilian Conservation Corps–era facilities at Death Valley. "When I came for my interview with [former maintenance chief] Jed Davis [in 1999]," chief of maintenance Wayne Badder remembered, "he said: 'Well, I'll take you up to the shop. I'm ashamed of it, but this is your shop up here.' So I went up there and looked at the shop and the ceilings were falling in, rat feces were everywhere, and it was just a complete and total mess. Every one of the buildings in this compound was like that, rat infested. We just [could not] keep them out."[5] In the oddest of fashions, the park's maintenance backlog, the single need weighing down Death Valley and most of the national park system, began in the park's maintenance shop.

An upgrade of the maintenance shop had been debated for more than twenty years. The lack of funding stymied previous proposals. Superintendent Edwin Rothfuss first programmed reconstruction of park facilities in the 1980s, but a decrepit maintenance facility awaited park superintendent Martin, who arrived in 1995. As was typical at Death Valley, the project did not find its way to the regional priority list. When Reynolds arrived, he learned that the park had under-taken some preliminary work, but Death Valley's budget was short of the funds necessary to complete the project. "The estimate on the maintenance facility was low," remembered Reynolds. "It was a class C old estimate, and it was not going to cover what really needed to be done."[6]

The park identified the actual cost of the project, including the premium that contractors often charged for working at Death Valley. In some cases, that amounted to 30 percent of the total cost. Inflation added even more, necessitat-ing a presentation to the Development Advisory Board, which oversaw capital expenditures. "We were a little over $2 million short," Reynolds said, shaking his head. "Utilizing photographs that I'd asked the staff to take of dilapidated, deplorable, third-world conditions, I wanted them to get a true sense of what was going on and [the consequences of] temperatures of 110 F in a maintenance facil-ity." Death Valley received the additional funding in part because of the presenta-tion but also because its compliance documents were complete. The park's ability to show its needs paid off.

And good things come to those who wait. Or so it seemed, for no sooner had the five-million-dollar project to overhaul the Cow Creek Maintenance Com-plex been completed in the mid-2000s than the park began to plan for and seek money to renovate its aging visitor center in Furnace Creek. Built in 1959 with Mission 66 funding, the center was badly in need of rehab; it was the most costly of its facilities to operate—its electric bills ran an estimated forty-five thousand dollars a year. A public-private partnership consisting of the park, the nonprofit Death Valley '49ers, and the State of California coordinated the planning pro-cesses, and with major funding from the American Recovery and Reinvestment Act of 2009, the project began in November 2010 and was opened to the public in mid-February 2012. Among its state-of-the-art features are a host of energy-efficiency elements and an impressive eight-hundred-thousand-dollar solar instal-lation (the Cow Creek Maintenance Complex also secured solar panels). Deriv-ing its energy from the sun, in a place of such intense light and heat, would seem noncontroversial, but it sparked debate nonetheless. This was a result of South-ern California Edison's slow-to-negotiate strategy over a federal requirement that prohibits agencies from signing contracts that could leave them liable for unknown or unpredictable damages because that would mean spending money that Congress has not allocated. Although the state's other major utility, Pacific Gas and Electric, had agreed to such terms for federal solar projects in its service area, the SCE had not. After intense, negative publicity, including what amounted to a public reprimand from Senator Barbara Boxer (D-CA), the SCE agreed to return to negotiations.[7]

For all the benefits to be won from flipping the switch to make the solar facilities at Death Valley operational—"We are purchasing electricity from SCE," declared park superintendent Woody Smeck in January 2012, "whereas we could be using renewable energy from the sun and returning power to the grid"—not all solar power is created equal. The massive solar plants that were being proposed for and constructed on land that the Bureau of Land Management manages in eastern California and southern Nevada were of considerable concern to the National Park Service. Conceding that the development of renewable energy "presents an important dimension to meeting our nation's energy needs in an innovative and environmentally responsible manner," the NPS argued in a 2009 interagency memorandum that the BLM should "consider the potential impacts to units of the National Park System that are located in the immediate vicinity of the proposed developments." Noting that most of "the areas in Nevada that have been identified on BLM maps as having the highest solar energy potential also tend to be areas of scarce water resources," hyperalert to threats to its water rights in Amargosa Valley and elsewhere, and recognizing that increased groundwater pumping required to sustain solar-concentration units—which consume large quantities of water for generation, cooling, and cleaning—posed significant threats to endangered species such as the Devil's Hole pupfish, the NPS asserted that it was not in the "public interest" for the BLM to approve permits for industrial-scale solar farms in the arid basins of southern Nevada if it did not factor in the rights, obligations, and responsibilities of other state and federal agencies. Three years later, after an exponential rise in the number of solar-power plants receiving BLM permits in the Amargosa Desert and Pahrump Valley, its protest was more direct: "NPS believes groundwater withdrawal for *water-cooled* solar thermal energy plants in the Amargosa Desert and Pahrump Valley is neither environmentally responsible nor sustainable. The water requirements of all solar projects, regardless of the technology they employ, need to be carefully considered with regard to their collective potential for aquifer depletion. Regional aquifer depletion is the biggest threat to the success of the endangered Devils Hole Pupfish, and it also threatens the health of other aquatic environments and communities in Death Valley NP."[8]

Like the ongoing battles over air and light pollution and those that sprawling residential development pose for desert parks, the solarization of the Mojave Desert is yet more evidence that the national parks across the West are "islands under siege." External threats to the integrity of the lands themselves had been of a much lower order and frequency in the NPS's first fifty years. Beginning in the 1960s, and accelerating ever since, regional populations have soared, and even once-modest-size cities have exploded in size and extent, a major human presence outside the parks that has complicated their internal management. Those pressures have only intensified as solar- and wind-energy farms, oil and gas drilling, and rare-earth mining have been approved near Death Valley, Joshua Tree, and other western parks, industrial activity that the first generations of NPS leaders and administrators never had to address.[9]

Faced with such difficult challenges, the current cohort of managers must do so with annual budgets constraining an individual park's actions. In 1981, for example, Death Valley's base budget was $2,175,200, with a total of $3,804,051 available to obligate as a result of soft-money funding for special projects. The base budget grew slowly throughout the 1980s, and the soft money fluctuated greatly. It became difficult for the park to determine how to deploy its inconsistent resources. The base budget did not adequately cover operations, and each year, the park had to compete for money for projects. An ongoing struggle over attainable objectives resulted, another example of the terrible difficulty at Death Valley. In the early to mid-1980s, when the national economy still wavered, base-budget increases were minimal. In fiscal year 1985, the base climbed to $2,719,490, with a total budget of $4,664,005, and that in 2004 stood at $6,778,000 (which, when factored for inflation, represented a *decline* in the park's real purchasing power). More concerning is that even the additional moneys over the past three decades were usually designated for one-year projects, limiting the park's ability to redress long-term patterns of neglect.[10]

This has meant that Death Valley has had to fulfill more of its obligations by competing for money from agency-wide pools rather than being able to secure major increases in its base budget, leading to perennial annual budget shortfalls. Each year, the increase in base budget did not cover the growing cost of agency operations and failed to make up for historic shortfalls. Death Valley had to devise other strategies to meet everything from statutory obligations to the cost of staffing the park. In some cases, the volunteers-in-the-park, or VIP, system has offset the lack of permanent staff. More often, the park has been compelled to cannibalize its staffing budget, shifting funds to underwrite a pressing or an emergency need that could not be funded in any other manner and then finding year-to-year money to fill the slot on the staff, and then hope for the best with the next budgetary cycle.

The advent of the Recreation Fee Demonstration Program in 1996 offered one such resolution. The National Park Service had charged fees at national parks almost since its inception, but until 1996 the revenue collected went to the US Treasury. Only part of it, roughly 20 percent, was returned to the individual parks. There had been a number of attempts to direct entrance fees back to the parks, the most prominent in the 1980s, when the Reagan administration sought to use entrance-fee money to decrease the parks' overall base budgets. In 1996 legislation permitted parks to keep 80 percent of the revenues they generated from entrance fees. The remaining 20 percent was earmarked for parks that did not charge entrance fees.[11] For Death Valley, "Fee Demo," as the program was soon labeled, offered some tantalizing possibilities and potential difficulties.

In one respect, the Fee Demo program was a veritable boon to the park. It functioned as a revolving fund, not limited to any specific fiscal year, and when base-budget money was added for a project, the Fee Demo resources could be moved to another pressing need. In fiscal year 2001, for instance, the park netted $1.2 million from the program, a stunning sum that let the park accomplish a range of projects and retain personnel in a number of areas. "We have gotten projects done we could never get done" without Fee Demo money, park budget officer Toni Moran indicated. Such projects included rehabilitation work on historic structures at Texas Springs and on the wagons at Harmony Borax, as well as on the exterior of a ranger station at Emigrant Spring and the boardwalk and exhibits at Badwater. Other beneficiaries were upgraded, including a heating, ventilation, and air-conditioning system for Scotty's Castle and essential mitigation of abandoned mining structures and lands.

Yet the Fee Demo program was not a permanent program, and the resources it offered encouraged the necessary but tricky process of transferring base-budget obligations—hard money—into soft money that the park had to scrounge for on an annual basis. The process was most pronounced in personnel matters. "This park has survived for years on [money from position] vacancies," Moran noted, and Fee Demo seemed to promote that process. The fear remained that the advent of such a pool of money might prompt Congress to reduce the base budget of parks and to insist that Fee Demo support all park activities and not special projects above and beyond the base budget. Nor did Fee Demo let the park increase staff, as its terms did not permit the hiring of permanent employees. "It would be very frightening if [Fee Demo] became a reduction in our base [budget] because it's limited in what we can do," Moran concluded. "We can't pay the superintendent's salary with it."[12]

With or without the Fee Demo program, the budget remained a major obstacle at Death Valley. Although in fiscal year 2001 the base budget had grown to

$6,551,115 with an additional $1.5 million in special money, and nine years later would stand at $8,902,000, these additional dollars still could not meet all of the park's statutory obligations and also support programming, maintenance, and rehabilitation. Despite its enormous size, Death Valley's base budget was roughly one-quarter of other major national parks. Nearby Sequoia National Park, with only 767,000 acres to manage compared to Death Valley's 3,340,410 acres, received almost four times the amount of the base budget. True, Death Valley's visitation remained far smaller than some parks with significantly larger budgets, and its numbers fell from 1,014,636 visitors in 2001 to 704,122 in 2007, a decline consistent with a post-9/11 travel-wary public. But visitation has since boomed, reaching 946,867 in 2011, renewing public demands on the land and its stewards. Add to this the fact that many of the National Park Service's statutory management obligations result from the amount of land the agency manages rather than the number of visitors who arrive. By that measure, Death Valley's relative lack of funding has crimped, and will continue to crimp, visitors' experiences.[13]

Law enforcement also remains a nagging issue for the national park. With expanded land and no commensurate increase in staff, park managers have found their protection resources spread even more thinly than before the park's change in status. The number of law enforcement positions had been reduced from twenty-three in the late 1990s to fifteen in 2004; there were two fewer in 2012. Diminished numbers of personnel left much of the park without consistent patrol or super-vision. From the perspective of park superintendent J. T. Reynolds, the situation was untenable. "Death Valley is about 95 percent wilderness area," Reynolds told the press. "We have over 600 miles of backcountry wilderness roads, and those areas get neglected—which means our core mission of resource protection, for the most part, is neglected."[14]

To counteract that situation, park managers got creative, tapping into funding associated with the Interagency Burned Area Emergency Response (BAER) budget. After the 2005 and 2006 fire seasons, in which 85,000 acres were burned in Death Valley National Park and nearby Mojave National Preserve, increased postfire patrols of the charred terrain had a marked impact on looting of archaeological sites and damage to other cultural and natural resources. BAER dollars provided aerial "maps of sensitive resource locations, specialized burned area patrol logs," and led to the installation and maintenance of "seismic ground sensors on roads. In addition, BAER funded use of the park aircraft at Death Valley National Park to more effectively patrol widely-spaced burned areas." This mechanism was a short-term solution that underscored the long-term need for sustained law enforcement budgets at the park.[15]

Changes in the nature of the crimes park rangers faced made their job more demanding still. Drug interdiction remained a priority obligation, a function of the growing methamphetamine plague that has scourged the nation and the need for complete solitude to obscure the smell and toxicity of the makeshift labs in which this toxic product was manufactured.[16]

Drug manufacture was only one dimension of the problem. A bizarre but timely issue came to the fore in March 2000, when a Nevada Highway Patrol officer stopped an old BMW with two men and a woman inside on US 95, south of Beatty, Nevada. The driver fired on the officer and fled to the north, firing at a Nye County, Nevada, sheriff's deputy who tried to stop the car in Beatty and, after they entered the park, at a California Highway Patrol officer who also responded to the call. Rangers scrambled as the trio headed toward Furnace Creek, where about three thousand visitors continued their leisurely activities. A park aircraft tracked the racing automobile, which turned off the main thoroughfare onto a park tour road. Law enforcement officials from a number of agencies set up roadblocks at both ends of the road as the aircraft searched for the trio. The car had become stuck in a salt pan; its occupants had abandoned it and headed west across Death Valley.[17]

As the fugitives trekked into the wilderness area, far from other visitors or any park facilities, law enforcement determined that observation and confinement of the suspects were the best strategy. More law enforcement personnel were sent to the scene. Some remained near the abandoned car and watched the trio with spotting scopes. The park's airplane circled; a US Army Blackhawk helicopter already in the park on an antidrug mission dropped five protection rangers and three officers, headed by park special agent Eric Inman, in advance of the fleeing felons. The park airport served as the incident command post. Soon a California Highway Patrol helicopter arrived and joined in the aerial surveillance. The three fugitives realized that they were surrounded. They dug a foxhole and began shooting at the two aircraft. When the CHP helicopter passed directly over the fugitives, two rounds hit it. The main oil line burst, endangering the two crewmen and forcing it to land within three-quarters of a mile of the bunker and vulnerable to the suspects' weapons. A Blackhawk helicopter with eight Inyo County SWAT-team members on board rescued the two shaken but unharmed CHP crewmen. A helicopter gunship from the San Bernardino Sheriff's Office arrived and joined the aerial surveillance. As the sun set, a stalemate existed.[18]

Night posed a problem: law enforcement expected that the fugitives would try to use the cover of darkness to escape. Keeping the three from reaching the populated Furnace Creek area was a priority. The combined law enforcement leadership decided to put the Inyo County SWAT team to the east of the fugitives, and five Death Valley rangers, all trained and equipped for night operations, stood guard on the west. Lake Mead chief ranger Dale Antonich's team was placed where they could support the Inyo County team and protect the downed CHP helicopter. A Kern County helicopter and a US Customs jet—each equipped with infrared observation equipment—flew to the park to provide additional surveillance, and other CHP units blocked park roads. Additional units were standing by, ready to move into Furnace Creek if the suspects escaped the law officers' net.[19]

At about eleven that night, the three suspects began to move toward Furnace Creek. Antonich's team confronted them, and after a very short, tense standoff, they surrendered without a shot fired. The three were heavily armed, carrying five handguns and two rifles, all loaded. In the abandoned car, officers found several handguns and rifles, hundreds of rounds of ammunition, antigovernment and anti–law enforcement literature, bomb-making manuals, and military operations manuals. One of the men was found to have a history of violence and sex crimes. A total of 113 law enforcement officers and rangers from ten local, state, and federal agencies were involved in the incident, which concluded without a single injury to law enforcement personnel or park visitors. The action represented a model response to a problem that seemed likely to loom larger as the once-remote desert becomes even more accessible.[20]

Ensuring the safety of law-abiding visitors has proved no less tricky. Tragically, some people's casual disregard for the valley's punishing heat and aridity, and the spatial disorientation that its vast size can produce on even the most cautious visitors, can lead to expensive and time-consuming search-and-rescue missions— and at times to fatalities. The discovery in 2009 of the remains of a German tourist, one of a family of four that had disappeared thirteen years earlier, reflected this park's dangerous nature. So did the death of six-year-old Carlos Sanchez in 2011, whose demise Death Valley wilderness coordinator Charlie Callagan attributed to what he called "Death by GPS": "People are renting vehicles with [a global positioning system] and they have no idea how it works and they are willing to trust the GPS to lead them into the middle of nowhere." Each of these episodes, and others like them, is a stark reminder of just how tough the Mojave Desert can be.[21]

Other issues have been as worrying. Even though it was more than one hundred miles from the Los Angeles basin, Death Valley National Park faced air-quality issues emanating from that distant, autocentric metropolis. As a Class II area in the federal air-monitoring system, Death Valley could be subjected to moderate increases in pollution without invoking federal statute. The park's air-quality management program at Cow Creek monitored ozone and particulate matter, the bane of desert air, and in 2002 there were plans to install wet and dry acid-deposition monitoring. The park and the surrounding environment were in perpetual nonattainment for particulate matter, a common condition throughout the desert. In response, Death Valley committed itself to reducing the problem and sought help not only within the federal system, but from its partners as well. In 2002, for example, the Ford Motor Company and the National Parks Foundation donated five hundred electric cars called TH!NK for use in the twenty-three national parks in California; twelve of these zero-emissions, low-speed, and quiet vehicles (which look like fancy golf carts) continue to operate in Death Valley, at Furnace Creek, and at other facilities. A small but symbolic innovation, the introduction of the fleet accentuated the possibility of maintaining good air quality and an enhanced visitor experience through technological means. Yet expanding on this possibility, in an era of tough budgeting, will depend on the generosity of the park's private partners.[22]

Wilderness was another persistent challenge and potential drain on the park's limited personnel and resources. Finally authorized in the California Desert Protection Act in 1994, Death Valley's wilderness area included 3,253,028 acres, more than 95 percent of the park. Death Valley responded with planning measures, but it lacked the resources to implement its plan. Early in 1995, the park appointed two wilderness coordinators. In 1996 they offered an action plan to initiate a wilderness program. A wilderness and backcountry management plan was the first step. Death Valley National Park staff assembled a planning team, and preliminary work began. In the late 1990s, the process progressed no further, as the park searched for funds for the task and redirected its energy toward its new *General Management Plan*. The GMP presented a broad outline for wilderness management, committing the park to the "maximum statutory protection allowed," and affirmed Death Valley's commitment to develop a wilderness and backcountry management plan. The park simultaneously pursued the wilderness and backcountry management plan; in 2001 it held eight planning meetings alone, from which emerged a draft outline and draft-scoping workbook; these background analyses provided the basis for its search for funding for a wilderness monitoring program and for a more complete plan for wildlands protection.[23]

Prior human use of the desert further complicated the issue of designated wilderness. The Mining Act of 1872 governed most public land claims, and its notoriously lax provisions allowed great leeway for prospective operators. In essence, anyone could simply make a claim and have nearly perpetual rights to a tract of public land. Claimants could leave such lands for a long time and still be able to recover their claim. The National Park Service had been able to dispense with many claims inside national monument boundaries through the Mining in the Parks Act, but the program was limited to lands under National Park Service jurisdiction. The new area contained many claims, most unpatented, and often these fell within designated wilderness. Some of these potentially posed severe management problems for the park.[24]

The transition in management added an additional facet to this concern. During the summer of 1994, the Bureau of Land Management approved a permit for the talc mining operation of Edward and Carol Baumunk and their partner, A. J. Jackson. The trio held a claim for the Rainbow Talc Mine, which they operated intermittently between 1952 and 1972. The request and the approval were hardly unusual. Despite a generation of complaints about the terms of the 1872 law, no superseding legislation had been introduced in Congress, much less passed. Even had the BLM sought to terminate such a claim, existing law gave that agency few options.[25]

Passage of the California Desert Protection Act later that year included the mining claim in a designated wilderness in a national park, creating a conundrum that simultaneously bound the National Park Service's hands and confounded its claimants. By its designation, wilderness was not supposed to have human influence. Rainbow Talc was a preexisting use with legitimate standing that the National Park Service could only hope to thwart. The change to wilderness status did not abrogate the partners' rights; it merely meant that operators had to conform to the more stringent National Park Service mining regulations. The agency had no legitimate legal way to stop the permit; it could only apply its regulations to the claim. If approved, the mine would have been the first inside a designated wilderness in a national park area. Almost a generation after the Mining in the Parks Act of 1976, the new Death Valley National Park faced its most invidious threat: the prospect of a new mining operation inside its boundaries.

Proponents swiftly articulated their position. "We've put our sweat and blood in this for 50 years," Jackson hyperbolically remarked about the mine, and the antigovernment forces prevalent in the era of the "Contract with America" Congress found a cause célèbre. They worked to cast the situation as an example of big government picking on the little guy, and the age of the protagonists helped fuel this image. "We're no spring chickens," seventy-nine-year-old Edward Baumunk told reporters, and he and the eighty-one-year-old Jackson provided sympathetic figures for those with pent-up animosity against federal agencies and government in general. Couched in the property-rights language of the 1990s, a characteristic of the antigovernment hostility that had become common in the West, the Rainbow Talc Mine posed an insidious threat to the park on more than one level.[26]

The opponents of the mine were numerous as well. "We've got piles of comments," park superintendent Richard Martin told reporters. Some organizations suggested strategies to influence decision making. The California Wilderness Coalition asked its members to "pressure the NPS to do their job." The organization believed that the National Park Service had not undertaken appropriate compliance work, typically an environmental impact statement or, in cases of lesser impact, an environmental assessment. Others challenged the National Park Service's record of protection of its parks, and a number tried to persuade their congressional representatives to retroactively change the offending 1872 Mining Act. A few even suggested that the claim was resuscitated in an attempt to compel the federal government to buy it out for an extravagant price.[27]

There was no easy resolution. The National Park Service was restricted to "willing seller" purchases of inholdings, and the Baumunks were willing sellers. But the National Park Service lacked the funds to purchase their claim. Kathy A. Davis, supervisor of the First District of San Bernardino County and a member of the Death Valley Advisory Commission, suggested an alternative. She believed a "cherry stem," a thin corridor that would include the mine and its approach road, an alternative eschewed in the 1999 draft general management plan, was a possible solution. "We disagree that proposing a cherry-stem through wilderness to the Rainbow Talc Mine would overcome the controversy surrounding this potential mine development," Martin responded. The issue was larger, definitive not only for Death Valley National Park but also for the National Park Service. Purchase remained the best option, and rather than allow the first mining operation in a National Park Service wilderness area, "instead, we bought it," recalled one park staff member.[28]

In many ways, the Rainbow Talc Mine controversy illustrated an ongoing theme in the New West. The end of the regional extractive economy had come in a hurry, and its replacement by recreation and tourism was almost complete. By 1994 only a handful of counties in the interior West made even 40 percent of their livelihood from extractive industries. Yet the legal mechanisms of American society favored this anachronistic form of production. Years after resolution of the Rainbow Talc situation, some public officials in desert California still clung to the vision of an extractive economy. In 2003 Bill Postmus, supervisor of San Bernardino County, told the US Congress that the sale of the Rainbow Talc Mine to the National Park Service prevented economic development in his district. "Sadly, it was a mine that could have generated income, property taxes, and employment," Postmus insisted with more faith than reason. "Instead, the agency spent public money to prevent its development."[29] Then, in 2007, the Environmental Working Group, citing government records indicating a major spike in mining claims within ten miles of such treasured public lands, asserted that once more, a "modern-day Gold Rush is threatening California's national parks, national monuments, wilderness and roadless areas." These incidents suggest that no matter how far the New West had come, some people still clung to the image of the Old.[30]

Another persistent concern that has dogged Death Valley National Park since its inception is how its staff can manage resources for present use while protecting them for the future. The agency has generally wrestled with this tension since 1916. In some eras, parks have leaned toward constituency management, which generally meant prioritizing present-day demands. Since 1978 and especially after the implementation of the 1991 Vail Agenda, the agency has stressed resource protection. But Death Valley (and other parks) suffered from what Reynolds described as "plural missions."[31]

The protection-access question remains unresolved. The growth of Las Vegas and Pahrump, Nevada, and the expansion of the Los Angeles basin's population into the Mojave have made Death Valley more accessible than ever before. Before the 1960s, the sheer difficulty of reaching the backcountry and the discomfort of staying there offered considerable protection for wilderness areas. Since then, energized public constituencies for all kinds of outdoor use, especially off-highway-vehicle users, have accelerated their use of these terrains and loudly promoted their right to use technology to do essentially as they pleased. With more lands and essentially the same budget with which to manage them, Death Valley National Park faced a conundrum. "We're not going to allow vehicles to run over Eureka Dunes, but they can still access a park that is 95 percent wilderness with over 600 miles of dirt four-wheel-drive roads," insisted Reynolds. "Maybe not the way they used to, but you can still access it."[32]

The battle for access to Surprise Canyon has been emblematic of this tension. The old road to Panamint City had been in use since the mining rush in the area in the late nineteenth century. By the 1970s, weekend desert recreational users used it to reach the ruins of the old mining town. A 1984 flash flood sunk the streambed as much as twenty feet in some places and entirely washed out the road, but the roadbed's absence served only to attract the attention of four-wheel-drive enthusiasts. They saw in the water-swept bedrock the opportunity to exercise their dreams. Within a few years, four-wheel-drive vehicles with battery-operated winches negotiated the streambed on a regular basis, using the winches to hoist vehicles straight up the waterfalls.[33]

The California Desert Protection Act redesignated the terrain that had been the off-roaders' playground, turning it into protected wilderness. The legislation included the canyon's upper reach in Death Valley National Park, while the lower area remained under the jurisdiction of the Bureau of Land Management as part of a wilderness area. The new law left a sixty-foot-wide corridor around the road, creating a "cherry stem" surrounded by wilderness in which off-roading continued. Yet by the time the National Park Service and BLM began to implement the CDPA, off-roaders had become a fixture in the canyon. "There were times it was bumper to bumper up there," said Rocky Novak, one of the only real residents of the area. Afterward, "the river was running mud for a month."[34]

Conservation organizations recognized the threat to the area and sought to restrict off-roaders' access to it. Water officials recognized the potential for degradation of water quality, and wildlife officials expressed concern about the destruction of habitat. The issue came to a head in May 2001, when the Tucson-based Center for Biological Diversity and other organizations filed a lawsuit charging that the BLM had let the area fall below its minimum standards. The BLM closed the area to vehicles by installing a gate. The user community was livid. "When I saw that gate, I cried," avid four-wheeler Marlin Czajkowski of Fresno said.[35]

Even those drivers of all-terrain vehicles who tended to obey the law pose dilemmas for park staff and other visitors. Automobile manufacturers are only too happy to have their tricked-out vehicles tested against the valley's legendary tough and brutal landscapes. Typical accounts read like this breathless title: "Sand Stormer—Chrysler's New Jeep Wrangler Rubicon Duels It Out with the Death Valley Outback." Its accompanying text is as hyped. "Death Valley is a wilderness of rocks and sand nearly the size of Connecticut, with topography as arid and mountainous as the Moroccan fringes of the Sahara. Since 1849 it's been notorious for waylaying travelers in wheeled vehicles. What better proving ground, then, for a factory-new 2012 Jeep Wrangler Rubicon?" Although the reporter put the "dozer"-colored jeep through its high-speed paces on roads paved and not, it made its mark when he pulled off-road: it "wasn't until we'd forded a stream, climbed a steep pile of mine tailings and performed a brush-crushing turnaround at a washout illuminated only by our headlights that we got a taste of what the Ruby could do." He meant how it handled in rough country, but from the park's perspective, what that particular vehicle did—and too many others like it—was to chew up the landscape, damage that the park has fought hard to limit. Noted ranger Kevin Emmerich, a sixteen-year veteran of Death Valley National Park: "In two decades of living in the Mojave Desert, I have witnessed harm to fragile desert ecosystems by increasing off-road vehicle use. I have recently seen a desert stream lose eighty percent of its vegetation and have seen the air quality of the desert in Amargosa Valley, Nevada be polluted because off-road vehicles have removed large tracts of vegetation and soil crusts. Clearly, off-roading on public lands needs more regulation."[36]

The Saline Valley provided another similar clash of values between some users of the park and the park's wilderness character. A collection of three primary natural hot springs, collectively known as Warm Springs, held the most significant example of Native American ranching added to the monument in 1994. A range of sites dotted with artifacts attest to a long presence, likely of a semino-madic character. Available evidence indicates that the valley was inhabited during autumn, winter, and spring. Summer heat drove the people to higher elevation. After the arrival of Euro-American settlers in the 1860s, Native peoples acquired agriculture and moved to a fertile tillable area west and north of their original settlement. This community, with as many as 125 people, became known as the Saline Valley Indian Ranch. It slowly declined during the twentieth century.[37]

As the ranch declined, automobile tourism brought new people to the Death Valley area. With its waters, the Saline Valley attracted new attention as early as 1940, when a group from nearby Deep Springs College camped there during its annual spring trip. The group encountered a bus full of students from a nearby junior college, a portent of the changes that soon followed. More people came to enjoy the therapeutic effects of the warm water, and by 1947, a small concrete tub had been constructed at Lower Warm Spring, most probably by cattlemen or sheepherders who sought to catch the runoff. Increased use led to visible evidence of human impact, and a countermovement to clean up the area began in 1964. By 1965 a new and larger tub that allowed as many as a dozen people to soak at one time had been constructed. The pool attracted growing numbers and acquired many of the characteristics of a small tourist destination. In the end, an array of facilities, including two airstrips, made the lower pool comfortable for even the most finicky arrival.[38]

About one-half mile above the lower spring lay Palm Spring, another source pool. Despite little cover from the wind and sun, Palm Spring grew in attrac-tiveness because of its pristine condition, beautiful views, and the increasing crowdedness of the lower spring. By 1968 the first soaking pool there had been constructed. Three miles above this spring lay the isolated Upper Warm Spring. Although the BLM fenced the area to prevent fouling by feral burros in the 1980s, no other facilities existed there. Its remote nature attracted a constituency that sought to avoid the commotion that increasingly characterized the lower two pools.[39]

A community formed around the springs. A loose collection of individuals regulated themselves in the vicinity of the springs, cared for the pools and their soaking tubs, and generally impressed a sense of order on the region. Among their members were some who did not follow either BLM or later National Park Service rules. At the same time, some who made the Saline Valley their own feared inter-vention by the National Park Service and other federal agencies. In response, they formed the Saline Valley Preservation Association to safeguard their interests. The growing population in the Saline Valley posed a range of management issues. Pot hunting took place with some regularity in the Saline Valley, prompting attention from National Park Service law officers. The Timbisha found development in the region offensive, for it was one of their sacred sites.[40] The springs had been one of their seasonal locales since prehistory, and Anglo habitation had likely destroyed not only consistent access, but possibly important cultural resources as well. The people who lived there had only tenancy to authenticate their right to remain, but culture and custom stood strong in the rural West.

A similar tenacity has marked the life of the Timbisha, an enduring force that continues to shape its internal relations and those with the National Park Service. No sooner had the Timbisha Homeland Act secured President Clinton's signature in 2000, for instance, when an internecine struggle erupted. Those living in and around Furnace Creek, which had long served as the crucible for Timbisha activism, found themselves confronted with challengers to their authority to speak for the tribe. Members residing in Bishop and other communities outside the park agitated for a per capita distribution of the tribe's share of money derived from the Indian Gaming Revenue Sharing Trust Fund rather than the encumbrance of those funds for economic development; they also pushed for the construction of a casino, disputed the leadership of Pauline Esteves (and voted her out of office), and in 2004 managed to grab the Furnace Creek office files and transport them to Bishop (a coup d'état that was reversed four years later). This power struggle, writes Theodore Catton, "was hugely destabilizing and sapped the Tribe's energy," and it complicated the working relationship between the Timbisha and the national park. Making headway in the fraught environment, he concluded, depended on the two parties recognizing the situation's limitations and prospects: "There is a need for realism and there is a need for patience."[41]

This measured response highlights the need for another: different constituencies have always sought to use the park's resources in their own way. In a manner that rarely occurred at Yosemite or Yellowstone, the public tolerated or advocated uses of Death Valley that it would not accept elsewhere in the national park system. Mining had been chief among them, a consequence of the nature of the monument's establishment. It was as if segments of the public did not regard Death Valley as a national park; even worse, for a long time, the National Park Service seemed to tacitly agree with such a critique. The consequences were apparent in budget and personnel shortfalls and, even after national park status was attained, in the way the agency funded Death Valley. The result created a perennial dilemma for park managers. Not only did they have to administer Death Valley National Park with fewer resources than at other national park areas, but they also had to constantly fight to ensure that the rest of the National Park Service recognized the park's singular value. Its quest for respect from its parent agency underpins everything else Death Valley has faced, and will continue to confront, across the twenty-first century.

In this, Death Valley National Park faces a future that is directly derived from its past. Since its founding in the 1930s, the park has struggled within the larger national park system. Often considered of a different order than the crown jewels of the national park system—such as the iconic Yellowstone, Grand Canyon, and Yosemite National Parks—Death Valley's human history and in particular the persistence of mining within its boundaries, combined with its desert character, have diminished the park in the eyes of NPS administrators. As a result, Death Valley received less than the park merited or needed to fulfill its multifaceted and complicated mission.

As the twenty-first century gathers momentum, however, there is little to suggest that this pattern will change. Curiously enough, this may mean that Death Valley National Park will serve as a bellwether for the rest of the system. With some exceptions, the American national parks have been facing hard times since the 1970s. Although there have been some brilliant revivals, the general trend has been to ask parks and their staffs to do more with less—with varying degrees of success. This management approach, and the uneven results that have come from it, have informed the most recent strategy that NPS director John Jarvis announced in August 2011, five years in advance of the agency's 2016 centennial. Park staff "must recommit to exemplary stewardship and public enjoyment of these places," and they will diligently "promote the contributions that national parks and our community assistance programs make to create jobs, strengthen local economies, and support ecosystem services." As a federal agency, Jarvis continued, the National Park Service will "integrate our mission across parks and programs and use their collective power to leverage resources and expand our contributions to society." Criticized for its boilerplate language—"This is another document looking for an idea, hence its cliché-riddled, shotgun approach," chided historian Al Runte—it was silent too about the costs that will surely be associated with its proposed recommitments, or the outlays that will come from the peculiar changes that a shifting climate will bring to its management of the system's cultural and natural resources, or the expenses that might arise as gasoline prices increase, thus challenging the ability of visitors to drive to such isolated parks as Death Valley.[42]

The irony is that of all the national parks, Death Valley may be in the best position to respond to these and other trials, current and potential. In an era of climate change, the nation's most arid park will be in a good position to help other entities anticipating less precipitation respond appropriately. In an era of cost-cutting, Death Valley, which has had to address fiscal difficulties and staffing problems from its creation, will be in a good position to advise other parks on difficult budgetary choices. If this park's past is a portent of what the future may hold for the national park system generally, then the resilience, flexibility, and inventiveness of the employees of Death Valley National Park will be of enormous value to their peers across the country. This is hardly an ideal situation, of course, and should this underfunded scenario come to be, it will also certainly complicate the National Park Service's second century of service and the conservation mission it has done so much to promote across the nation and around the world.

NOTES

INTRODUCTION

1. David Darlington, *The Mojave: A Portrait of the Definitive American Desert* (Henry Holt: New York, 1996), 1–6.

2. John Muir, *A Thousand-Mile Walk to the Gulf* (San Francisco: Sierra Club Books, 1991), 41–66; Michael P. Cohen, *The Pathless Way: John Muir and American Wilderness* (Madison: University of Wisconsin Press, 1984), 1–37.

3. Jared Diamond, *Guns, Germs, and Steel: The Fates of Human Societies* (New York: W. W. Norton, 1997), 13–35; Alfred W. Crosby, *Ecological Imperialism: The Biological Expansion of Europe, 900–1900 AD* (New York: Cambridge University Press, 1986), 1–32; James L. Newman, *The Peopling of Africa: A Geographic Interpretation* (New Haven, CT: Yale University Press, 1997), 15–24; Joseph E. Inkori and Stanley L. Engerman, *The Atlantic Slave Trade: Effects on Economies, Societies, and Peoples in Africa, the Americas, and Europe* (Durham, NC: Duke University Press, 1994), 3, 7.

4. Roderick Nash, *Wilderness and the American Mind* (New Haven, CT: Yale University Press, 1967), 1–16; Patricia Nelson Limerick, *Desert Passages: Encounters with the American Desert* (Albuquerque: University of New Mexico Press, 1985), 165–77.

5. Robert G. Elston, "Prehistory of the Western Area," in *Handbook of North American Indians: Great Basin,* edited by Warren L. D'Azevedo, 11:135–48 (Washington, DC: Smithsonian Institution Press, 1986); David H. Thomas, Lorann S. A. Pendleton, and Stephen C. Cappanati, "Western Shoshone," in ibid., 262–83; Maurice Zigmond, "Kawaiisu," in ibid., 398–411; Sven Liljeblad and Catherine S. Fowler, "Owens Valley Paiute," in ibid., 412–34; Lawrence Hogue, *All the Wild and Lonely Places: Journeys in a Desert Landscape* (Washington, DC: Island Press, 2000), 3–9; Vincent Bugliosi with Curt Gentry, *Helter Skelter: The True Story of the Manson Murders* (New York: W. W. Norton, 1974), 75–81.

6. Edward H. Spicer, *Cycles of Conquest: The Impact of Spain, Mexico, and the United States on the Indians of the Southwest, 1533–1960* (Tucson: University of Arizona Press, 1962), 1–262. Although Spicer pays scant attention to Death Valley and the Mojave, the model he presents contributes to an understanding of the circumstances and predicament of Native peoples in the Mojave.

7. Steven J. Crum, *The Road on Which We Came: Po'i Pentun Tammen Kimmappeh: A History of the Western Shoshone* (Salt Lake City: University of Utah Press, 1994), 66–70; "Technical Reports Regarding the Death Valley Timbi-Sha Shoshone Band of Death Valley, California," L30 Land Use—Indian Village, 1981–82, PRG 8-8, Death Valley National Park archives (hereafter Death Valley archives).

8. John Perlin, *A Forest Journey: The Role of Wood in the Development of Civilization* (New York: W. W. Norton, 1989), 1–25; Frederick Merk, *History of the Westward Movement* (New York: Alfred A. Knopf, 1978), 229–52; David M. Wrobel, *Promised Lands: Promotion,*

Memory, and the Creation of the American West (Lawrence: University Press of Kansas, 2002), 1–18.

9. Richard E. Lingenfelter, *Death Valley and the Amargosa: Land of Illusion* (Berkeley: University of California Press, 1986), 50–51.

10. Thomas W. Brooks, *By Buckboard to Beatty: The California-Nevada Desert in 1886,* edited by Anthony L. Lehman (Los Angeles: Dawson's Book Shop, 1970), 24.

11. Wallace E. Stegner, *The Big Rock Candy Mountain* (New York: Hill and Wang, 1943), 13–22; Wallace E. Stegner, *Where the Bluebird Sings to the Lemonade Springs* (New York: Random House, 1987), 34–44.

12. J. Smeaton Chase, *California Desert Trails* (Boston: Houghton Mifflin, 1919), 1–14; 37; Edna Brush Perkins, *The White Heart of the Mojave: An Adventure with the Outdoors of the Desert* (New York: Boni and Liveright, 1922), 9–19, 87–95. Other writers who lived in the region and wrote compellingly about its life and folkways were Mary Austin, *Land of Little Rain* (Boston: Houghton Mifflin, 1903); and Dix Van Dyke, *Daggett: Life in a Mojave Frontier Town,* edited by Peter Wild (Baltimore: Johns Hopkins University Press, 1997).

13. A. Constandina Titus, *Bombs in the Backyard: Atomic Testing and American Politics* (Reno: University of Nevada Press, 1986), 1–35; Michon Makedon, *Bombast: Spinning Atoms in the Desert* (Reno, NV: Black Rock Institute Press, 2010); John A. Findlay and Bruce Hevly, *Atomic Frontier Days: Hanford and the American West* (Seattle: University of Washington Press, 2011).

14. Darlington, *Mojave,* 1–4; Edward Abbey, *Desert Solitaire: A Season in the Wilderness* (New York: McGraw-Hill, 1968). GPS technology can also be confused by Death Valley's vast extent, leading to fatalities that park rangers call "Death by GPS."

CHAPTER 1 : BEFORE THE MONUMENT

1. Jesse D. Jennings, "Prehistory: Introduction," in *Handbook of North American Indians,* edited by D'Azevedo, 11:113, 115 (see introduction, n. 5); C. Michael Barton, *Archeological Survey in Northeastern Death Valley National Monument,* Western Archeological and Conservation Center Publications in Anthropology, no. 23 (Tucson, AZ: Western Archeological and Conservation Center, National Park Service, 1983), 15–16; Elizabeth von Till Warren et al., *A Cultural Resources Overview of the Colorado Desert Planning* (Riverside: California Desert District, Bureau of Land Management, US Department of the Interior, 1981), 19–20; Claude N. Warren and Robert H. Crabtree, "Prehistory of the Southwestern Area," in *Handbook of North American Indians,* edited by D'Azevedo, 11:183–84.

2. Barton, *Archeological Survey,* 16–17; Warren et al., *Cultural Resources Overview,* 33.

3. Barton, *Archeological Survey,* 17–18; Warren et al., *Cultural Resources Overview,* 35–44; Warren and Crabtree, "Prehistory of the Southwestern Area," 184–87.

4. Barton, *Archeological Survey,* 20–21; Warren et al., *Cultural Resources Overview,* 49–52; Warren and Crabtree, "Prehistory of the Southwestern Area," 189–91.

5. Gary B. Coombs, *The Archaeology of the Northeast Mojave Desert,* with contributions by Robert Crabtree and Elizabeth Warren (Washington, DC: US Bureau of Land Management, 1979), 22; Barton, *Archeological Survey,* 21–23; William James Wallace and Edith

Wallace, *Ancient Peoples and Cultures of Death Valley National Monument* (Ramona, CA: Acoma Books, 1978), 129–34.

6. Lingenfelter, *Death Valley and the Amargosa*, 29–30 (see introduction, n. 9); David Roberts, *A Newer World: Kit Carson, John C. Frémont, and the Claiming of the West* (New York: Simon and Schuster, 2000), 127–39.

7. John Charles Frémont, *Report of the Exploring Expedition to the Rocky Mountains in the Year 1842, and to Oregon and North California in the Years 1843–'44* (Washington, DC: Gales and Seaton, 1845), 261–65.

8. Lingenfelter, *Death Valley and the Amargosa*, 40–42. Benjamin Levy's map of the probable routes for these parties indicates that the Jayhawkers and the Manly-Bennett Party entered Death Valley near Furnace Creek.

9. William Lewis Manly, *Death Valley in '49* (Chicago: R. R. Donnelley and Sons, 1927), 210–17; Lingenfelter, *Death Valley and the Amargosa*, 46–51; William H. Goetzmann, *Exploration and Empire: The Scientist and the Explorer in the Winning of the American West* (New York: Alfred A. Knopf, 1966), 177, 471–74.

10. *Draft Environmental Impact Statement and General Management Plan: Death Valley National Park* (Washington, DC: National Park Service, 1998), 135; Charles B. Hunt, *Death Valley: Geology, Ecology, Archaeology* (Berkeley: University of California Press, 1975), 174–81; Benjamin Levy, *Death Valley National Monument Historical Background Study* (Washington, DC: National Park Service, 1969), 35–39.

11. Lingenfelter, *Death Valley and the Amargosa*, 80–82; *Draft Environmental Impact Statement*, 135–37; Phillip W. Powell, *Death Valley* (private printing, 1936), 51–60.

12. Lingenfelter, *Death Valley and the Amargosa*, 91–97; Goetzmann, *Exploration and Empire*, 469–73; George M. Wheeler, *Preliminary Report upon a Reconnaissance Through Southern and Southeastern Nevada, Made in 1869* (Washington, DC: Government Printing Office, 1875), 64–70.

13. Levy, *Historical Background Study*, 77–82; Lingenfelter, *Death Valley and the Amargosa*, 96–97; Goetzmann, *Exploration and Empire*, 472–75.

14. *1998 Draft Environmental Impact Statement;* Powell, *Death Valley*, 14–17; Barton, *Archeological Survey*, 24–25.

15. Levy, *Historical Background Study*, 7–16.

16. Carling I. Malouf and John M. Findlay, "Euro-American Impact Before 1870," in *Handbook of North American Indians*, edited by D'Azevedo, 11:512–15.

17. Ibid., 514–20; Crum, *Road on Which We Came*, 24–28 (see introduction, n. 7); Levy, *Historical Background Study*, 101–3, 163–64; United States Treaty with the Western Shoshoni, October 1, 1863, 18 *Statutes at Large* 689.

18. Robert P. Palazzo, "Darwin's Boom Period, 1974–1878" and "The Relationship Between Darwin, California, and Death Valley," in *Proceedings: Third Death Valley Conference on History and Prehistory, January 30–February 2, 1992,* edited by James Pisarowicz (Death Valley, CA: Death Valley Natural History Association, 1992), 57–79.

19. After a bitter mining dispute, assailants ambushed and killed Johnson. Lingenfelter, *Death Valley and the Amargosa*, 164–72; Crum, *Road on Which We Came*, 98.

20. Russell Elliott with William Rowley, *History of Nevada* (Lincoln: University of Nebraska Press, 1987), 162–79.

21. Lingenfelter, *Death Valley and the Amargosa,* 113–34; Levy, *Historical Background Study; 1998 Draft Environmental Impact Statement,* 138–39.

22. Lingenfelter, *Death Valley and the Amargosa,* 173–75; *Draft Environmental Impact Statement,* 138–39; Robert Shankland, *Steve Mather of the National Parks* (New York: Alfred A. Knopf, 1970), 22–23.

23. Lingenfelter, *Death Valley and the Amargosa,* 177–79.

24. Ibid., 175–85; Levy, *Historical Background Study,* 121–28; Alan Hensher, "Bonanza Days at Resting Spring," in *Proceedings: Second Death Valley Conference on History and Prehistory, January 21–25, 1988,* edited by Jean Johnson and Jim Pisarowicz (Death Valley, CA: Death Valley Natural History Association, 1991), 64–68.

25. George Hildebrand, *Borax Pioneer: Francis Marion Smith* (San Diego: Howell-North Books, 1982), 21–41; Lingenfelter, *Death Valley and the Amargosa,* 182–86, 380–90; Cynthia Woo, "The Bay Area World of Borax Smith," in *Proceedings: Third Death Valley Conference,* edited by Pisarowicz, 80–88.

26. Gordon Chappell, "The First Ryan: A Borate Mining Camp of the Amargosa," in *Proceedings of the Fourth Death Valley Conference on History and Prehistory, February 2–5, 1995,* edited by Jean Johnson (Death Valley, CA: Death Valley Natural History Association, 1996), 94–109; Hildebrand, *Borax Pioneer,* 98–115.

27. Lingenfelter, *Death Valley and the Amargosa,* 385–96.

28. Rhyolite became the largest of Death Valley's Gold Rush towns, reaching a population of more than ten thousand in just two years. Lingenfelter, *Death Valley and the Amargosa,* 284–300.

29. Linda W. Greene and John A. Latschar, *Historic Resource Study: A History of Mining in Death Valley National Monument* (Denver: Department of the Interior, 1981), 2:510–34; Levy, *Historical Background Study,* 101–59; Linda Greene to Gordon Chappell, April 19, 1978, N30 Historic Sites and Structures—Management 1978–80, Death Valley National Park archives (hereafter Death Valley archives).

30. Lingenfelter, *Death Valley and the Amargosa,* 275–77.

31. Ibid., 276–78.

32. Ibid., 286–99; Greene and Latschar, *Historic Resource Study,* 1:608–62; Levy, *Historical Background Study;* "Characters in Death Valley History, Death Valley National Monument," National Park Service fact sheet, Death Valley archives; Donald L. Fife, "Mesothermal Gold Mineralization: Skidoo–Del Norte Mines, Death Valley," *California Geology* (April 1987): 87–93.

33. Lingenfelter, *Death Valley and the Amargosa,* 428–29.

34. Jules Tygiel, *The Great Los Angeles Swindle: Oils, Stocks, and Scandal During the Roaring Twenties* (New York: Oxford University Press, 1994), 132–33.

35. Lingenfelter, *Death Valley and the Amargosa,* 424–36; Greene and Latschar, *Historic Resource Study,* 2:187–210; Tygiel, *Great Los Angeles Swindle,* 149, 156.

36. Russell Elliott, *Nevada's Twentieth Century Mining Boom: Tonopah, Goldfield, Ely*

(Reno: University of Nevada Press, 1966), 1–25; Rodman W. Paul, *Mining Frontiers of the Far West, 1848–1880* (New York: Holt, Rinehart, and Winston, 1963), 1–14.

37. Lingenfelter, *Death Valley and the Amargosa*, 242–45.

38. Ibid., 252–57.

39. Ibid., 242–74; Susan Buchel, "Death Valley Scotty's Place in Twentieth Century Popular Culture," in *Proceedings: Second Death Valley Conference,* edited by Johnson and Pisarowicz, 96–97; R. Patrick McKnight, "Death Valley Scotty: The Wild West Years," in *Proceedings: First Death Valley Conference on History and Prehistory, February 8–11, 1988,* edited by Richard Lingenfelter and Jim Pisarowicz (Death Valley, CA: Death Valley Natural History Association, 1991), 1–9.

40. National Park Service, *Historic Structure Report: Death Valley Scotty Historic District Main House and Annex* (National Park Service, September 1991), 83–85; letter quoted in National Register of Historical Places Inventory, "Death Valley Scotty Historic District," Death Valley archives; Susan Buchel, "Albert Johnson's Pursuit of a Death Valley Dominion," in *Proceedings: First Death Valley Conference,* edited by Lingenfelter and Pisarowicz, 12–19; for Pratt, see Hal K. Rothman, *Promise Beheld and the Limits of Place: A Historic Resource Study of Carlsbad Caverns and Guadalupe Mountains National Parks* (Santa Fe, NM: National Park Service, 1998); for Paepcke, see James Sloan Allen, *The Romance of Commerce and Culture: Capitalism, Modernism, and the Chicago-Aspen Crusade for Cultural Reform* (Chicago: University of Chicago Press, 1983).

41. Lingenfelter, *Death Valley and the Amargosa*, 447–48.

42. Ibid., 455–64; Buchel, "Johnson's Pursuit," 12–15.

43. Buchel, "Johnson's Pursuit," 14–19; Buchel, "Death Valley Scotty's Place," 97.

44. Ibid.

45. Lingenfelter, *Death Valley and the Amargosa*, 291–92, 442.

46. Marguerite Shaffer, *See America First: Tourism and National Identity, 1880–1940* (Washington, DC: Smithsonian Institution Press, 2001), 93–129; Hal K. Rothman, *Devil's Bargains: Tourism in the Twentieth-Century American West* (Lawrence: University Press of Kansas, 1998), 143–67.

47. Lingenfelter, *Death Valley and the Amargosa*, 449–56; L. Burr Belden, *Old Stovepipe Wells* (Death Valley, CA: Death Valley '49ers, 1968), 1–5.

48. Lingenfelter, *Death Valley and the Amargosa*, 453–54; Ron Miller, *Fifty Years Ago at Furnace Creek Inn* (Death Valley, CA: Death Valley '49ers, 1977), 1–16.

49. Lingenfelter, *Death Valley and the Amargosa*, 454–56.

50. Miller, *Fifty Years Ago*, 6–9; Shankland, *Steve Mather*, 65–71, 120–27, 133–40, 145–52; Donald C. Swain, *Wilderness Defender: Horace M. Albright and Conservation* (Chicago: University of Chicago Press, 1970), 130–34.

CHAPTER 2 : ON THE PERIPHERY

1. Barbara Novak, *Nature and Culture: American Landscape, 1825–1862* (New York: Oxford University Press, 1980), 1–15.

2. Alfred Runte, *National Parks: The American Experience,* 2nd ed. (Lincoln: University

of Nebraska Press, 1987), 33–79; Stephen J. Pyne, *How the Canyon Became Grand* (New York: Viking, 2000), 1–16.

3. Runte, *National Parks,* 109–12; Horace M. Albright as told to Robert Cahn, *The Birth of the National Park Service: The Founding Years, 1913–1933* (Salt Lake City: Howe Brothers Press, 1986), 275–78; Perkins, *White Heart of the Mojave* (see introduction, n. 12).

4. Shankland, *Steve Mather,* 170–90 (see chap. 1, n. 22); Hal K. Rothman, " 'A Regular Ding-Dong Fight': Agency Culture and Evolution in the Park Service–Forest Service Dispute, 1916–1937," *Western Historical Quarterly* 20, no. 2 (1989): 41–60.

5. Shankland, *Steve Mather,* 56, 220–24; Lingenfelter, *Death Valley and the Amargosa,* 464 (see introduction, n. 9); David H. Stratton, *Tempest over Teapot Dome: The Story of Albert B. Fall* (Norman: University of Oklahoma Press, 1998), 222–24.

6. Lingenfelter, *Death Valley and the Amargosa,* 452–54; Shankland, *Steve Mather,* 276–78; Hal K. Rothman, *Preserving Different Pasts: The American National Monuments* (Urbana: University of Illinois Press, 1989), 188; Albright as told to Cahn, *Birth of the National Park Service,* 275–78.

7. Albright as told to Cahn, *Birth of the National Park Service,* 275–76; Shankland, *Steve Mather,* 276; Swain, *Wilderness Defender,* 311 (see chap. 1, n. 50); Death Valley Master Plan 1960, vol. 3, sec. A, 2, Death Valley National Park archives (hereafter Death Valley archives).

8. Swain, *Wilderness Defender,* 311–13; Albright as told to Cahn, *Birth of the National Park Service,* 278.

9. Horace M. Albright, *Origins of National Park Service Administration of Historic Sites* (Philadelphia: Eastern National Park and Monument Association, 1971), 16–17; Albright as told to Cahn, *Birth of the National Park Service,* 278–80.

10. Swain, *Wilderness Defender,* 178–206; David Harmon, Francis P. McManamon, and Dwight T. Pitcaithley, eds., *The Antiquities Act: A Century of American Archaeology, Historic Preservation, and Nature Conservation* (Tucson: University of Arizona Press, 2006).

11. Roger W. Toll to the Director, National Park Service, April 23, 1931, File 11568, Death Valley archives; Horace M. Albright, "The Creation of the Death Valley Monument and Death Valley 'Scotty,' " H30 Area and Service History, 1953–62, Box 1-11, Death Valley archives.

12. Edwin L. Rothfuss, "The Making of a National Park," in *Proceedings: Fourth Death Valley Conference,* edited by Johnson (see chap. 1, n. 26); John White to the Director, National Park Service, February 21, 1931, Situation Reports, A2623 38-31, Death Valley archives; Albright, "Creation of the Death Valley Monument"; Swain, *Wilderness Defender,* 311–16. Although the proclamation that created Death Valley National Monument banned new mining claims, even that constraint was deleted that June through congressional mandate: 48 Stat. 139; 16 USC 447.

13. Swain, *Wilderness Defender,* 183–98, 217.

14. Albright, *Administration of Historic Sites,* 13–17; Rothman, *Preserving Different Pasts,* 68–69, 224, 236; Barry Mackintosh, *The National Parks: Shaping the System* (Washington, DC: National Park Service, 1997), 18–25; Swain, *Wilderness Defender,* 202, 217, 276–78.

15. White to the Director, April 7, 1933, May 18, 1934, Situation Reports, A2623 38-31, Death Valley archives.

16. Ibid., May 18, 1934; T. R. Goodwin to Hon. Harry L. Eaglebright, March 19, 1935; "Death Valley National Monument Resume for the Year Ending September 30, 1933," Situation Reports, A2623 38-31, Death Valley archives.

17. Administrative Plan, Death Valley National Monument, 1934–35, Situation Reports, A2623 38-31, Death Valley archives; Rothman, *Preserving Different Pasts*, 89–118.

18. Rothman, *Preserving Different Pasts*, 119–39; Ronald Foresta, *America's National Parks and Their Keepers* (Washington, DC: Resources for the Future, 1980), 30–42.

19. William Leuchtenberg, *Franklin D. Roosevelt and the New Deal, 1932–1940* (New York: Harper and Row, 1963), 1–26; Samuel P. Hays, *Conservation and the Gospel of Efficiency* (Cambridge, MA: Harvard University Press, 1959), 36–69; Harold K. Steen, *The United States Forest Service: A History* (Seattle: University of Washington Press, 1976), 98–100; Rothman, *Preserving Different Pasts*, 68; Richard Lowitt, *The New Deal and the West* (Bloomington: Indiana University Press, 1984), 1–9.

20. John Paige, *The Civilian Conservation Corps and the National Park Service, 1933–1942: An Administrative History* (Washington, DC: Government Printing Office, 1985), 1–13.

21. T. R. Goodwin to Hon. Harry L. Eaglebright, March 19, 1935, Situation Reports, A2623 38-31, Death Valley archives.

22. Death Valley National Monument Annual Report, 1934, Death Valley archives; White to the Director, May 18, 1934, and Goodwin to the Director, July 10, 1937, Situation Reports, A2623 38-31, Death Valley archives.

23. T. R. Goodwin to John White, March 31, 1934, LL417 DEVA Boundaries, 1933–34, Death Valley archives.

24. Death Valley National Monument annual reports 1937, 1938, 1939, 1942, 1937, 1938, 1939, 1942, Death Valley archives. There is some discussion about Goodwin's position description and the dates of his residency in the park. Rothfuss, "Making of a National Park," suggests that Goodwin's tenure as superintendent began in November 1937. The National Park Service directory of officials from 1991 gives his title as "superintendent" beginning on April 15, 1938.

25. Duane A. Thompson, "Mining in National Parks and Wilderness Areas: Policy, Rules, Activities," Congressional Research Service Report for Congress, February 12, 1996, 4–7; Gordon Morris Bakken, *The Mining Law of 1872: Past, Politics, Prospects* (Albuquerque: University of New Mexico Press, 2008).

26. J. H. Favorite to Bradley B. Smith, January 28, 1936; Arno B. Cammerer to Goodwin, February 16, 1938; Arno B. Cammerer to the Commissioner, General Land Office, February 16, 1939, all Box 279, File 609-01 Mining, National Archives and Record Administration, Pacific Region–San Bruno (hereafter NARA-SB); Heather Abel, "Blasting from the Past," *High Country News*, June 23, 1997; Robert McClure and Andrew Schneider, "The General Mining Act of 1872 Has Left a Legacy of Riches and Ruins," *Seattle Post-Intelligencer*, June 11, 2001.

27. John White to the Director, National Park Service, March 2, 1938, Box 279, File

609-01 Mining, NARA-SB; Hal K. Rothman, "The History of National Parks and Economic Development," in *National Parks and Rural Development,* edited by Gary Machlis and Donald Field (Washington, DC: Island Press, 2000), 36–52; Shankland, *Steve Mather,* 181–82.

28. Abraham Lincoln signed the Homestead Act in 1862. A homesteader had only to be head of a household and at least twenty-one years old to claim a 160-acre parcel. Each homesteader had to live on the land, build a home and other improvements, and farm for five years before becoming eligible to "prove up." The act remained in effect until 1935, but Congress extended it to 1976 in a few circumstances. In Alaska homesteading was legal into the 1980s. E. Louise Peffer, *The Closing of the Public Domain: Disposal and Reservation Policies, 1900–50* (Stanford, CA: Stanford University Press, 1950), 22–51.

29. George F. Whitworth to Regional Director, Region Four, January 10, 1958, Death Valley files, Box 95 File 1-1-54 to 12-31-59, L3031 vol. 1 "Areas," NARA-SB.

30. Ibid.

31. T. R. Goodwin, "Report, Privately Owned Lands and Their Acquisition, Death Valley National Monument," July 3, 1934, 4–9.

32. John White to the Director, National Park Service, May 16, 1934, L1417 DEVA Boundaries, 1933–34, Death Valley archives; "Park Origin and Land Status," Silver File "History of Death Valley," Death Valley archives; H.R. 2476; the congressional action for Scotty's Castle was 54 Stat. 1193; Master Plan for Death Valley National Monument, Mission 66 Edition, D18 Master Plan, January 1960, PRG 1-7, vol. 3, sec. A, 2, Death Valley archives.

33. *Environmental Impact Statement,* 21–22, Death Valley archives; Proclamation 2961, Addition of Devil's Hole to Death Valley National Monument, L48 Wilderness Areas and Research Reserves, 1981–83, PRG 8-9, Death Valley archives; Superintendent, Death Valley, to Regional Director, Region Four, April 7, 1952, L1417 Boundaries (Extension), 1933–52, Death Valley archives.

34. Superintendent, Death Valley, to Regional Director, Region Four, June 27, 1952; Assistant Regional Director, Region Four, to Director, June 2, 1952; Acting Assistant Director to Regional Director, Region Four, July 11, 1952, all Death Valley files, Box 279, File 609-01 "Mining," NARA-SB.

35. Superintendent, Death Valley, to Regional Director, Region Four, July 21, 1952; Acting Assistant Regional Director to the Director, July 25, 1952, Death Valley files, Box 279, File 609-01 "Mining," NARA-SB.

36. Swain, *Wilderness Defender,* 236, 302; Albright as told to Cahn, *Birth of the National Park Service,* 312–13.

37. "Chronology Data on Proposal, Subdocumented in 'For Construction of New Airport at Furnace Creek, California,'" Death Valley files, Box 56, File 601-02 "Airfield," NARA-SB.

38. Susan Schrepfer, *The Fight to Save the Redwoods: A History of Environmental Reform, 1917–1978* (Madison: University of Wisconsin Press, 1983), 74–78, 104–5; Mark Harvey, *A Symbol of Wilderness: Echo Park and the American Environmental Movement* (Albuquerque: University of New Mexico Press, 1994), 1–15.

39. John Ise, *Our National Park Policy* (Baltimore: Johns Hopkins University Press, 1961), 486–87; Conrad L. Wirth, *Parks, Politics, and the People* (Norman: University of Oklahoma Press, 1980), 237–66.

40. Superintendent, Death Valley, to Regional Director, January 11, 1952, Death Valley files, File 501-05, NARA-SB; "Chronology Data on Proposal."

41. "List of the Superintendents of Death Valley," Reference Material, A2615, Death Valley archives; Rothfuss, "Making of a National Park"; "Chronology Data on Proposal."

42. Foresta, *America's National Parks*, 80–94.

43. Ibid.; Wirth, *Parks, Politics, and the People*, 251–81.

44. Hal K. Rothman, *Devil's Bargains: Tourism in the Twentieth-Century West* (Lawrence: University Press of Kansas, 1998), 55–80; Diane Thomas Darnall, *The Southwestern Indian Detours: The Story of the Fred Harvey/Santa Fe Railway Experiment in Detourism* (Phoenix: Hunter, 1978), 317–25.

45. National Park Service, "Death Valley National Monument (Profile)," January 31, 1993, Death Valley archives.

46. "List of the Superintendents of Death Valley"; Rothfuss, "Making of a National Park"; "Chronology Data on Proposal."

CHAPTER 3 : CHANGING THE MEANING OF DESERT

1. Richard West Sellars, *Preserving Nature in the National Parks: A History* (New Haven, CT: Yale University Press, 1999), 212–22; A. Starker Leopold et al., "Wildlife Management in the National Parks," in *Transactions of the Twenty-Eighth North American Wildlife and Natural Resources Conference,* edited by James B. Trerethren (Washington, DC: Wildlife Management Institute, 1963); National Academy of Sciences, National Research Council, "A Report by the Advisory Committee to the National Park Service on Research," typescript, August 1, 1963.

2. Hal K. Rothman, *Saving the Planet: The American Response to the Environment in the Twentieth Century* (Chicago: Ivan R. Dee, 2000), 109–14; Walter A. Rosenbaum, *Environmental Policy and Politics,* 2nd ed. (Washington, DC: Congressional Quarterly Press, 1991), 35–42.

3. Roderick Nash, *Wilderness and the American Mind,* 2nd ed. (New Haven, CT: Yale University Press, 1983), 1–8; Runte, *National Parks,* 240–41 (see chap. 2, n. 2); Foresta, *America's National Parks,* 69–70 (see chap. 2, n. 18).

4. Sellars, *Preserving Nature,* 191–96; William C. Everhart, *The National Park Service* (Boulder, CO: Westview Press, 1983), 91–99; David Louter, *Windshield Wilderness: Cars, Roads, and Nature in Washington's National Parks* (Seattle: University of Washington Press, 2006); Paul S. Sutter, *Driven Wild: How the Fight Against Automobiles Launched the Modern Wilderness Movement* (Seattle: University of Washington Press, 2002).

5. Annual Superintendent's Report, Death Valley National Park, 1975; "List of the Superintendents of Death Valley" (see chap. 2, n. 41). The *Death Valley Wilderness Proposal* is essentially the plan adopted in the Desert Protection Act, language that became law on October 31, 1994. For the Desert Protection Act, see http://www.nps.gov/legal/parklaws/3 /volume_3-03_natlparks.pdf.

6. Rothman, *Saving the Planet,* 131–41; Rothman, *Preserving Different Pasts,* 102–3, 133 (see chap. 2, n. 6).

7. Superintendent's Monthly Report, December 1969, Death Valley National Park archives (hereafter Death Valley archives); Superintendent's Monthly Report, June 1970, Death Valley archives.

8. Superintendent's Monthly Report, November 1970, Death Valley archives; James Barker, telephone conversation with Hal K. Rothman, September 17, 2002; Briefing Statement, Death Valley National Monument, January 1993, Death Valley archives; Robert D. McCracken, *A History of the Amargosa Valley, Nevada* (Tonopah, NV: Nye County Press, 1990), 91–92.

9. "Fourth Meeting, Western Regional Advisory Committee, Death Valley National Monument, October 4–6, 1973, Current Legislation," A18, Western Regional Advisory Committee, Death Valley archives.

10. Ibid.

11. Superintendent's Monthly Report, June 1972, May 1972, January 1973, Death Valley archives.

12. Superintendent's Annual Report, 1975, 11, Death Valley archives.

13. James Barker to Hal K. Rothman, private communication, September 11, 2002; R. A. Walters, "Tenneco Oil's Colemanite Milling Operations Near Lathrop Wells, Nevada," Special Report 26, February 1977, Nevada Bureau of Mines and Geology, Reno; Superintendent's Annual Report, 1974 and 1975, Death Valley archives.

14. Rothman, *Saving the Planet,* 158–60; Steven C. Schulte, *Wayne Aspinall and the Shaping of the American West* (Boulder: University Press of Colorado, 2002), 3–15, 177–90.

15. "Dispute Heats Up in Death Valley: Mining Profits vs. Environment," *Petaluma Argus-Courier,* February 4, 1976.

16. Barker, telephone conversation with Rothman, September 17, 2002; Death Valley National Monument Annual Report, 1976, 3, Death Valley archives.

17. Mining in the Parks Act, PL 94-419, 16 USC 1901.

18. Rothfuss, "Making of a National Park" (see chap. 2, n. 12); Barker, telephone conversation with the author, September 17, 2002; Lingenfelter, *Death Valley and the Amargosa,* 394 (see introduction, n. 9); Duane A. Thompson, "Mining in the National Parks and Wilderness Areas: Policies, Rules, Activities," Congressional Research Service, 96-161 ENR, February 12, 1996, 2.

19. Superintendent's Annual Report, 1975, 11, Death Valley archives; "List of the Superintendents of Death Valley"; Rothfuss, "Making of a National Park," 152–70.

20. *United States v. American Borate Corporation,* CIV 76-206, August 3, 1977; Superintendent's Annual Report, 1977, 2, Death Valley archives.

21. Superintendent's Annual Report, 1997, 3, Death Valley archives; "List of the Superintendents of Death Valley"; Rothfuss, "Making of a National Park," 152–70.

22. Superintendent's Annual Report, 1978, 13–15, Death Valley archives; Superintendent's Annual Report, 1979, 15–19, Death Valley archives.

23. Superintendent's Annual Report, 1981, 22–29, Death Valley archives; "List of the Superintendents of Death Valley"; Rothfuss, "Making of a National Park," 152–70.

24. McCracken, *History of the Amargosa Valley,* 93–94.

25. Monthly Report, Death Valley National Monument, August 1971, Death Valley archives; "Significant Events in December 1971," December 29, 1971; "Significant Events in November 1971," December 7, 1971; Record of Significant Events, I&RM Spec. 2-12/71, A2615, Death Valley archives; McCracken, *History of the Amargosa Valley,* 93–94.

26. James E. Deacon and Cynthia Deacon Williams, "Ash Meadows and the Legacy of the Devils Hole Pupfish," in *Battle Against Extinction: Native Fish Management in the American West,* edited by W. L Minckley and James E. Deacon (Tucson: University of Arizona Press, 1991), 69–92.

27. "Remarks of James T. McBroom, Former Chairman of the Now Dissolved Interior Department Pupfish Task Force, at the Third Annual Symposium on Rare and Endangered Fishes of the Death Valley System, Furnace Creek, California, November 16, 1971," Animal Life—Fish, Pupfish, 10-12/71, N1423 (1-28), Death Valley archives.

28. McCracken, *History of the Amargosa Valley,* 94; "Remarks of James T. McBroom."

29. US Department of the Interior, "A Progress Report on the Interior Task Force for Preserving Desert Pupfish" (Department of the Interior, June 1971), 10; T. R. Goodwin, "Public Reaction to the Death Valley Region," Situation Reports, A2623, 38-31, Death Valley archives; "Cranston Introduces Bill to Save Unique Fish for Science," *Sacramento Bee,* June 30, 1971; "Ranch to Quit Pumping Water to Save Death Valley Pupfish," *Las Vegas Review-Journal,* September 3, 1971; Elsie Carper, "Devils Hole Pupfish Granted Reprieve," *Washington Post,* September 3, 1971.

30. April Perry, "Devils Hole and the Implied Reservation of Water Rights Doctrine" (unpublished paper, copy in possession of the author). The Winters Doctrine, *Winters v. U.S.,* 207 US 564 (1908), had established the principle of unreserved water rights designated by the government for use in the terms of an executive order or congressional legislation.

31. *Francis Leo Cappaert et al. v. United States,* 426 U.S. 128, N1423, Death Valley archives; Perry, "Devils Hole"; Linda Mathews, "Justices Back Rare Pupfish," *Los Angeles Times,* June 8, 1976.

32. J. R. McCloskey, cited in "Over the Line: Nevada News," *Inyo Independent,* July 15, 1976; G. Michael McCarthy, *Hour of Trial: The Conservation Conflict in Colorado and the West, 1891–1907* (Norman: University of Oklahoma Press, 1977), 236–52; R. McGreggor Cawley, *Federal Land, Western Anger: The Sagebrush Rebellion and Environmental Politics* (Lawrence: University Press of Kansas, 1993), 15–70.

33. Darlington, *Mojave,* 1–11 (see introduction, n. 1); Rothman, *Saving the Planet,* 158–65.

34. Edwin Rothfuss, interview by Hal K. Rothman, August 6, 2002.

35. Ibid.

36. Ibid.

37. Ibid.; George B. Hartzog, *Battling for the National Parks* (Mt. Kisco, NY: Moyer Bell, 1988), 159–81. Hartzog's description of the North Cascades, which he fought successfully to secure for the park system, reflects his philosophical take on what constituted a real park: "The North Cascades is the last place in the lower 48 where the Lord put His hand

on the land to make it a thing of majesty and beauty. There is certainly a park there—and all that remained was to identify it" (164–65).

38. Edwin Rothfuss, interview by Hal K. Rothman, August 6, 2002; Schrepfer, *Fight to Save the Redwoods,* 44–64 (see chap. 2, n. 38); John Jacobs, *A Rage for Justice: The Passion and Politics of Phillip Burton* (Berkeley: University of California Press, 1995), 211–14, 353–55. As an analogue to the NPS's perception of Death Valley being outside agency norms was the similar response in the late 1970s and 1980s to the inclusion of the flat tundra in Alaska: many in the agency believed this treeless, oft-frozen terrain "would be unworthy additions to the System because they lacked scenic appeal." Foresta, *America's National Parks,* 115.

39. Rothfuss, interview, August 6, 2002.

40. Ibid.

41. Ibid.

42. Edward Abbey, *Postcards from Ed: Dispatches and Salvoes from an American Iconoclast* (Minneapolis: Milkweed Press, 2008), 175.

43. Darlington, *Mojave,* 7–9; Hal K. Rothman, *The Greening of a Nation? Environmentalism in the U.S. Since 1945* (Fort Worth, TX: HarBrace Books, 1997), 177–78.

44. Darlington, *Mojave,* 8; Frank Wheat, *California Desert Miracle: The Fight for Desert Parks and Wilderness* (San Diego: Sunbelt, 1999), 2–5.

45. Charles F. Wilkinson and H. Michael Anderson, *Land Resource and Planning in the National Forests* (Washington, DC: Island Press, 1988), 64–65; 4; James M. Ridenour, *The National Parks Compromised: Pork Barrel Politics and America's Treasures* (Merrillville, IN: ICS Books, 1994), 85–87; Hunter S. Thompson, *Fear and Loathing in Las Vegas* (New York: Random House, 1971), 47–79.

46. National Park Service, "Wilderness, Boundary Adjustments, and Name Change to National Park Status," January 1993, 104th Congress Issues Briefing Statement, Death Valley archives; Superintendent's Annual Report, 1986, Death Valley archives.

47. Superintendent's Annual Report, 1986, Death Valley archives; National Park Service, "Briefing Statement: General Information, Death Valley National Monument"; Superintendent, Death Valley, to Regional Director, Region Four, November 10, 1993, L1417 Central Files, Calif. Desert Protection Act, Death Valley archives.

48. Rothman, *Saving the Planet,* 149.

49. National Park Service, "Wilderness, Boundary Adjustments, and Name Change," briefing statement, January 1993, Death Valley archives; Superintendent's Annual Report, 1986, Death Valley archives; James Richardson, *Willie Brown: A Biography* (Berkeley: University of California Press, 1996), 160; Eleanor Fowle, *Cranston: The Senator from California* (San Rafael, CA: Presidio Press, 1980), 15–27.

50. James V. Hansen to Edwin Rothfuss, October 27, 1993; Rothfuss to Hansen, November 10, 1993; Superintendent, Death Valley, to Director, National Park Service, June 1, 1994; Death Valley National Park, boundary description, May 1995, L1417 Central Files, Calif. Desert Protection Act, Death Valley archives; Wheat, *California Desert Miracle,* 297–303; Harlan D. Unrau, *A History of the Lands Added to Death Valley National Monument by the California Desert Protection Act of 1994* (Washington, DC: National Park Service, 1997), 4–9.

51. Wheat, *California Desert Miracle*, 158–303.

52. "New National Preserve Embraces NRS Site," University of California Office of the President, 1996; Wheat, *California Desert Miracle*, 287–304; Wilkinson and Anderson, *Land Resource and Planning*, 64–65, 233–37.

CHAPTER 4 : NATIVE AMERICANS AND THE PARK

1. Robert Keller and Michael Turek, *Native Americans and National Parks* (Tucson: University of Arizona Press, 1998), 2–26; Mark D. Spence, *Dispossessing the Wilderness: Indian Removal and the Making of the National Parks* (New York: Oxford University Press, 1999), 3–8, 41–62; Karl Jacoby, *Crimes Against Nature: Squatters, Poachers, Thieves, and the Hidden History of American Conservation* (Berkeley: University of California Press, 2001); Marguerite Shaffer, "Performing Bears and Packaged Wilderness: Reframing the History of National Parks," in *Cities and Nature in the American West*, edited by Char Miller (Reno: University of Nevada Press, 2010), 137–53.

2. Barbara Novak, *Nature and Culture: American Landscape and Painting, 1827–1875* (New York: Oxford University Press, 1996), 1–6; Runte, *National Parks*, 35–40 (see chap. 2, n. 2).

3. Swain, *Wilderness Defender*, 61–90 (see chap. 1, n. 50); Spence, *Dispossessing the Wilderness*, 133–39; Keller and Turek, *Native Americans and National Parks*, 232–40; Theodore Catton, *Inhabited Wilderness: Indians, Eskimos, and National Parks in Alaska* (Albuquerque: University of New Mexico Press, 1997); Jacoby, *Crimes Against Nature*, 1–7; Louis Warren, *The Hunter's Game: Poachers and Conservationists in Twentieth-Century America* (New Haven, CT: Yale University Press, 1997), 1–21; Philip Burnham, *Indian Country, God's Country: Native Americans and the National Parks* (Washington, DC: Island Press, 2000), 19–29.

4. Crum, *Road on Which We Came*, 1–16 (see introduction, n. 7); "Technical Reports Regarding the Timbi-Sha Shoshone Band" (see introduction, n. 7); Burnham, *Indian Country, God's Country*, 295–96.

5. "Technical Reports Regarding the Timbi-Sha Shoshone Band"; Julian Steward, "Basin-Plateau Aboriginal Sociopolitical Groups," *Bureau of American Ethnology Bulletin* 119 (1938).

6. "Technical Reports Regarding the Timbi-Sha Shoshone Band"; Steward, "Basin-Plateau Aboriginal Sociopolitical Groups."

7. Memorandum to Those Attending October 18, 1975, Meeting in Death Valley National Monument, L30 Land Use—Indian Village, 1970–77, Death Valley National Park archives (hereafter Death Valley archives); "Technical Reports Regarding the Timbi-Sha Shoshone Band"; Steward, "Basin-Plateau Aboriginal Sociopolitical Groups."

8. Pauline Esteves and Grace Goad, interviews by Hal K. Rothman, December 9, 2002.

9. "Technical Reports Regarding the Timbi-Sha Shoshone Band."

10. Ibid.; Charles E. Kelsey, *Census of Non-reservation California Indians, 1905–1906* (Berkeley: University of California Archaeological Research Facility, 1906).

11. Frederick Hoxie, *A Final Promise: The Campaign to Assimilate the Indians, 1880–1920* (Lincoln: University of Nebraska Press, 1984), 1–14; David Wallace Adams, *Education for*

Extinction: American Indians and the Boarding School Experience, 1875–1928 (Lawrence: University Press of Kansas, 1995), 1–9.

12. "Technical Reports Regarding the Timbi-Sha Shoshone Band"; Christopher H. Peters, "Land Acquisition and Needs Assessment for the Timba-Sha Shoshone Band of Indians" (Eureka, CA: Peters, Matilton), L30 Land Use—Indian Village, 1983, PRG 8-8, Death Valley archives; Crum, *Road on Which We Came,* 75.

13. "Technical Report Regarding the Timbi-Sha Shoshone Band," 14–17.

14. Bishop Agency, Annual Reports of the Superintendent, 1911–1926, NARS microfilm, 301, R. 3, and Carson Indian Agency, Carson Indian School Student Folders, 1920–1960, National Archive and Records Center–Santa Barbara, Calif. (hereafter NARA-SB), R.G. 75, cited in "Technical Reports Regarding the Timbi-Sha Shoshone Band"; Adams, *Education for Extinction,* 205–12.

15. Esteves, interview, December 9, 2002.

16. Albright as told to Cahn, *Birth of the National Park Service,* 271–98 (see chap. 2, n. 3), provides the best description of the National Park Service's goals and objectives during the early 1930s.

17. Burnham, *Indian Country, God's Country,* 300–305; Spence, *Dispossessing the Wilderness,* 115–32; Jacoby, *Crimes Against Nature,* 121–70.

18. Crum, *Road on Which We Came,* 112; Albright as told to Cahn, *Birth of the National Park Service,* 279; Esteves, interview, December 9, 2002.

19. "Technical Report Regarding the Timbi-Sha Shoshone Band," 16–18.

20. Lawrence C. Kelly, *The Assault on Assimilation: John Collier and the Origins of Indian Policy Reform* (Albuquerque: University of New Mexico Press, 1983), 42–65; Kenneth R. Philp, *John Collier's Crusade for Indian Reform, 1920–1954* (Tucson: University of Arizona Press, 1977), 13–37.

21. John R. White to Alida C. Bowler, February 11, 1936; T. R. Goodwin to Alida C. Bowler, March 11, 1936; White to Bowler, March 15, 1936, all L30 Land Use—Indian Village, 1933–39, Death Valley archives; Bowler to Goodwin, March 30, 1936, DEVA General Correspondence, NARA-SB. Spence, *Dispossessing the Wilderness,* 124–27, describes twelve cabins for sixty-six people at Yosemite.

22. White to Bowler, March 15, 1936, L30 Land Use—Indian Village, 1933–39, Death Valley archives.

23. Jacoby, *Crimes Against Nature,* 187–91; Hal K. Rothman, *Devil's Bargains: Tourism in the Twentieth Century West* (Lawrence: University Press of Kansas, 1998), 74–77.

24. Memorandum to Those Attending October 18, 1975, Meeting.

25. "Trust Agreement for Rehabilitation Grant to Unorganized Tribe," November 3, 1936, L30 Land Use—Indian Village, 1933–39, Death Valley archives.

26. "Technical Reports Regarding the Timbi-Sha Shoshone Band," 19–21.

27. Esteves, interview, December 9, 2002; Perry Gage to John R. White, August 28, 1936; John Bergen to Chief Architect, May 28, 1936, all L30 Land Use—Indian Village, 1933–39, Death Valley archives.

28. Esteves, interview, December 9, 2002; Goad, interview, December 9, 2002.

29. "Technical Reports Regarding the Timbi-Sha Shoshone Band," 19–21; Adams, *Education for Extinction,* 13–23.

30. Lingenfelter, *Death Valley and the Amargosa,* 449–53 (see introduction, n. 9); Darlington, *Mojave,* 8, 273 (see introduction, n. 1).

31. Alida C. Bowler to Commissioner of Indian Affairs, January 23, 1939; T. R. Goodwin, Memorandum for the Director, August 15, 1939; Fred H. Daiker to Don C. Foster, November 7, 1939, all L30 Indian Village, Death Valley archives.

32. Memorandum for the Director, August 15, 1939; Daiker to Foster, November 7, 1939, both L30 Land Use—Indian Village, 1970–77, Death Valley archives.

33. J. Collier, Memorandum for Indian Organization, October 23, 1939, cited in "Technical Reports Regarding the Timbi-Sha Shoshone Band."

34. Ibid.

35. Ibid.

36. Ibid., 20; Esteves, interview, December 9, 2002.

37. Richard Drinnon, *Keeper of Concentration Camps: Dillon S. Myer and American Racism* (Berkeley: University of California Press, 1987), 233–48; Donald L. Fixico, *Termination and Relocation: American Indian Policy, 1945–1960* (Albuquerque: University of New Mexico Press, 1986), 1–23; Kenneth R. Philp, *Termination Revisited: American Indians on the Trail to Self-Determination, 1933–1953* (Lincoln: University of Nebraska Press, 1999), 1–15.

38. Hoxie, *Final Promise,* 1–25.

39. Superintendent, Death Valley, to Assistant Regional Director, March 23, 1951, Death Valley files, Box 279, File 610: Private Holdings, NARA-SB; letter to Ralph Gelvin, March 24, 1947, L30 Land Use—Indian Village, 1940–49, Death Valley archives.

40. Spence, *Dispossessing the Wilderness,* 129–31; Peters, "Land Acquisition and Needs Assessment." It is telling that most histories of the national parks do not even mention termination.

41. Superintendent, Death Valley, from Regional Director, Region Four, October 31, 1956; Death Valley Indian Village Housing Policy, May 9, 1957; Memorandum to Those Attending October 18, 1975, Meeting; Director from Regional Director, Region Four, May 17, 1957, all L30, Land Use—Indian Village, 1950–59, PRG 8-8, Death Valley archives.

42. Esteves, interview, December 9, 2002.

43. Goad, interview, December 9, 2002

44. Staff Anthropologist to Chief Anthropologist, January 13, 1983, L30 Land Use—Indian Village, 1983 (Folder 3), PRG 8-8, Death Valley archives.

45. Roger Ernst to R. Graham, April 18, 1958; Superintendent, Death Valley, to Files, July 31, 1981, both L30 Land Use—Indian Village, 1981–82 (Folder 2), PRG 8-8, Death Valley archives.

46. The self-determination movement found symbolic manifestation in the Indian occupation of Alcatraz Island in 1969 when members of a number of Indian peoples seized the old prison island and occupied it for nineteen months. Memorandum to Those Attending October 18, 1975, Meeting.

47. Executive Assistant to the Regional Director, Western Region, to Regional Director,

Western Region, February 6, 1975, H-22 Archaeological, Historical Research General, 1973–1975, Death Valley archives.

48. Superintendent, Death Valley, to Regional Director, Western Region, October 29, 1975, L30 Land Use—Indian Village, 1970–77, Death Valley archives; Memorandum to Those Attending October 18, 1975, Meeting; Goad, interview, December 9, 2002.

49. Dick Ditlevson to Files, October 22, 1975, L30 Land Use—Indian Village, 1970–77, Death Valley archives.

50. Ibid.

51. William E. Finale to Alice Eben, August 24, 1977, L30 Land Use—Indian Village, 1970–77, Death Valley archives; Peters, "Land Acquisition and Needs Assessment," 3.

52. Superintendent, Central California Agency, Bureau of Indian Affairs, to Donald Spalding, March 21, 1977; Chief Ranger to Files, May 27, 1977, L30 Land Use—Indian Village, 1970–77, Death Valley archives.

53. C. D. Newell to Cecil D. Andrus, December 22, 1977; Stephen V. Quesenberry to James A. Joseph, January 20, 1977, both L30 Land Use—Indian Village, 1970–77, Death Valley archives; Superintendent, Death Valley, to Regional Director, Western Region, June 20, 1979, H4217, Historic Preservation, Native America Religious, 1978–1980, Death Valley archives.

54. Foresta, *America's National Parks,* 59–90 (see chap. 2, n. 18); Andrew Gulliford, *Sacred Objects and Sacred Places: Preserving Tribal Traditions* (Boulder: University Press of Colorado, 2000), 185–243.

55. Staff Anthropologist to Chief Anthropologist, January 13, 1983, L30 Land Use—Indian Village, 1983 (Folder 3), Death Valley archives; Esteves, interview, December 9, 2002; Goad, interview, December 9, 2002.

56. Susan Sorrells, "Out of Tourists' Sight, Death Valley Indians Battle for Their Homes," K34 News Media, Newspaper Clippings 1978–80, Death Valley archives; Superintendent, Death Valley, to Files, July 31, 1981; Acting Associate Regional Director, Resources Management, to Regional Director, Region Four, December 2, 1981; Superintendent, Death Valley, to Regional Director, March 25, 1977, all L30 Land Use—Indian Village, 1983, PRG 8-8, Death Valley archives.

57. Esteves, interview, December 9, 2002.

58. 25 CFR 84, January 4, 1983; Deputy Assistant Director, Indian Affairs (Operations), to Assistant Director, Indian Affairs, February 9, 1982, L30 Land Use—Indian Village, 1981–82, PRG 8-8, Death Valley archives; "Death Valley Timbi-Sha Shoshone Band of California; of Final Determination for Federal Acknowledgment," October 6, 1982, *Federal Register,* vol. 47, no. 214.

59. Summary: National Park Service Timbi-Sha Tribe Relationships Issues Meeting, June 14, 1983, L30 Land Use—Indian Village, 1983, PRG 8-8, Death Valley archives.

60. Superintendent, Death Valley National Monument, to Western Regional Director, March 17, 1983; Staff Anthropologist to Chief Anthropologist, January 13, 1983, both L30 Land Use—Indian Village, 1983 (Folder 3), PRG 8-8, Death Valley archives.

61. Staff Anthropologist to Chief Anthropologist, January 13, 1983; Superintendent, Death Valley, to Regional Director, June 10, 1983; David Geissinger to Regional

Director, Western Region, June 27, 1983, all L30, Land Use—Indian Village, Death Valley archives.

62. Superintendent, Death Valley National Monument, to Western Regional Director, March 17, 1983; Deputy Assistant Director, Indian Affairs (Operations), to Assistant Director, Indian Affairs, February 9, 1982; Edwin L. Rothfuss to Pauline Esteves, November 2, 1983; Larry Beal, preparer, "Task Directive: Timbi-Sha Planning Alternatives Study," Package no. 360, August 1983, 2, all L30 Land Use—Indian Village, 1983, PRG 8-8, Death Valley archives.

63. Director to Regional Director, Region Four, June 8, 1983, L30 Land Use—Indian Village, 1983, PRG 8-8, Death Valley archives.

64. Superintendent, Death Valley, to Regional Director, Region Four, June 10, 1983, L30 Land Use—Indian Village, 1983, PRG 8-8, Death Valley archives; Esteves, interview, December 9, 2002.

65. Beal, "Task Directive."

66. California Desert Protection Act of 1994 (PL 103-433), Section 705B; *Draft Legislative Environmental Impact Statement: Timbisha Shoshone Homeland* (April 2000), Death Valley archives; Darlington, *Mojave*, 7–9, 313–14.

67. Linda Greene, interview by Hal K. Rothman, March 22, 2004.

68. "Urgent Request for Support: Death Valley Shoshone California Timbisha Shoshone Tribe Face Eviction," ca. 1996; Timbisha Shoshone, Death Valley Land Restoration Project, "Secretary Babbitt Promises to Throw the Timbisha Shoshone Off Its Ancestral Tribal Homeland in Death Valley," American Indian Liaison Office, National Park Service, Timbisha Shoshone Homeland Act Records; Steven Haberfeld, "Government-to-Government Negotiations: How the Timbisha Shoshone Got Its Land Back," *American Indian Culture and Research Journal* 24:4 (2000): 127–65.

69. "Timbisha Shoshone Death Valley Land Restoration Project"; Haberfeld, "Government-to-Government Negotiations," 133–36; Robert J. Paton, "Landless California Tribe May Get a Home," *Indian Country Today,* July 13, 1995; Martin Forstenzer, "Indian Tribe Challenges Plan for Gold Mine," *Los Angeles Times,* July 20, 1995, 17.

70. *Draft Legislative Environmental Impact Statement,* 5; Frank Clifford, "Tribes Bid to Control Parks," *Los Angeles Times,* November 25, 1995; Frank Clifford, "U.S., Death Valley Indians Strike a Unique Land Deal," *Los Angeles Times,* February 25, 1999; "Dividing Death Valley," *Sacramento Bee,* August 7, 1999; Haberfeld, "Government-to-Government Negotiations," 149–59; Greene, interview, March 22, 2004.

71. *Draft Legislative Environmental Impact Statement,* 5; William Claiborne, "Bigger Role for Death Valley Tribe," *Washington Post,* April 6, 1999; "Timbisha Shoshone Can Return to Homelands," *Indian Country Today,* April 26, 1999.

72. Linda Saholt, "Timbisha Celebrate Victory," *Native News,* January 21, 2001; "Timbisha Celebration and General Council Meeting a Success," *Nagkawittu,* special edition (February 2001): 1.

73. Esteves, interview, December 9, 2002; Greene, interview, March 22, 2004.

1. J. T. Reynolds, interview by Hal K. Rothman, July 25, 2002.

2. Hartzog, *Battling for the National Parks,* 1–11 (see chap. 3, n. 37); Foresta, *America's National Parks,* 71–74 (see chap. 2, n. 18).

3. Bob Murphy, *Desert Shadows: A True Story of the Charles Manson Family in Death Valley* (Morongo Valley, CA: Sagebrush Press, 1993), 1–11, 78–96; Vincent Bugliosi, *Helter Skelter: The True Story of the Manson Murders* (New York: W. W. Norton, 1974), 123–34.

4. Murphy, *Desert Shadows,* 71–78.

5. Death Valley National Monument, Drug Interdiction, 102nd Congress Issues Briefing Statement, January 1991, Department of the Interior, National Park Service, Silver Box: Management, Subject: Briefing Statements, 102nd Congress, Death Valley, Death Valley National Park archives (hereafter Death Valley archives); Superintendent's Annual Report, 1991, Death Valley National Monument, Death Valley archives, 4.

6. Superintendent's Annual Report, 1991, Death Valley National Monument, Death Valley archives, 4, 25; Superintendent's Annual Report, 1992, Death Valley National Monument, Death Valley archives, 29; Death Valley National Monument, Drug Interdiction, 104th Congress Issues Briefing Statement, January 1993, Department of the Interior, National Park Service, Silver Box: Management, Subject: Briefing Statements, 102nd Congress, Death Valley, Death Valley archives.

7. Shannon Peterson, *Acting for Endangered Species: The Statutory Ark* (Lawrence: University Press of Kansas, 2002), 3–38; Walter A. Rosenbaum, *Environmental Politics and Politics,* 5th ed. (Washington, DC: Congressional Quarterly Press, 2002).

8. Benjamin Levy, *Death Valley National Monument Historical Background Study* (Washington, DC: Government Printing Office, 1969); *Management Options for Natural and Cultural Resources, Death Valley National Monument: Environmental Assessment* (Death Valley, CA: National Park Service, 1976); Linda W. Greene and John A. Latschar, *Historic Resource Study: A History of Mining in Death Valley National Monument,* 4 vols. (Denver: National Park Service, 1981).

9. "Death Valley in the Movies (and on Television)," http://www.nps.gov/deva/Pdf/DVmovies.pdf.

10. Keith Bradsher, "Have Camera, Will Spy: Trying to Get the Drop on Detroit's Latest Designs," *New York Times,* April 7, 2001.

11. "Marines Prepare for Trek," *New York Times,* July 12, 1959; "Hikers in 4th Day in Desert," *New York Times,* August 29, 1966.

12. Kirk Johnson, "A Will to Suffer Draws Runners to the Desert," *New York Times,* July 15, 1998; Samantha Stevenson, "A Run Good for the Spirit, but Torture for the Body," *New York Times,* July 18, 1998.

13. National Park Service, *Death Valley National Monument: Final Environmental Impact Statement General Management Plan* (Death Valley, CA: National Park Service, 1989); Edwin L. Rothfuss to General Management Planning Process Participant, April 25, 1989, D16 L76, Death Valley archives.

14. US Department of the Interior, "Record of Decision, General Management Plan,

Death Valley National Monument, Inyo and San Bernardino Counties, California; Esmerelda and Nye Counties, Nevada," attached to Rothfuss to General Management Plan Process Participants, April 25, 1989.

15. "Interagency Desert Management Plan Northern and Eastern Mojave Desert Inyo and San Bernardino Counties, CA; Intent to Prepare an Environmental Impact Statement," September 5, 1995, *Federal Register,* vol. 60, no. 171, 46132–33.

16. Vicki Warren, "The Southern California Deserts," ATV *Connection,* October 6, 2001; Off-Road Business Association, ORBA *Newsletter,* June 2001; Reynolds, interview, July 25, 2002; Darlington, *Mojave,* 248–312 (see introduction, n. 1).

17. Krista Deal, *Draft Cultural Resource Management Plan for Death Valley National Monument* (Denver: Technical Information Center, Denver Service Center, 1987), 19–24, DEVA D-149.

18. Superintendent's Report, January 1949, January 1950, Death Valley archives; Superintendent's Annual Report, 1942, Death Valley archives; Draft 1987 Cultural Resources Management Plan (Denver: Denver Service Center-Technical Information Center), DEVA D-149, 7, Death Valley archives.

19. Paul Fagette, *Digging for Dollars: American Archaeology and the New Deal* (Albuquerque: University of New Mexico Press, 1996), 19–98; C. W. Ceram, *The First American: A Story of North American Archaeology* (New York: Harcourt, Brace, Jovanovich, 1971), 106–58.

20. Park Naturalist to Superintendent, Death Valley National Monument, August 18, 1950, Death Valley files, Box 281 File DNM 620-46, Museum, National Archives and Record Administration, Pacific Region–San Bruno (hereafter NARA-SB).

21. C. W. Meighan, *Archeological Survey in Death Valley* (Denver Service Center, Technical Information Center, 1953), Death Valley archives, D-83.

22. Superintendent's Monthly Report, February 1953, January 1953, November 1954; Acting Superintendent to Director, Annual Report of Officials in Charge of Field Areas, May 30, 1953, A2683, Death Valley archives.

23. "Master Plan for Death Valley National Monument, Mission 66 Edition," January 1960, D18 Master Plan, January 1960, PRG 1-7, Death Valley archives.

24. Foresta, *America's National Parks,* 132–36; Lary M. Dilsaver, ed., *America's National Park System: The Critical Documents* (Lanham, MD: Rowman and Littlefield, 1994), 302–8; Runte, *National Parks,* 219–20 (see chap. 2, n. 2); Barry Mackintosh, *The National Historic Preservation Act and the National Park Service: A History* (Washington, DC: Government Printing Office, 1986), 1–4.

25. Gordon Chappell, interview by Hal K. Rothman, December 12, 2002; Executive Order 11593, "Protection and Enhancement of the Cultural Environment," May 13, 1971, in *America's National Park System,* edited by Dilsaver, 377–78.

26. Chappell, interview, December 12, 2002.

27. Regional Historical Architect, Western Region, to Regional Director, Western Region, March 30, 1977, H30 Skidoo, 1973–77, Death Valley archives; Department of the Interior, "Proposed Regulation of Mining in the Skidoo National Historic Register; Property," H30 Skidoo, 1973–77, Death Valley archives, 5–6; Chappell, interview, December 12, 2002.

28. Death Valley National Monument, "Proposed Regulation of Mining Within the Skidoo National Historic Register Property, Death Valley National Monument, California, 1975," 1–4; Bakken, *Mining Law of 1872* (see chap. 2, n. 25).

29. Regional Historical Architect to Regional Director, Western Region, March 30, 1977, H30 Skidoo, 1973–77, Death Valley archives; Superintendent's Report, 1984, Death Valley archives.

30. Gordon Chappell to Hal K. Rothman, December 5, 2002.

31. Death Valley National Monument, "Environmental Assessment: Proposed Regulation of Mining in the Skidoo National Historic Register Property," H30 Skidoo, 1973–77, Death Valley archives; Briefing Statement—General Information, Death Valley National Monument, January 1993, Death Valley archives; Donald L. Fife, "Mesothermal Gold Mineralization: Skidoo–Del Norte Mines, Death Valley," *California Geology* (April 1987): 86–93; Superintendent's Annual Report, 1992, Death Valley archives; Harlan D. Unrau, "Preliminary Historic Structure Report, March 1998: Skidoo Mill/Mine, Death Valley National Park," 1–4, Death Valley archives; Chappell to Rothman, December 6, 2002.

32. Rothman, *Preserving Different Pasts* (see chap. 2, n. 6); Archaeological Resources Protection Act 1979, 93 Stat. 721; Dilsaver, *America's National Park System,* 371–73.

33. Superintendent's Annual Report for 1991, Death Valley National Monument, 13, Death Valley archives; Rothman, *Preserving Different Pasts,* 1–66.

34. Todd Swain, "Operation Indian Rocks," January 21, 2004, http://www.death-valley .us/article907.html.

35. Kelly Turner, comments, Death Valley National Park Draft Administrative History, May 2005, Death Valley archives.

36. Mel Essington, interview by Hal K. Rothman, July 25, 2002; Linda Greene, interview by Hal K. Rothman, July 25, 2002; Sellars, *Preserving Nature,* 234–35 (see chap. 3, n. 1); Mackintosh, *National Historic Preservation Act,* 88–93. Death Valley National Park calls its unit the "Resources Management Division." I have held to the park's nomenclature when describing the unit, following the larger agency guideline in generic references.

37. Superintendent's Annual Report, 1985, 12, Death Valley archives; Superintendent's Annual Report, 1984, Death Valley archives; Superintendent's Annual Report, 1989, Death Valley archives.

38. Superintendent's Annual Report, 1984, 5, Death Valley archives; Superintendent's Annual Report, 1985, 13, Death Valley archives; Essington, interview, July 25, 2002.

39. Disturbed Lands Restoration Program, "Reclamation Summary of Abandoned Mineral Lands in the National Park Service" (Washington, DC: Geologic Resources Division, 2001), 1–3; Keane Wonder Mine Aerial Tramway Stabilization, April 2011, http://www.cfr.washington.edu/research.cesu/reports/J8W07090003_final_report.pdf.

40. "Timbisha Design Guidelines Meeting, 2/5/01," Cultural Resource Management Files, Death Valley National Park, Death Valley archives; Greene, interview, March 22, 2004.

41. Shankland, *Steve Mather,* 111–13 (see chap. 1, n. 22); Sellars, *Preserving Nature,* 56–57, 89–90; Runte, *National Parks,* 105–8; Horace M. Albright and Marian Albright Schenk, *Creating the National Park Service: The Missing Years* (Norman: University of Oklahoma

Press, 1999), 274–85; National Park Service, *National Parks for the 21st Century: The Vail Agenda* (Post Mills, VT: Chelsea Green, 1991).

42. White to Director, June 6, 1933; Goodwin to White, November 16, 1934; White to Director, December 5, 1934, all Death Valley files, Box 280, File 610: Nevares, NARA-SB; 1998 General Management Plan, Death Valley archives; Pauline Esteves, interview by Hal K. Rothman, December 12, 2002; Lingenfelter, *Death Valley and the Amargosa*, 14 (see introduction, n. 9). The best account of the fecundity of feral pigs comes from Alfred Crosby, *Ecological Imperialism: The Biological Expansion of Europe, 900–1900 AD* (New York: Cambridge University Press, 1986), 173–76.

43. Goodwin to White, October 18, 1935; White to Goodwin, October 24, 1935; White to Office of Chief Engineer, November 18, 1935; White to Nevares, December 23, 1935; Nevares to White, December 23, 1935; Demaray to White, December 21, 1935; White to Goodwin, February 5, 1936; Goodwin to White, February 18, 1936; White to Nevares, March 11, 1935; Nevares to White, March 14, 1936; White to Nevares, April 21, 1936; White to Director, May 20, 1936, all Death Valley files, Box 280, File 610: Nevares, NARA-SB.

44. Hillory A. Tolson to Superintendent, June 5, 1936; White to Director, June 15, 1936; Ernest Dawson to White, June 14, 1936; William E. Colby to White, June 18, 1936; Cammerer to Superintendent, June 23, 1936; White to Director, June 29, 1936, all Death Valley files, Box 280, File 610: Nevares, NARA-SB; Norris Hundley Jr., *The Great Thirst: Californians and Water, a History*, rev. ed. (Berkeley: University of California Press, 2001), 71–97, 422.

45. White to Nevares, June 30, 1936; Memorandum of Conference, from F. A. Kittredge, September 11, 1936; Kittredge to White, September 11, 1936; Joseph E. Taylor to Merriam, September 15, 1936, all Death Valley files, Box 280, File 610: Nevares, NARA-SB; Hundley, *Great Thirst*, 71–97, 422.

46. Taylor to White, January 20, 1937; A. E. Demaray to Acting Superintendent, Sequoia National Park, October 7, 1936; White to Director, September 9, 1937; Demaray to White, September 24, 1937; White to Nevares, September 30, 1937; Nevares to White, October 10, 1937; White to Nevares, October 19, 1937; White to Director, October 19, 1937; White to Nevares, November 5, 1937; White to Colby, November 13, 1937; White to Nevares, November 13, 1937; White to Director, November 5, 1937; Telegram to White, November 12, 1937; Kittredge to Director, November 9, 1937; White to Wirth, October 25, 1937; Taylor to Director, November 3, 1937; Wirth to White, November 9, 1937; Demaray to White, November 9, 1937, all Death Valley files, Box 280, File 610: Nevares, NARA-SB.

47. Goodwin to Director, April 22, 1940; H. Donald Curry to Superintendent, May 16, 1940; Goodwin to Regional Director, December 30, 1940; Appraisal Sheet, prepared by T. R. Goodwin, June 7, 1940; A. van V. Dunn to Regional Director, October 7, 1940, all Death Valley files, Box 280, File 610: Nevares Part II, NARA-SB.

48. A. L. Hickson to Bates Booth, November 6, 1940; Memorandum for Chief Counsel, March 4, 1941; Notes on Testimony, February 28, 1941; Memorandum for Associate Attorney Johnson, March 21, 1941; Memorandum for the Director, April 2, 1941; Memorandum for Associate Attorney Albert A. Johnson, April 8, 1941; Memorandum for the Regional Director, Region IV, May 10, 1941; R. Neil Grunigen, Report of Work Performed by the National Park Service, July 5, 1941, all Death Valley files, Box 280, File 610: Nevares,

NARA-SB; Chronology of Events File 1, LI425 Private Holdings, Nevares IV, 1951–52, PRG 1-23, Death Valley archives.

49. Chronology of Events File 2, LI425 Private Holdings, Nevares IV, 1951–52, PRG 1-23, Death Valley archives.

50. Chronology of Events File 2; *U.S. v. 320 Acres of Land,* LI425 Private Holdings, Nevares IV, 1951–52 PRG 1-23, Death Valley archives.

51. Hal K. Rothman, "Urban Oasis: Why Desert Cities Won't Run Out of Water—and Why They Shouldn't," *Urban Ecology* (Spring 2001): 14–22.

52. Michael Weissenstein, "The Water Empress of Las Vegas," *High Country News,* April 9, 2001.

53. Terry Fisk, interview by Hal K. Rothman, July 24, 2002; Hal K. Rothman, *Neon Metropolis: How Las Vegas Started the Twenty-First Century* (New York: Routledge, 2002), 157–86.

54. John G. Edwards, "Pahrump's Progress: Competition Is Heating Up in What Was Once a One-Casino Town," *Las Vegas Review-Journal,* November 10, 1997. Pahrump's population has long been the subject of dispute. In 1997 Nye County, where the town is located, claimed a population of 27,460, and Pahrump comprised the overwhelming majority. The people of Pahrump claimed foul, saying that their own numbers showed as many as 30,000, and the state demographer's estimate for the county in July 1999, 33,000, confirmed the city's claim.

55. Michael Weissenstein, "Boomtown Faces Slowdown: Pahrump Growth Falters," *Las Vegas Review-Journal,* January 7, 2001.

56. *National Park Service Briefing: Renewable Energy Projects,* Death Valley National Park, February 2012, Death Valley archives.

57. Reynolds, interview, July 25, 2002; *Draft Environmental Impact Statement,* III–14 (see chap. 1, n. 10); McCracken, *History of Amargosa Valley,* 2, 16, 29 (see chap. 3, n. 8).

58. A. Costandina Titus, *Bombs in the Backyard: Nuclear Testing and American Politics* (Reno: University of Nevada Press, 1987); Cabell Phillips, "Huge Blasts Claim Growing Atomic Power," *New York Times,* February 4, 1951, "Atomic Age Reaches Old Nevada Town," *New York Times,* May 7, 1967; Anthony Ripley, "Underground Blast Fired in Nevada," *New York Times,* March 27, 1970; Iver Peterson, "Issue of National Nuclear Waste Dump Polarizes Three States," *New York Times,* January 25, 1985, A10; Matthew L. Wald, "Work Is Faltering on U.S. Repository for Atomic Waste," *New York Times,* January 17, 1989; Matthew L. Wald, "Finding a Burial Place for Nuclear Wastes Grows More Difficult," *New York Times,* December 15, 1989, C1; William J. Broad, "A Mountain of Trouble," *New York Times Magazine,* November 18, 1990, 36–40, 80–82; Matthew L. Wald, "Doubt Cast on Prime Site as Nuclear Waste Dump," *New York Times,* June 20, 1997, A12.

59. Martin Forstenzer, "Concerns Arise over Aquifer Near Nuclear Test Site," *New York Times,* March 21, 2000, F2; Reynolds, interview, July 25, 2002.

60. Edwin L. Rothfuss, *An Administrative History of the Removal of Feral Burros from Death Valley National Monument,* March 1990, DEVA Cat. 63356, 1–4, Death Valley archives.

61. Sellars, *Preserving Nature,* 82; R. Gerald Wright, *Wildlife Research and Management in the National Parks* (Urbana: University of Illinois Press, 1992), 36–38, 97–98; Michael

F. Anderson, *Living at the Edge: Explorers, Exploiters, and Settlers of the Grand Canyon Region* (Grand Canyon, AZ: Grand Canyon Association, 1998), 58–61.

62. Annual Report, 1937, Death Valley archives; 1947 Wildlife Conservation Report, Death Valley files, Box 285, File 700-01 Nature Study, NARA-SB; Monthly Report, February 1948; Monthly Report, December 1944; Monthly Report, August 1942; Annual Report, 1934, Death Valley archives.

63. Rothfuss, *History of the Removal of Feral Burros,* 5–9.

64. Ibid., 1–10.

65. Fred Binnewies to Horace M. Albright, April 21, 1959, Death Valley, H14, L2023, Death Valley archives; Rothfuss, *History of the Removal of Feral Burros,* 4.

66. E. Lowell Sumner, "The Effects of Wild Burros on Bighorns in Death Valley National Monument," *Transactions of the Desert Bighorn Council* 3 (1959): 4–9.

67. Rothfuss, *History of the Removal of Feral Burros,* 6.

68. Robert J. Murphy, "Burro Management Plan, Death Valley National Monument," 1970, Death Valley archives.

69. Rothman, *Saving the Planet,* 170–75; Sellars, *Preserving Nature,* 258–59.

70. Rothfuss, *History of the Removal of Feral Burros,* 9–10; Superintendent's Annual Report, 1981, Death Valley archives.

71. Wright, *Wildlife Research and Management,* 97–98; Sellars, *Preserving Nature,* 258–59.

72. 1998 Draft General Management Plan, Death Valley National Monument, Death Valley archives; Rothfuss, *History of the Removal of Feral Burros,* 15–17; Scott R. Abella, "A Systematic Review of Wild Burro Grazing Effects on the Mojave Desert USA," *Environmental Management* 41 (2008): 809–19.

73. 1998 Draft General Management Plan; Frank Wheat, *California Desert Miracle: The Fight for Desert Parks and Wilderness* (San Diego: Sunbelt Publications, 1999), 158–212.

74. Annual Performance Plan for Death Valley National Park, Fiscal Year 2001–2002, 1, http://www.death-valley.us/article202.html; NPS Burro Management Plan, 2003, http://www.docstoc.com/docs/18493267/NPS-Burro-Management-Plan—2003; "BLM Schedules Beatty Wild Burro Gather in Late March," *Pahrump Valley Times,* February 29, 2012, http://pvtimes.com/news/blm-schedules-beatty-wild-burro-gather-in-march/; John Janiskee, "Feral Burros Are 'Equina Non Grata' in the National Parks," April 18, 2009, http://www.nationalparkstraveler.com/2009/04/creature-feature-feral-burros-are-equina-non-grata-national-parks; Thomas J. McGill, "Feral Equine Management at the Naval Weapons Center," *Proceedings of the Eleventh Vertebrate Pest Conference,* 1984, http://digitalcommons.unl.edu/cgi/viewcontent.cgi?article=1023&context=vpc11.

75. Crosby, *Ecological Imperialism,* 145–70.

76. Theodore A. Kerpez and Norman S. Smith, *Saltcedar Control for Wildlife Habitat Improvement in the Southwestern United States,* Resource Publication 169 (Washington, DC: US Department of Interior, Fish and Wildlife Service, 1987), 1–16; John G. Carman and Jack D. Brotherson, "Comparison of Sites Infested and Not Infested with Saltcedar (*Tamarix pentandra*) and Russian Olive (*Elaeagnus angustifolia*)," *Weed Science* 30 (1982): 360–64.

77. John H. Bergen, "Final Report to the Chief Architect, N.P.S.," 1934, Death Valley

archives; Final Report to the Chief Architect, NPS, PRG 1-11, Death Valley archives, 6–7; W. G. Carnes to Director, June 2, 1954, Final Report to the Chief Architect, NPS, PRG 1-11, Death Valley archives; "General Information—Death Valley National Monument: Briefing Statement," January 1993, Death Valley archives.

78. Memorandum for the Superintendent, May 8, 1947; Lowell Sumner, "A Special Report on the Relation of Salt Brush to Hay Fever in the Wildrose Area, Death Valley National Monument," May 5, 1947, both Death Valley files, Box 285 File 701: Flora, NARA-SB.

79. Master Plan for Death Valley National Monument, Mission 66 Edition, D18 Master Plan, January 1960, PRG< 1-7, vol. 3, sec. D, 27–29, Death Valley archives.

80. Superintendent's Monthly Report, July 1970, July 1971, Death Valley archives; "List of the Superintendents of Death Valley" (see chap. 2, n. 41); Superintendent's Annual Report, 1992, Death Valley archives.

81. Northern and Eastern Mojave Planning Effort, Update, June 22, 2001, Death Valley archives.

82. *Death Valley Draft Environmental Impact Statement/General Management Plan,* 59, 69, Death Valley archives.

83. "Principles for Wilderness Management in the California Desert," *Death Valley Draft Environmental Impact Statement/General Management Plan,* 294–311, Death Valley archives.

84. Death Valley General Management Plan, 2002, 18–37, Death Valley archives; *Mapping Wilderness Character in Death Valley National Park,* Natural Resource Report NPS/DEVA/NRR—2012/503 (Fort Collins, CO: US Department of the Interior, 2012); Mark Henry and Leslie Armstrong, *Mapping the Future of America's National Parks: Stewardship Through Geographic Information Systems* (Redlands, CA: ESRI Press, 2004); Richard Lake, "UNLV Students Discover New Scorpion Species," *Las Vegas Review-Journal,* May 13, 2012, http://www.lvrj.com/news/unlv-students-discover-new-scorpion-species-151285715 .html; Eyrn Brown, "New Species of Scorpion Found in Death Valley National Park," *Los Angeles Times,* March 24, 2012, http://articles.latimes.com/2012/mar/24/local/la-me -0324-new-scorpion-20120324.

CHAPTER 6 : DEATH VALLEY IN THE TWENTY-FIRST CENTURY

1. National Park Service, *National Parks for the 21st Century,* 3, 13–19 (see chap. 5, n. 41).

2. Rep. Sidney Yates to Bruce Babbitt, January 20, 1995; Bob Krumenaker, "Are We Flourishing Yet?," in *Natural Resources Year in Review* (Washington, DC: National Park Service, 1997), D-1182; Department of the Interior, *FY 1995 DOI Annual Report* (Washington, DC: Department of the Interior), 12–13.

3. Peter E. Thorsett, "Reorganizing the U.S. National Park Service" (unpublished paper, University of Tennessee, Knoxville), 3–16; Department of the Interior, Order 3189, May 25, 1995, "Reorganizing the National Park Service."

4. Melody Webb to Hal K. Rothman, June 20, 2003, in possession of the author; Krumenaker, "Are We Flourishing Yet?"

5. Wayne Badder, interview by Hal K. Rothman, July 29, 2002.

6. J. T. Reynolds, interview by Hal K. Rothman, July 25, 2002.

7. Edwin Rothfuss, interview by Hal K. Rothman, August 6, 2002; Reynolds, interview, July 25, 2002; Architectural Resources Group, Historic Structure Report prepared for Cow Creek Historic District, Death Valley National Park, February 2000, 1–3, Death Valley National Park archives (hereafter Death Valley archives), 8374; Death Valley National Park Annual Report, 2001, 32, TIC 143/D-220, Death Valley archives; "Remodeled Visitor Center to Reopen in Death Valley National Park," *Las Vegas Review-Journal,* February 15, 2012, http://www.lvrj.com/news/remodeled-visitor-center-to-open-in-death valley-national-park-139396593.html; "Renewable Energy Projects in California Go Unused," *Los Angeles Times,* January 9, 2012, http://articles.latimes.com/2012/jan/09/local/la-me-parks-solar-20120109; Char Miller, "Sun Stroke: SoCal Edison and the Battle over Solar Power," February 1, 2012, http://www.kcet.org/updaily/the_back_forty/commentary /golden-green/sun-stroke-socal-edison-and-the-battle-over-solar-power.html; "Boxer Calls on Southern California Edison to End Delay in Connecting Renewable Energy Projects to Electric Grid," January 12, 2012, http://boxer.senate.gov/en/press/releases/011212.cfm.

8. Jarvis Solar Energy Memo, February 6, 2009, http://www.nationalparkstraveler. com/files/Jarvis-Solar_Energy_Memo.pdf; *National Park Service Briefing: Water Resources in Death Valley National Park,* December 2011; *National Park Service Briefing: Renewable Energy Projects,* Death Valley National Park, February 2012, Death Valley archives.

9. John C. Freemuth, *Islands Under Siege: National Parks and the Politics of External Threats* (Lawrence: University Press of Kansas, 1991). Protecting the park's dark skies from light pollution emanating from onsite resort facilities, nearby urbanization, and solar and wind farms outside the park's boundaries has become a key issue. *National Park Service Briefing: Night Sky Designation,* Death Valley National Park, February 2012, Death Valley archives.

10. Superintendent's Annual Report, Death Valley National Park, FY 1982, 42, Death Valley archives; Annual Report, Death Valley National Park, FY 1983, appx. 1, 2, Death Valley archives; Superintendent's Annual Report, Death Valley National Park, FY 1985, 23, Death Valley archives.

11. Barry Mackintosh, *Visitor Fees in the National Park System: A Legislative and Administrative History* (Washington, DC: Government Printing Office, 1983), 72–80; US Stat. at Large, PL 104-134, 16 U.S. Code 4601–6a; Toni Moran, interview by Hal K. Rothman, July 29, 2002.

12. Mackintosh, *Visitor Fees,* 72–75; Moran, interview, July 29, 2002. Underscoring some of the problems that can come from the impermanence of the NPS Fee Demo program is the Ninth Circuit Court of Appeals' rejection in February 2012 of the Forest Service's application of its similarly framed "user fee" program: *Adams v. U.S. Forest Service,* http://www.ca9.uscourts.gov/datastore/opinions/2012/02/09/10-16711.pdf; Char Miller, "Fee Simple," http://www.kcet.org/updaily/the_back_forty/commentary/golden-green /fee-simple-why-we-need-to-pay-to-hike-boat-fish-camp-and-just-plain-recreate-on-the -national-forests.html.

13. National Park Budget (California), 2010, http://home.nps.gov/applications /budgetweb/FY2010/sbtoc.htm.

14. Zachary Coile, "National Parks Cut Visitor Services: Watchdogs Say Jobs, Visitor Center Hours Are Being Reduced," *San Francisco Chronicle,* May 28, 2004; Blair Davenport to Char Miller, e-mail, May 14, 2012.

15. National Fire Plan Success Story, 2007, http://www.forestsandrangelands.gov /success/stories/2007/nfp_2007_q4_ca_nps_moja_rehab.shtml. Making this same case is Tom Knudsen, "Thieves at Work in Death Valley National Park," *Sacramento Bee,* June 2, 2010, http://blogs.sacbee.com/the-public-eye/2010/06/thieves-at-work-in-death-valley -national-park.html.

16. Stephen Lyons, "Meth Invasion," *High Country News,* August 14, 2000.

17. Division of Ranger Activities, Washington Office, "National Park Service Morning Report, March 20, 2000."

18. Ibid.; Dale Antonich, interview by Hal K. Rothman, April 14, 2002.

19. Ibid.

20. Division of Ranger Activities, Washington Office, "National Park Service Morning Report, March 20, 2000."

21. "Search Ends for Four German Tourists," *Los Angeles Times,* October 31, 1996, http: //articles.latimes.com/1996-10-31/news/mn-59804_1_german-tourists; Associated Press, "Death Valley Bones Linked to German Tourists," November 13, 2009, http://www. msnbc.msn.com/id/33919797/ns/us_news-life/t/death-valley-bones-linked-german -tourists/#.T4TBHNkQByI; "'Death by GPS' in the Desert," *Desert Independent,* February 11, 2011, http://www.thedesertinde.com/Articles-2011/Death-by-GPS-in-desert-0211 .html.

22. General Management Plan, 2002, 18–19; Joseph Siano, "Parks Take Steps to Clean Air," *New York Times,* August 25, 2002; "Ford Donates 500 Vehicles to Calif. Nat'l Parks," *Road and Travel Magazine,* http://www.roadandtravel.com/newsworthy/Newsworthy2002 /deathvalleythink.htm.

23. Death Valley National Park Annual Report, 2001, 28, Death Valley archives; Death Valley General Management Plan, Inyo and San Bernardino Counties, California, and Esmerelda and Nye Counties, Nevada, April 2002, 62–64.

24. Bakken, *Mining Law of 1872* (see chap. 2, n. 25).

25. Mitch Tobin, "Mining the Crown Jewels," *High Country News,* August 17, 1998; Stephanie Simon, "Dust Up over Death Valley Talc," *Seattle Times,* February 22, 1998, http://community.seattletimes.nwsource.com/archive/?date=19980222&slug=2735892.

26. Simon, "Dust Up over Death Valley Talc."

27. Helen Wagonvoord, "Mine Threatens Death Valley," *Wilderness Record,* October 1997.

28. Death Valley Draft General Management Plan; Kathy A. Davis to Richard Martin, January 12, 1999, Superintendent's Files, Death Valley National Park, Death Valley archives.

29. Bill Postmus, "Statement of Supervisor Bill Postmus, First District of San Bernardino County Board of Supervisors, Before the Subcommittee on National Parks, Recreation & Public Lands of the House Committee on Resources," August 18, 2003; Patricia Limerick et al., *Atlas of the New West* (New York: W. W. Norton, 1997).

30. "The New Gold Rush," *Environmental Working Group,* October 15, 2007, http://www.ewg.org/release/new-gold-rush-surge-mining-claims-threatens-california-s-national-parks-wilderness.

31. Reynolds, interview, July 25, 2002.

32. Ibid.

33. Lee Romney, "Off-Roaders in Uphill Fight on Canyon," *Los Angeles Times,* June 23, 2003.

34. Linda Greene, interview by Hal K. Rothman, June 26, 2003; Romney, "Off-Roaders in Uphill Fight on Canyon."

35. Center for Biological Diversity, "BLM Closes Surprise Canyon to Off-Road Vehicles to Protect Rare Species, Wilderness Values, and Water Quality," May 29, 2001, http://www.peer.org/news/news-releases/2001/05/29/blm-closes-surprise-canyon-to-off-road-vehicles/; Romney, "Off-Roaders in Uphill Fight on Canyon."

36. David Page, "Sand Stormer," *Hemisphere Magazine,* April 2012, 30–32.

37. Harlan D. Unrau, *A History of the Lands Added to Death Valley National Monument by the California Desert Protection Act of 1994* (Denver: National Park Service, 1997), 138–39.

38. Death Valley Management Plan, 2002, 39; Unrau, *History of the Lands Added,* 141–43.

39. Death Valley Management Plan, 2002, 40.

40. Ibid.

41. Theodore Catton, "To Make a Better Nation: An Administrative History of the Timbisha Shoshone Homeland Act," report prepared under cooperative agreement with Rocky Mountain Cooperative Ecosystem Studies Unit for Death Valley National Park, California, October 2009, 93–101.

42. "A Call to Action: Preparing for a Second Century of Stewardship and Engagement," August 25, 2011, http://www.nps.gov/calltoaction/PDF/Directors_Call_to_Action_Report.pdf; "National Park Service Issues 5-Year 'Call to Action' Plan for Moving Toward Its Second Century," http://www.nationalparkstraveler.com/2011/08/national-park-service-issues-5-year-call-action-plan-moving-toward-its-second-century8687.

INDEX

condemnation (land acquisition), 116–17
confirmed patents, 38
copper mining, 21–22
Cow Creek, 114–17
Cranston, Alan, 57, 64
CR Briggs Mine, 94
criminal activity, 98–99, 139–40
Crocker, M. D., 53
Cry California, 56
cultural resource management: efforts to
    identify and evaluate historic sites, 107–10;
    impact of Timbisha homeland on, 113;
    limited emphasis prior to 1966, 104–7; 1980s
    changes in strategy, 111–12; problem of pot
    hunting, 110–11

Daiker, Fred H., 79, 82, 83
Daunet, Isadore, 18
Davis, Kathy A., 143
Dawes Act of 1887, 80–81
Deacon, James, 56
Death Valley: as a desert landscape, 1–2; early
    human habitation, 8–10; entry into national
    park system, 28–32; European entry into,
    10–12; history of mining and prospecting
    in, 11–12, 15–23; Native inhabitants, 3–4 (*see
    also* Timbisha Shoshones); origin of name,
    4, 11–12; rise of tourism in, 5–6, 25–27, 29;
    role of "Death Valley Scotty," 23–25; US
    government mapping of, 12–14. *See also*
    Mojave Desert
Death Valley Coyote, 23
Death Valley Hotel Company, 26
"Death Valley Indian Village Housing Policy,"
    85–87
Death Valley National Monument: air access
    and airports as key issues, 41–43; air-quality
    issues, 102–3; budgetary challenges, 136;
    creation of, 28–32; cultural and historical
    resources (*see* cultural resource manage-
    ment); early management of, 33–36; expan-
    sion of boundaries, 35–36, 39; impact of
    Civilian Conservation Corps, 34–35; impact
    of Mission 66, 43–45; land claims and
    inholdings, 36–41, 44–45, 59, 114–17; late-
    twentieth-century management challenges,
    97–104; mining claims and related issues
    (*see* mining and prospecting); personnel and
    facilities issues, 59–62; politics of wilderness

designation, 47–48, 65; resource manage-
    ment issues (*see* resource management);
    struggle for park status, 63–67; struggles of
    Timbisha within (*see* Timbisha Shoshones);
    visitation levels, 35, 43; water claims and
    related issues (*see* water issues)
Death Valley National Park: air-quality issues,
    102–3, 140–41; as a bellwether for national
    park system, 148–49; budgetary challenges,
    136–38; creation of Timbisha homeland,
    93–96; cultural and historical resources (*see*
    cultural resource management); as a desert
    landscape, 1–2; devaluing by National Park
    Service, 60–61, 147–48; facilities-related
    challenges, 133–35; late-twentieth-century
    management challenges, 67–68, 97–104; law
    enforcement issues, 138–40; legacy of mining
    in (*see* mining and prospecting); protection-
    access question, 144–47; resource manage-
    ment issues (*see* resource management);
    struggle for park status, 63–67; visitation
    levels, 138; water claims and related issues
    (*see* water issues); wilderness management
    issues, 129, 141–42
"Death Valley Scotty," 23–25, 32
Death Valley Shoshones. *See* Timbisha
    Shoshones
"Death Valley Special School," 76
Death Valley Wilderness Proposal, 48
Delamar, J. R., 21
Denton, William, 13
Desert Parks Conference, 61
deserts: early tourists in, 5–6; Native inhabitants
    of, 3–4; Old World views of, 2–3, 4; as places
    of refuge, 3; transforming attitudes toward,
    6–7, 62
Desert Solitaire: A Season in the Wilderness
    (Abbey), 7
Devils Hole, 55–58
"dollar-a-year men," 33
Doty, Captain Edward, 11
*Draft Legislative Environmental Impact State-
    ment,* 95
Dresselhaus, Carl, 110
drug interdiction, 99, 139
Drury, Newton B., 42
Dunne, Jim, 100
Dutton, Clarence, 28

Eagle Borax Works, 18
East Mojave National Scenic Area, 67
Eichbaum, Helene, 38
Eichbaum, Herman W. "Bob," 26, 32
Embrey, Frank, 111
Emergency Conservation Work (ECW), 34
Emmerich, Kevin, 145
Endangered Species Act, 51
endurance training, 101
Engle, Clair, 43
environmental revolution, 46–47
Esteves, Pauline, 76, 80, 86, 90, 96
Etcharren, Domingo, 21
exotic plant species, 126–28
extractive industries. *See* mining and prospecting
extreme sports, 101

federal educational programs, 75–76
Federal Land Policy and Management Act
   (FLPMA), 63
"Fee Demo," 137
Feinstein, Dianne, 66
Files, Kathy, 64
filming, 100
Fisk, Terry, 118
Flores, Gabriel, 101
Foreman, George, 88
Fred Harvey Company, 44
Frémont, Captain John C., 11
French, E. Darwin, 15
Furnace Creek, 72–73
Furnace Creek Airport, 43
Furnace Creek Inn, 26
Furnace Creek Ranch airstrip, 41–43

Garrett, Billy, 113
Geissinger, David, 90
General Authorities Act, 101
General Mining Act of 1872, 36
George, Samuel G., 15
Gilbert, Charles H., 14
global positioning systems (GPS), 7, 140
Goad, Grace, 80, 86, 88
Goddard, George H., 13
gold mining and prospecting, 11–12, 20–21
Goldwater, Barry, 49
Goodwin, Theodore R., 33–36, 39–40, 78, 82,
   114–15, 157n24
Gore, Al, 68

Gospel Foundation, 25, 45, 59
Great Basin, 9
"great survey" era, 13–14
Greene, Bruce, 88
Greene, Linda W., 96, 100, 113
Gypsum period, 10

Hansen, George, 16
Hansen, James, 65
Hanson, George, 75, 79
Harmony Borax Works, 18, 106
Harris, Frank "Shorty," 20
Hartzog, George B., Jr., 61
Hedges, Patty, 64
Historical Resources Management Plan, 107–8
*Historic Resource Study: A History of Mining in
   Death Valley,* 100
Holland, Ross, 108
homesteading, 16, 158n28
homestead patents, 38
Hoover, Herbert, 30, 32
Hudson River School, 28
Hungry Bill, 16, 74
Hunter, William L., 16

Indian George, 16
Indian Reorganization Act (IRA) of 1934, 78,
   81, 83
Indians. *See* Native Americans; Timbisha Sho-
   shones; Western Shoshones
*Interagency Desert Management Plan: Northern
   and Eastern Mojave,* 103
invasive plants, 126–28
Inyo County, 81
Ives, Lieutenant Joseph Christmas, 13

Jackson, A. J., 142
James, George Wharton, 8
Jarvis, John, 148
Jayhawkers, 11–12
"Jazz Baby," 22
Jenifer, Frank, 26
Johnson, Albert, 23–25
Johnson, Bessie, 24, 25
Johnson, William, 16
Jones, John P., 17
Jordan, Charlotte, 5
Joshua Tree National Park, 67
Julian, C. C., 22

129, 141–42; protection-access question, 144–47; provision of Depression-era relief to Timbisha, 77–79; resource management issues (*see* resource management); water issues (*see* water issues)

National Park Service (NPS), parent agency: air access and airports as key issues, 41, 42; as a beneficiary of the New Deal, 34; devaluing of Death Valley and other desert parks, 60–61, 147–48; disregard for Native Americans in creating national parks, 69–70, 77; early emphasis on "scenic parks," 28–29; early emphasis on visitor services, 26–27; implementation of Mission 66, 43–44; land-claim and -use issues, 37; 1995 reorganization, 131–33; role in promoting Death Valley and establishing Death Valley National Monument, 26–27, 28–32; support for Death Valley park status, 65; twenty-first-century park system challenges, 148–49; views on wilderness designation, 47–48

National Register of Historic Places, 107–8

Native Americans: disregarded by creators of national parks, 69–70, 77; as early inhabitants of Death Valley, 3–4, 8–10; tensions with miners, 15–16. *See also* Timbisha Shoshones; Western Shoshones

natural resource management. *See* resource management

Nature Conservancy, 58

Nevada Territory, 13

Nevada Test Site, 119–20

Nevares, Adolphus, 38–39, 114–17

New Deal, 34

Northern and Eastern Mojave Planning Effort, 128

Novak, Rocky, 144–45

NPS. *See* National Park Service, Death Valley; National Park Service, parent agency

nuclear tests, 6

Obama, Barack, 6

off-roading, 144–45

Ogden, Peter Skene, 11

Ogston, Edward E., 40

open-pit mining, 49–53

Operation Indian Rocks, 111

O'Sullivan, Timothy, 14

Pacific Coast Borax Company, 19, 29–30, 35, 41–42, 80, 106

Paepcke, Walter, 24

Pahrump, 7, 117, 118–19, 172n54

Paiute, 10, 71

Panamint City, 17

Panamint Joe, 74

Panamint Mining Company, 17

Panamint Shoshones, 10, 71. *See also* Timbisha Shoshones; Western Shoshones

Panamint Tom, 16, 74

Parcher, Frank, 83

Patrick, L. L., 21

Peeler, David, 111

Perkins, Edna Brush, 5–6, 8

Pinkley, Frank "Boss," 34

Pinto Basin Complex, 9–10

Pinto period, 9–10

plainwares, 10

planners and planning, 101–4

pluvial lakes, 9

population growth, 7, 58–59

Postmus, Bill, 143

pot hunting, 110–11

Powell, Major John Wesley, 13

Pratt, Wallace, 24

"prior appropriation" doctrine, 40, 57, 115

prospecting. *See* mining and prospecting

protection-access question, 144–47

pupfish, 55–56

"radioactive politics," 6

railroad surveys, 12–13

Rainbow Talc Mine, 142–43

Raines, Eliphalet P., 17

Ramsey, John L. "Harry," 21

recreation, 97–98

Recreation Fee Demonstration Program, 137

Reid, Harry, 6

resource management: of cultural assets (*see* cultural resource management); forging a twenty-first-century management plan, 128–30; management and removal of burros, 120–26; management and removal of exotic plant species, 126–28; planning as a new focus of, 101–4; water-supply issues, 113–20

Reynolds, J. T., 97, 119, 120, 133–34, 138, 144

Rhyolite, 4, 20

Ridenour, James M., 64